Adventures in Hemi-Sync® Consciousness:
Related Feedback, Experiences and Benefits

Edited by Susan Smily, MA (Ed)

Adventures in Hemi-Sync® Consciousness: Related Feedback, Experiences and Benefits

Edited by Susan Smily, MA (Ed)

First Edition – March, 2016
Second Edition – June 2016
Revised Edition – August 2017

ISBN-13:978-1523751273
ISBN-10:1523751274

Printed in the United States of America

Dedication

This book is dedicated to all the people who took the time to share their stories,
and to the Professional Division members of The Monroe Institute
for being the conduit between TMI and their patients, clients, and students.

Thank you.

Table of Contents

The Forest, Not the Trees

by Bob Monroe

(TMI Focus, Vol. XV, No. 4, Fall, 1993)

It is astounding how intense concentration can divert attention away from the obvious. Only very recently were we made aware of the broad view of our work these many years. It may well be extremely important—far more than any single event that has taken place.

As you may already know, back in 1956, my company began a small R&D program into the possibility of data learning by rote during the sleep state. The first problem encountered was that of getting the subject to sleep when needed for testing, without the use of medication. As the parent company was one of the nation's leaders in the use of sound to evoke emotional states, it was relatively easy to develop audio patterns that performed the sleep-inducing function.

We gave it the label Frequency Following Response (FFR) when EEG studies showed similar brain-wave patterns appeared concurrently or soon after the sound stimulus was heard. Early results were quite successful. However, the project was diverted in 1958 when it was discovered that such waveforms with variations could evoke states of expanded consciousness far different from the normal waking state.

It was exciting, even frightening at times back in those early days, because what was taking place among our subjects was completely new to us and beyond our knowledge and experience. Conventional studies brought out nothing remotely close to our findings. Unorthodox areas such as meditation, hypnosis, trance states, and the like offered points of similarity, but there were differences that could not be ignored.

We continued our exploration. It was too fascinating to dismiss. We began to develop methods to induce certain repeat- able states of consciousness. We gave them our own labels because we couldn't find appropriate I.D.s in scientific literature or in esoteric areas. None seemed to fit closely our results.

Through the years, assorted researchers, psychologists, philosophers, scientists, and others somehow heard of our work and came to visit or participate in our exploration. With this came much improvement and sophistication in our methods and techniques, including measurement, most of them from scientific and medical sources. We probably would have remained a quiet and obscure research facility had it not been for a single event.

In the mid-seventies, Esalen Institute at Big Sur in California heard of our work and invited us to conduct a workshop there, using the methods we had developed. After that, evidently the word spread and we found ourselves with an opportunity to see the results with a wide range of subjects, far more than the eighteen we had at the time. Bullish, we called it the M-5000 Program. Later, we changed the name to the

GATEWAY VOYAGE®, sure that we would never reach such an optimistic goal. (It passed the 5,000 mark in 1987.)

All of this is an explanation or apology for missing the Broad View.

It happened when someone suggested a simple "teaser" line on the outside of a new brochure we were preparing:

NOW!

Learn to Control the OTHER THIRD of Your life!

SLEEP! That other third of our lives. Mysterious for the most part. Very little scientific knowledge about it except for body biological and electrical data, conflicting dream studies, variegated theories as to what really happens, and uncontrollable in most instances.

The revelation: Virtually all of the Monroe Institute activities involve constructive use of the various stages of sleep.

During planned exercises, in states physiologically identifiable as the four stages of sleep, TMI participants access and communicate with what might be identified as the unconscious, subconscious, ID, superego, autonomic system, and other areas of the human mind yet to be labeled. Until recently, the process of going to sleep and waking up had long been relegated to a secondary interest, it was so easy to establish. The prime interest has been the exploration of self under the simple condition code: Mind Awake/Body Asleep.

Under this Broad View, the Institute recognizes that it possesses only the tools and limited experience to approach such a massive undertaking as total control and constructive use of this "Other Third" of our lives. Therefore, we invite the participation and cooperation, one way or another, of sleep authorities, researchers, technicians, organizations, associations, and others in this new project.

The potentials for change in human consciousness are enormous from this Broad View.

Not the trees! The Forest!

Foreword

This book grew out of a desire to provide Professional Members and Outreach Trainers of The Monroe Institute with a guide of sorts – something that could be grabbed on the run in order to find out what exercise went with what real-life application.

I also wanted a place to put all the feedback that had been reported in the Hemi-Sync Toolkits about various real-life applications of Hemi-Sync, and possibly some of the other feedback reported in the various journals.

The information from the Toolkits forms the substance of Part I of this book. Following each section, I have added a list of the Hemi-Sync Exercises that relate to the particular application – the list is up to date with the 2015 catalog.

Part 2 is a reverse reference. There I have listed every Hemi-Sync product, given the basic information about the CD, and then noted all the applications where that particular item has been found to be helpful.

Part 3 contains some feedback reported in the early journals produced by TMI – going back to 1983. I found it interesting to see some of the early reports of the uses of both the Metamusic and the H-Plus programs that were being developed.

But all in all, this is a book about "The Forest, not the Trees." And from my perspective, all of the products are the Trees, but Hemi-Sync is the Forest.

What Is Hemi-Sync®?

by Leslie France, Director, Professional Division
(TMI Focus, Vol. XII, No. 4, Fall 1990)

[Ed. Note: Since this article was first published in 1990, Interstate Industries, Inc., has been granted legal ownership of the trademark Hemi-Sync®, and the sole production rights. Therefore, all references in the article to The Monroe Institute as the producer of Hemi-Sync should be considered to be references to Interstate Industries.]

In response to this question, The Monroe Institute has published quantities of explanatory literature over the years. By now, most people with a lively curiosity about mind-brain technology know that:

1. Hemi-Sync is a noninvasive technology based on two fundamental, naturally occurring auditory phenomena: frequency following response (FFR) and binaural beat stimulation.

2. FFR is essentially a process of entrainment whereby, when a listener's audio environment is dominated by sounds of specific frequencies, the listener tends to reproduce those frequencies within his/her own physiology. Further, the listener can become entrained to the state of awareness engendered by those frequencies. Over time, individuals can learn to reproduce the state at will without continuous external audio stimulation.

3. Binaural ("two-ears") beats are produced within the physiology of a listener when different audio frequencies are introduced into each ear. The brain-mind discerns this difference and strives to bridge the gap. It therefore produces a third frequency, which is the difference between the two, and which is not an actual sound but may be perceived as an oscillating sound. To cite the usual example: If 100 Hz (cycles per second) is introduced into the left ear, and 104 Hz is introduced into the right, the binaural beat frequency will be 4 Hz.

4. The beauty of a binaural beat system is that:(a) it provides the opportunity for a listener to be influenced by frequencies below the threshold of normal human hearing (we generally have trouble hearing sounds below 40 Hz) and, (b) it tends to stimulate a state of low-frequency brain-wave interhemispheric synchronization. The results of such synchrony include an amplification in the attention a listener is able to apply while in this state. Although interhemispheric synchronization occurs naturally, it is usually intermittent and of limited duration. Binaural beat stimulation aids the listener to sustain it, thereby greatly increasing one's ability to maintain a unique focus of attention over relatively long periods of time.

5. The sounds which are used to stimulate binaural beats (in the example above, the 100 Hz and 104 Hz frequencies) are called "carrier frequencies."

6. The Monroe Institute works with beat frequencies primarily in the Beta, Alpha, Theta, and Delta ranges.

Add to these basics the fact that certain frequency combinations have been identified as conducive to stimulating various, specific mind-brain states. To review, this process quickly guides an individual into a targeted, sustained state of awareness, within which s/he is able to apply a unique focus of attention toward achieving his/her desired outcome. Furthermore, s/he learns to reproduce the state at will. This, then, is the common knowledge—the body of technical components which support the spirit of the Hemi-Sync systems. Entrainment to sound frequencies and binaural beat stimulation are neither patented nor copyrighted by The Monroe Institute. They occur naturally and spontaneously; they were not invented, but rather harnessed and directed by the Institute.

Perhaps an appropriate question to pose at this juncture is: What is not Hemi-Sync? Due to the burgeoning interest in current brain-mind technology over the last decade or so, including a proliferation of hardware, a list of what is not Hemi-Sync would fill a small telephone book. Suffice it to say, only those systems designated with one or more of the Institute's registered trademarks are Hemi-Sync. Any programs, tapes, hardware, or software bearing a registered Hemi-Sync trademark or tradename of The Monroe Institute or Interstate Industries, Inc., without authorization of The Monroe Institute or Interstate Industries, Inc., are in violation of copyright law.

The importance of making this distinction far exceeds any legal implications. You need to know that, when you choose to utilize Hemi-Sync, you are taking advantage of more than a quarter-century of research and development that have brought The Monroe Institute's sound technology to its present level of evolution. Inherent in this advantage is the spirit of Hemi-Sync—the precisely identified, controlled, and proven complex frequency combinations themselves.

Within the carrier and beat frequency ranges out of which Hemi-Sync signals are selected, are a virtually limitless sea of individual frequencies from which to choose. Through meticulous, provocative, and sometimes boring research and trial and error at the Institute laboratory, specific combinations were discovered to elicit certain results; some beneficial, some ineffective, and others that were found to be potentially harmful. Beneficial frequency combinations were refined further and integrated into larger systems. These became Hemi-Sync frequencies. Ineffective patterns were discarded, and potentially harmful signals were noted as such and avoided. This process of identification, classification, and evaluation continues today.

The process, while ultimately resulting in the compilation of a vast inventory of highly effective signal patterns, is analogous to emptying the sea with a bucket. The nature of the water remaining in the sea is anybody's guess. Some will eventually become a part of the Hemi-Sync inventory. Many will not pass the Institute's evaluation standards.

Since the late 1950s we have been accumulating the body of knowledge which allows us to configure sound wave forms accurately into the subtle and powerful consciousness tools you are using. Following the frequency evaluation, the architecture of the Hemi-Sync sound patterns is designed. The relationships between the beat and carrier frequencies are identified and fine-tuned; the number, positions, and amplitudes of the superimposed frequencies are determined. Finally, the flow of merging and separation of these complex combinations is established depending upon the purpose of a particular exercise. All of these contributing details eventually culminate in a Hemi-Sync tape.

Herein lies the essence of what Hemi-Sync is and is not. Hemi-Sync is: complex combinations of sound frequencies which have been found to be beneficial and which are subsequently utilized within Hemi-Sync systems designed and produced by The Monroe Institute. Hemi-Sync is not: any combination of binaural beat and carrier frequencies, either purposefully or randomly selected, by other than The Monroe Institute.

We offer this information to the Institute's position within the growing industry of brain-mind research and technology. Throughout the past twenty-five years we have witnessed the cultural perception of this arena change from considering such research as occult-inspired phenomenology to the wave of the future. We are proud to be one of the pioneers in this field. And, we are pleased to share this valuable work with the many others who are attracted by its potential.

Part 1: Experiences by Topic

Accelerated Learning

Experiences Related to Accelerated Learning

This information has been reported to Monroe Products and The Monroe Institute by individuals and/or by professional practitioners about the use of Hemi-Sync.

A thirty-year-old dyslexic called to say that *Hemi-Sync* is like a "shot in the arm." After only a month of using the *PAL Executive Package, Attention, Synchronizing,* and *Think Fast*, he's aware of a noticeable improvement in cognitive ability. This has made a big difference in on-the-job effectiveness, and has changed his self-image from someone with a handicapping condition to that of a self-directed achiever.

***

I was worried about passing the test I would soon have to take to become a court reporter. I had been studying hard, but my speed wasn't what it needed to be. After I started using the *PAL Student Package* for practice sessions, my speed picked up. I knew I'd pass, and I did so in a relaxed and confident manner.

Hemi-Sync Exercises Related to Accelerated Learning

Hemi-Sync Series
PAL Executive Package
PAL Student Package
LEK: Learning Enhancement Kit

Human Plus Titles
Attention
Buy the Numbers
Imprint
Think Fast

LightSOURCE Arts
Blossoming Lotus

Metamusic Titles
Baroque Garden
Breakthrough
Einstein's Dream
Golden Mind
Guitarra Clásica

Illumination
Indigo
Lightfall
Remembrance
Seasons at Roberts Mountain

Mind Food Titles
Concentration
Retain-Recall-Release

Addictions

Experiences Related to Addictions

This information has been reported to Monroe Products and The Monroe Institute by individuals and/or by professional practitioners about the use of Hemi-Sync.

***

Alcohol and drug abuse led to a very long, downhill slide. She began listening to *Hemi-Sync* and found herself making better choices, about little things and big things, on a daily basis. After a while it became apparent that her whole life style had turned around. *Deep 10 Relaxation* was her favorite tape for nighttime use, and she listened to *Remembrance* during the day.

***

All of our patients have successfully quit smoking and all report that the *De-Hab* tape is a key factor. The tape is also something they can review when necessary to reinforce their belief that they are indeed nonsmokers.

***

Report from the attending physician at a rehabilitation center for alcohol and drug abuse: I introduced *Hemi-Sync* as an adjunct to a traditional twelve step treatment program, with results that suggest a substantial increase in recovery for addicted patients using *Hemi-Sync.* Direct action of *Hemi-Sync* on the brain provides an excellent therapeutic tool. The experience of positive states of mind, not achieved by alcohol or drugs, reinforced the patient's ability to cope with stress and the craving for alcohol and drugs.

***

I've been working with the *De-Hab* tape to cut back on my smoking habit. During the first week I went from an average of 10 to 12 packs a week to 7 packs. Now I'm down to 3-4 packs a week, and feel really good about it.

***

I was telling a friend about my discouragement over several failed attempts to stop smoking. She turned me on to *Hemi-Sync* and—smart lady that she is—suggested I start with the *Catnapper* tape to learn the effectiveness of the Monroe method through my own experience. After a week of marveling at the restful breaks the tape provided in my busy days, I knew I had finally found the tool that would help me quit, and ordered *De-Hab.* It sure helped to have those cues when the urge to smoke was strong, and I continued to use *Catnapper* to help me handle the big change in my life.

***

For most of my adult life I've been a two-pack-a-day smoker, and smoke even more as a response to the stress and discomfort of having MS. I started to cut down with the use of *Möbius West* and soon cut back to four cigarettes a day.

***

I was introduced to *Hemi-Sync* during the early stages of my recovery from drug and alcohol addiction. My counselor and I both agree that the tapes made a positive impact with the recovery process. I listen to *De-Hab* and *De-Tox: Body* to aid in replacing old emotional and physical patterns with healthier ones. *Morning Exercise* gives me an optimistic outlook to begin my day with, and *Deep 10 Relaxation* really helps me deal with stress related issues. Your tapes have been a strong source of support in my new life.

***

Although I have been drug and alcohol free for several years, I still have difficulty with negative thought patterns creeping in. The *Reset* and *De-Hab* tapes have helped me to quickly change my attitude at times when I need to most.

Hemi-Sync Exercises Related to Addictions

Human Plus Titles
De-Hab
De-Tox: Body
Let Go
Möbius West
Reset

Mind Food Titles
Breaking Free from Addictions
Catnapper
Claiming Your Self
Creating Success
Deep 10 Relaxation

Emerging from Depression
Hemi-Sync Nap
Morning Exercise
Total Relaxation
Weight Loss

ADD/ADHD

Experiences Related to ADD/ADHD

This information has been reported to Monroe Products and The Monroe Institute by individuals and/or by professional practitioners about the use of Hemi-Sync.

An investigation into the relevance of Hemi-Sync binaural beat signals for use with ADHD populations supported the conclusion that the audio signals facilitate the ability to attend and persevere at routine motor tasks and facilitate improved attention.

***

I played *Cloudscapes* for my grandson with ADD every night when he went to bed during the entire summer. When school started in the fall, teachers couldn't believe how much his reading skills had improved. They assumed he had spent the summer reading (which he didn't).

***

Our teenager has processing deficits and a short attention span. We're not sure if it is ADD or the effects of institutionalization (she was adopted from an orphanage). "They work, these tapes are good," she says, and she puts on a Hemi-Sync tape to go to sleep with.

***

The 14-year-old with ADHD loved to listen to the Prep Side of any H+ tape, saying, "It calms me and helps me focus." He browsed the Hemi-Sync Catalog to choose other tapes for himself, and selected Buy the Numbers. His math grades improved. The family started playing Remembrance in the car for him and his brother, and reported that it was very effective in keeping the friction down.

***

A psychiatrist called to report her great appreciation for *Remembrance*. "I've always been like a grasshopper in my personal life," she said, "always jumping from one thing to another. This tape has an amazing effect in helping me sustain my attention."

***

My eight-year-old daughter was having a very hard time both at home and at school. In terms of her ability to deal with sensory stimuli, she tested at a four-year-old level, and was constantly interacting with her environment. It was exhausting for her and for us. Since we learned about Hemi-Sync at an Autism Society Conference, we've been playing *Surf* and *Remembrance* for her during the day and *Sandman Suites* (no longer available) at night. The improvement is remarkable.

***

An orphanage in Rumania was home for our daughter's first 2 1/2 years. When we first saw her she was in a "cage," penned up with other children who were never held, never bathed, only given bottles. In the five years since we adopted her, we've made the rounds of every possible treatment and facility from sensory training to neuropsychiatric wards. Her behavior constantly shifted between super passive and super aggressive and back again. After learning about Hemi-Sync through a support group for parents of post-institutional children we bought *Surf, Midsummer Night, Sandman Suites* (no longer available), and *Remembrance* and kept one of the tapes playing all the time. We saw immediate results and, over time, her behavior has evened out. It feels like a miracle.

***

Some hyperactive children have a range of socially unacceptable habits and behaviors. To build rapport with these clients as quickly as possible, we suggest trying some relaxation to help them feel more comfortable. This is where Hemi-Sync comes in. Hemi-Sync with music or surf is played while we use guided imagery (i.e., a walk on the beach, etc.) to produce a relaxed state that then enables us to reach the clients on a subconscious level to make the fastest changes. When dealing with hyperactive children, this is the most effective way I have found to calm them and gain their attention.

***

Hemi-Sync tapes were used in a study conducted by the International Biomedical Center in the Netherlands. The Director reports that children with Attention Deficit Disorder were treated combined with amino acid therapy. The children, aged from five to thirteen years, all had attention and learning disorders accompanied by hyperactivity. The findings, which were confirmed by standard psychological tests, showed patients to be less tired and hyperactive at school and at home. Behavior usually improved within two to three weeks. The Center describes Hemi-Sync tapes as a "help to improve cerebral function in both children and adults."

***

Listening to Hemi-Sync has had a positive impact on my son, who has been hyperactive with numerous behavioral problems. When Hemi-Sync tapes were first recommended for my hyperactive son, I was extremely skeptical. In desperation, I finally decided to try, and I can now say that Hemi-Sync dramatically improved my son's life. Right away I noticed the calming effect while the tape was playing. Even better: my son can now usually recreate that calm state whenever he chooses to do so. It's as if his brain learned how to experience calmness while he listened to the tape, and now he can move into that mental state by himself.

***

I recommend your tapes for the treatment of ADHD as well as for dealing with the emotional problems that are a result of the ADHD effect. We use *De-Hab* to return some useful self-esteem to the patient and to remove those thought programs which have highlighted their apparent mental ineptitude. Watching the twisted, angry face of a past ADHD child turn into a sunny smiling face has a value beyond description.

***

My ADHD kid started out listening to *Remembrance* daily, and now plays it voluntarily on his own once or twice a week. He seems to be happier at home - much less angry.

***

A psychologist reports excellent results from using *Super Sleep* for children with learning disabilities and/or attention deficits. With *Super Sleep* playing all night, parents and teachers observe better concentration and less irritability during the day.

***

Hemi-Sync is an excellent example of the sensory integrative process of the brain. Two independent auditory signals are integrated in a way that produces a whole (i.e., Hemi-Sync) which is different from each of the separate parts. Initial processing and integration occurs in the brain stem. In addition, the tendency toward synchronization of the right and left hemispheres appears to enhance attention, sensory and extrasensory awareness, and intuitive processing, and to increase successful adaptation to personal experiences.

***

Remembrance has made a big difference for our son, who has been diagnosed with ADD. He puts on earphones and sits drawing happily for the whole tape, something he could not have sustained before.

***

Since 1981 I have been using Hemi-Sync with young children who experience sensory motor and sensory integrative disabilities. Both clinical experience and preliminary research indicate that the addition of Hemi-Sync signals (containing frequencies which produce more theta patterns in the brain) to background music increases the child's focus of attention, calms the emotions, and creates a mental set of open receptivity. Hemi-Sync signals enhance the child's ability to organize and integrate sensory information. This results in an increased ability to focus attention, to discriminate specific sensory properties, and to filter unwanted sensory input.

***

Homework time meant a daily struggle with my easily distracted seven-year-old until I introduced her to the *Concentration* tape. Now she goes into her room on her own, puts on either *Concentration* or *Surf*, and contentedly gets to work. I'm grateful for the improved grades, of course, and even more for the improved atmosphere.

***

A special education director reports: "*Remembrance* is very effective in facilitating enhanced attention for students of high school and college age. The tape is appropriate for use at home while during homework. A student with ADHD may also benefit from listening to the tape on a portable cassette player with headphones in a classroom setting. Youngsters with neurological delays, problems with cortical function, and developmental lags may be helped by Hemi-Sync tapes. The sleep tapes for children ease them into sleep comfortably and happily-a boon for parents. After listening to Hemi-Sync over time, youngsters seem to develop a greater neurological capacity to integrate. It seems they no longer need the external stimulus of Hemi-Sync to access certain brainwave states."

***

A three-year-old boy I'd been treating in play therapy for several months had finally been asked to leave his daycare, because of his sporadic, violent behavior. In our regular session, after asking him if he'd like to hear some special music, I gave him headphones and played *Remembrance*. While listening, he became very calm, his eyes widened and he smiled vibrantly. He turned to his mother and said, "Listen, Mommy-it's the angels!"

***

A fourteen-year-old client was in a foster home and having problems adjusting. She was always in motion during our sessions and had great difficulty focusing for more than a couple of minutes on any topic. Since she began using Hemi-Sync tapes she is able to stay focused on the internal work we are doing with guided imagery. We have used *Winds Over the World, Cloudscapes, Remembrance* and *Surf* with wonderful results. She can be completely still and relaxed now, and does not need to constantly check on me or her surroundings.

***

The Director of the International Biomedical Center in the Netherlands reports on a study that combined amino acid therapy tapes for children with Attention Deficit Disorder (ADD). The children, aged from five to thirteen years, all had attention and learning disorders accompanied by hyperactivity. During their treatment they received amino acid supplementation in combination with vitamin B6 and with restriction of refined carbohydrate consumption. The findings, which were confirmed by standard psychological tests, showed patients to be less tired and hyperactive at school and at home. Behavior usually improved within two to three weeks.

***

Super Sleep, played continually throughout the night with an auto-reverse player, was highly successful in modifying a 3-year-old's disturbed sleeping behavior and helping him sleep through the night. Additionally, the child worked harder and more persistently at tasks, spoke more clearly, and accepted correction of his speech more readily, listened better, and was less easily frustrated, started to enjoy books and to sit still for stories to be read to him.

***

A pre-school teacher says, "School hours were especially trying with a difficult group of hyperactive children. The classroom was always chaotic, and I hadn't been able to get the children down for a nap all year. I was totally frustrated, unable to do what I was trained to do. The first time I played a tape from *Sandman Suites* (no longer available) at nap-time the children settled down almost immediately. It was like a miracle. I play different Metamusic tapes now as background for various activities, and find a completely different level of comfort in the room. Obviously, it's good for the children. And I know it's great for me."

***

Homework time meant a daily struggle with my easily distracted seven-year-old until I introduced her to the *Concentration* tape. Now she goes into her room on her own, puts on either *Concentration* or *Surf*, and contentedly gets to work. I'm grateful for the improved grades, of course, and even more grateful for the improved atmosphere.

Hemi-Sync Exercises Related to ADD/ADHD

Hemi-Sync Series
LEK: Learning Enhancement Kit

Human Plus Titles
Buy the Numbers
De-Hab

Metamusic Titles
Baroque Garden
Breakthrough

Cloudscapes
Einstein's Dream
Elation
Golden Mind
Guitarra Clásica
Indigo
Lightfall
Midsummer Night
Remembrance

Seasons at Roberts Mountain
Winds Over the World

Mind Food Titles
Concentration
Sleep Deeply
Soft and Still
Surf
Super Sleep

Aging

Experiences Related to Aging

This information has been reported to Monroe Products and The Monroe Institute by individuals and/or by professional practitioners about the use of Hemi-Sync.

Positively Ageless is, perhaps, the most complete series dedicated solely to the rejuvenation and regeneration of a person's body, mind and spirit. A solid five out of five stars! Patty's soothing voice coupled with the special sound effects sends me to a deep, comfortable level where all mind-chatter ceases. I find it very easy to follow her instructions, which then allows information from my inner-self to come through and guide me to areas that need attention. When it is time to return to Awake and Alert, I am craving for more, but pleased to know there are four additional sessions to choose from and continue my journey.

***

I listen almost daily to *Rejuvenation*–I think it's my favorite….it surely has an impact on me. I wake renewed and ready to take on the new day. I have solved many problems during my meditation and slumber which then become solutions the following morning. I can't tell you how much I enjoy that meditation session.

Hemi-Sync Exercises Related to Aging

Heart-Sync Titles
Transforming Life's Challenges

Hemi-Sync Series
Positively Ageless
LEK: Learning Enhancement Kit

Human Plus Titles
Buy the Numbers
De-Hab
Tune-Up

Metamusic Titles
Baroque Garden
Breakthrough
Einstein's Dream
Elation
Golden Mind
Guitarra Clásica

Mind Food Titles
Concentration
Sleep Deeply

Illumination
Indigo
Lightfall
Remembrance
Seasons at Roberts Mountain
Winds Over the World

Soft and Still
Surf
Super Sleep

Aids/HIV

Experiences Related to Aids/HIV

This information has been reported to Monroe Products and The Monroe Institute by individuals and/or by professional practitioners about the use of Hemi-Sync.

An HIV positive patient reports: "The H+ tapes work for me as a direct mind-to-body experience. All have something to offer, and I believe each person who uses them regularly will develop a combination that works best for him or her. Initially I used one or two tapes every day. Now I listen when I feel the need and don't have a regular schedule. The tape I use and the time I use it is determined by my own sense."

***

Hemi-Sync tapes were part of an eight-week (24-hour) seminar attended by eight HIV positive men. Among the results: all noted an overall improvement in sleep patterns; two with pain noted a total cessation of symptoms; two reported a substantial (200+) increase in T4 cell levels; all noted significant changes related to well-being and physical relaxation. There was a noticeable reduction of general anxiety and tension, increased permission to explore options for change, increase in commitment to improve the quality of their lives, increase in personal energy conveyed and enthusiasm expressed in body posture and general attitude.

***

The *Positive Immunity Program* is a weekend course (also available as an album for home use) that incorporates tapes from the *Gateway Experience* Waves I and II and selected H+ tapes. Transformative changes begin early in the workshop. Some people experience a physical cleansing and display such symptoms as aching and cramping muscles, headaches, nausea, and back pain as toxins are cleansed from the body, and mental and emotional shifts take place. Powerful changes occur and are evidenced by dramatic differences in complexion, muscular relaxation, and actual reduction in AIDS symptoms. One participant suffered from Karpose's sarcoma lesions that had moved into his sinuses. He had received radiation therapy, causing the tissue around his eyes to swell severely and turn dark purple. By the workshop's end, this swelling was visibly reduced and the discoloration had shifted to pink.

Such comments as "I have never felt so relaxed," "I haven't had this much energy in months," and "I am leaving with tools that I can really use on my own," are characteristic. *Hemi-Sync* is a coping tool for those struggling with this new way of living. It opens doors to transformation and can be used to help create a harmonious release from a body stricken with AIDS. It is a most vital tool for the journey of those facing life with AIDS.

***

Susan contracted the AIDS virus through a transfusion of contaminated blood during a routine surgical procedure five years ago. She is a person who has an open mind and helps herself, given the tools. She is using *Immunizing, Imprint, Energy Walk, The Visit,* and *Focus 10 (Gateway)*, and tells that *Hemi-Sync* gives her necessary support to make her able to continue leading a normal life.

Hemi-Sync Exercises Related to Aids/HIV

Gateway
Gateway Experience

Hemi-Sync Series
The Positive Immunity Program

Human Plus Titles
Circulation
Immunizing
Imprint
Let Go

Lungs: Repair and Maintenance
(H+ Lungs: Repair and Maintenance works well for people with AIDS-related pneumonia.)
Off-Loading
Reset
Restorative Sleep
Tune-Up

Metamusic Titles
Cloudscapes
Inner Journey
Prisms
Sleeping Through the Rain
Transformation

Mind Food Titles
Energy Walk
Journey Through the T-Cells
The Visit

Allergies

Experiences Related to Allergies

This information has been reported to Monroe Products and The Monroe Institute by individuals and/or by professional practitioners about the use of Hemi-Sync.

For years I had regular headaches as a result of a sinus problem caused by allergies. Since using H+ *Tune-Up*, I haven't had one. At worst, there has been some general sinus discomfort, but this hasn't reached the level of pain. I have not used even an aspirin for pain since starting.

***

My allergy symptoms are less severe since I started using the method taught on *De-Tox: Body* and *Tune-Up* tapes. In just a few minutes, I can enhance my body's ability to discharge substances that normally cause a reaction. This is great, especially during the Spring and Fall allergy seasons.

***

The *Positive Immunity Program* has been very powerful and effective for a variety of ailments. I had been plagued with a "swimmers ear" type of infection, used the *FF-12* and *Patterning* concepts in the series, and saw dramatic results within 24 hours. I had also been taking prescription drugs for stomach pain and cramps for 3 years, and no longer use it, nor do I need the medication I had used for allergies. I attribute all of this to the *Positive Immunity Program.*

***

I've used *De-Tox: Body* to get rid of bothersome allergies which used to cause a constant runny nose in the Spring and Fall. The *Tune-Up* tape function command works well with both the *De-Tox: Body* and the *De-Discomfort* commands to get rid of allergies, headaches, and head cold problems.

Hemi-Sync Exercises Related to Allergies

Human Plus Titles
Circulation
De-Tox: Body
Lungs: Support & Maintenance
(Digital Download only)

Restorative Sleep
Tune-Up

Mind Food Titles
Energy Walk
Healing Journeys Support

Alzheimer's

Experiences Related to Alzheimer's

This information has been reported to Monroe Products and The Monroe Institute by individuals and/or by professional practitioners about the use of Hemi-Sync.

It began with my playing *Metamusic* tapes for the nursing home patients I met with in their rooms. The nurses liked what they were hearing and borrowed tapes from me. The area around the nurses' station was often noisy and hectic, crowded with anxious patients repeating demands that could not be satisfied. With *Metamusic* playing at the nurses' station, the whole atmosphere changed, becoming a place of calm and relaxation.

***

The patient spent long hours roaming the nursing home corridors, confused and anxious, not knowing where her room was. At mealtime she wouldn't stay at the table long enough to eat. The nurses were unable to get her to stay in one place. On one of her wanderings she fell, was badly bruised, and needed pain meds, though the nurses were reluctant to give her too much. I led her to her room and played *Sleeping Through the Rain* for her. She fell asleep, went to the dining room for dinner and ate a good meal. "The tape didn't do a bit of good," she complained to me. In the background, the nurse gave me a thumbs up sign.

***

My mother has Alzheimer's disease, does not speak, and did not respond in any noticeable way to people who visited her. Since we started playing *Metamusic* tapes for her we seem able to read expressions on her face.

Hemi-Sync Exercises Related to Alzheimer's

Metamusic Titles
Cloudscapes   Sleeping Through the Rain

Anger

Experiences Related to Anger

This information has been reported to Monroe Products and The Monroe Institute by individuals and/or by professional practitioners about the use of Hemi-Sync.

I cannot tell you what it means to me to be able to go inside with the help of the cassettes and slowly find my find way. I am learning more about balance. Huge bags of anger, revenge, hatred and resentments are slowly letting go. I am no longer afraid of getting stuck in a slow, downward spiral. All this has happened in such a short while of using *Hemi-Sync*.

***

Working with the *Discovery (Gateway)* tapes, I've been feeling generally more relaxed and more comfortable, as if I'm somehow "above" my usual bad feelings. There's a new sense of coming together with myself. Things can be going on all around me without my being disturbed. The first time I listened to the tapes, I was upset and angry at my partner. After the tape was over the anger just was no longer with me, and I was able to sincerely apologize for having been so snappy earlier.

Hemi-Sync Exercises Related to Anger

Heart-Sync Titles	**Human Plus Titles**	Off-Loading	**Mind Food Titles**
Transforming Life's Challenges	Attention	Relax	Deep 10 Relaxation
	De-Hab	Reset	Guide to Serenity
	Eight-Great		Surf
Hemi-Sync Series	Let-Go		Total Relaxation
Opening the Heart			

Anxiety

Experiences Related to Anxiety

This information has been reported to Monroe Products and The Monroe Institute by individuals and/or by professional practitioners about the use of Hemi-Sync.

My nursing home patient's panic disorder had been causing a great deal of somatic stomach pain, so much so that the nurses said her call light was almost constantly lit. She also had severe hearing loss. When I started playing *Pain Management* at her bedside she said, "Honey, I can't hear it."

"It doesn't matter," I told her, "just relax and I'll check back with you in ten minutes."

When I looked in on her, she was deeply asleep. Later on, waking from the best nap she had had in weeks, she said, "I didn't hear a thing but I feel wonderful."

***

Regular use of *Hemi-Sync* tapes trains patients with multiple anxiety related symptoms to achieve Alpha and Theta states easily. These states are useful in psychotherapy to inhibit the presence of anxiety. *Metamusic* tapes reduce the generalized anxiety level very quickly and qualitatively better than do psychotropic drugs. The most logical interpretation is that these tapes very definitely and quickly help the mind/body unity to return much closer to homeostasis, the ideal state of mental and physical equilibrium.

***

The 61-year-old woman was admitted to the hospital with severe emphysema, congestive heart failure, and depression. She was very anxious and struggling to breathe. Within 24 hours after I began using *Deep 10 Relaxation* with her, the staff was reporting a significant reduction in her anxiety level.

***

Report from a psychologist. The patient was experiencing intense anxiety about an upcoming MRI test, which involves the person remaining motionless inside a very cramped tube for hours as the machine takes pictures of the brain. Anesthesia cannot be used for this procedure. The medical team reported that no one who was even moderately claustrophobic had ever completed the MRI test. After three weeks of working with the H+ tapes *Relax*, *Let Go* and *Off-Loading* and the **Mind Food** tapes *Energy Walk* and *Morning Exercise*, the day for the MRI test came. She successfully entered into a very relaxed state and eventually went to sleep during the three-hour procedure.

***

A Clinical Psychologist reported on a patient whose extreme anxiety was causing her to resist the surgery that would relieve her extensive pain from cervical nerve damage. After following his recommendations to listen to *Metamusic* tapes continuously at home, she agreed to undergo the surgery on condition that the neurosurgeon permit her to listen to *Hemi-Sync* throughout the operation. The doctor complied, and she underwent the procedure without difficulty.

***

A college teacher reports on the use of *Hemi-Sync* in a variety of courses to allay anxiety, enhance cognitive learning and mental imagery, to promote creativity. All of these uses, he says, depend upon focusing attention. This is accomplished by *Hemi-Sync*'s auditory stimuli at frequencies which induce the brain into an appropriate state while simultaneously synchronizing the hemispheres to eliminate hemispheric rivalry.

***

The Department of Surgery at Columbia Presbyterian Hospital uses *Hemi-Sync* tapes in conjunction with other therapies to help patients heal more quickly and with less anxiety and pain.
My constant anxiety was very tough for me to live with. I was anxious about going out, anxious about staying home, anxious about going to sleep, anxious about not sleeping, anxious about everything. The tapes you recommended (*Relax*, *Sleeping Through the Rain*, *Let Go* and *Möbius West*) are helping me lead a more normal life. For the first time in a long while, I'm optimistic about the future.

Hemi-Sync Exercises Related to Anxiety

Human Plus Titles	**Metamusic Titles**	**Mind Food Titles**
Let Go	Sleeping Through the Rain	Deep 10 Relaxation
Möbius West		Energy Walk
Off-Loading		Morning Exercise
Relax		Pain Management
		Total Relaxation

Asthma

Experiences Related to Asthma

This information has been reported to Monroe Products and The Monroe Institute by individuals and/or by professional practitioners about the use of Hemi-Sync.

It's been interesting to note how *Hemi-Sync* helps families who have a child with asthma. Not only is an attack a scary event, but there's often a tension connected to anticipation of the next attack that might indeed stimulate the next attack. I've recommended to several such families that they keep *Hemi-Sync* playing at home day and night. *Remembrance* or *Concentration* during the day and any of the sleep tapes for nighttime use. This seems to have a cumulative effect over time, with the entire family calming down.

***

A psychologist reports using *Lungs: Support & Maintenance* with five asthmatic children and adults with excellent success. For example, one woman had difficulty climbing a short flight of stairs and was using her inhaler approximately six times per day. Within three weeks she was swimming a third of a mile daily and using her inhaler only twice per week. This gain remained consistent over a one-year period.

***

I've had a very bad asthmatic condition for years. After a co-worker told me how much *Lungs: Support & Maintenance* had helped another asthma sufferer, I began to listen to it each night when I went home from the office. After a few times I could actually feel my lungs and chest opening up. When I feel tightness in my chest at night, I just use the function command and get immediate relief.

***

Asthma has been a problem for me during most of my life. Since working with *Lungs: Support & Maintenance*, the attacks have lessened in number, and severity has decreased whenever I use the verbal cue of the tape. I've also noticed a gigantic improvement in my overall health.

Hemi-Sync Exercises Related to Asthma

Human Plus Titles	**Metamusic Titles**	**Mind Food Titles**
Lungs: Support & Maintenance	Remembrance	Concentration

Autism

Experiences Related to Autism

This information has been reported to Monroe Products and The Monroe Institute by individuals and/or by professional practitioners about the use of Hemi-Sync.

The two-year-old had limited eye contact, disliked touch, engaged in rocking and flapping his hands, was either fussy and irritable, or withdrawn into his internal world. After his first listening to a relaxed *Metamusic* tape, he accepted touch, initiated eye contact and smiling, and appeared to be calm and peaceful.

***

The results of introducing *Hemi-Sync* to children in a special education setting were incredible. *Hemi-Sync* seemed to stimulate cortical integration and whole-brain learning. One autistic child was able to sleep at night for the first time, with the *Surf* tape, which also improved the ability of an emotionally-impaired six-year-old to relate interpersonally.

***

As the years have passed, many of my earlier problems with Autism are gone, but it manifests in different ways now. I am often anxious and compulsive, feeling the need to check the doorknob or stove several times to make sure they are OK. I also had trouble sleeping. While at a local Autism Society meeting, I was introduced to *Sleeping Through the Rain* and *Inner Journey*. Since working with these tapes, my sleep is much better and I feel calmer, yet highly aware of everything during the day. I am more sensitive to sounds, am better able to solve problems, and come up with creative solutions. I also feel more optimistic, as though all things will really continue to work out for the best.

***

The combination of *Brain: Repair & Maintenance*, *Think Fast*, *Eight-Great*, *Möbius West* and *Options* has had a very powerful effect on the symptoms of my Autism. I am not picking at my fingers very much anymore and I am hardly making the tongue noises, either. I also use the *Gateway Experience* tapes. *Hemi-Sync* is by no means a cure for Autism, but it may be a way to help the individual tap into his or her brain's potential to facilitate growth and change, and so that treatments won't be necessary.

***

The therapist's videotape of a session with an autistic child illustrated dramatic change once *Hemi-Sync* was introduced into the environment. Early on, the child shrunk back with extreme defensive reactions. Contact was intolerable. After some moments of listening to *Metamusic* the child visibly relaxed and focused, and reached out to give the therapist a hug.

***

My eight-year-old daughter was having a very hard time both at home and at school. In terms of her ability to deal with sensory stimuli, she tested at a four-year-old level, and was constantly interacting with her environment. It was exhausting for her and for us. Since we learned about *Hemi-Sync* at an Autism Society Conference, we've been playing *Surf* and *Remembrance* for her during the day and *Sandman Suites (no longer available)* at night. The improvement is remarkable.

***

An orphanage in Rumania was home for our daughter's first 2 1/2 years. When we first saw her she was in a "cage," penned up with other children who were never held, never bathed, only given bottles. In the five years since we adopted her, we've made the rounds of every possible treatment and facility from sensory training to neuropsychiatric wards. Her behavior constantly shifted between super passive and super aggressive and back again. After learning about *Hemi-Sync* through a support group for parents of post- institutional children we bought *Surf, Midsummer Night, Sandman Suites (no longer available)*, and *Remembrance* and kept one of the tapes playing all the time. We saw immediate results and, over time, her behavior has evened out. It feels like a miracle.

***

All members of the group I am working with have children who, for one reason or another, are more difficult than "usual." Their children are all now listening to *Hemi-Sync* tapes with good results. One child, labeled "autistic," has been using tapes for about six weeks. Her cranial osteopath told her that the two halves of the brain are now working together when previously they were not.

***

Although some of the symptoms of Autism had been overcome through years of training, I was still anxious and compulsive, and had a great deal of difficulty sleeping. At an Autism Society workshop I heard my first *Hemi-Sync* tape, *Inner Journey*, and for the next few nights slept better than I had in a long time.

***

I was born with Congenital Rubella, and as a result, I have suffered with Autism. Cataract lenses were removed from my eyes, an open-heart valve was repaired, and nerve damage, resulting in deafness in my right ear is still present. Although many of my earlier problems with Autism are gone, it manifests itself in different ways now. I am often anxious and compulsive, feeling the need to check the stove or doorknob several times to insure things are OK. I also have a great deal of difficulty sleeping, due to my inability to discharge excess energy early enough in the evening. I often woke up tired and groggy as a result.

***

While speaking at a workshop for the local Autism Society office, a woman played a tape with beautiful music. When asked what it was, she showed me the *Hemi-Sync* tape, titled *Inner Journey*. I was given a copy, and for the next few nights, I slept better than I ever have. I've been using *Inner Journey* and *Sleeping Through the Rain* since, with remarkable results. I realize these tapes are helping me to obtain the most refreshing sleep I've ever experienced, with the added benefit of feeling less anxious during the day.

Hemi-Sync Exercises Related to Autism

Gateway
Gateway Experience

Human Plus Titles
Brain: Support
 and Maintenance
Eight-Great

Möbius West
Options
Think Fast

Metamusic Titles
Inner Journey

Midsummer Night
Remembrance
Sleeping Through the Rain

Mind Food Titles
Surf

Behavior Change

Experiences Related to Behavior Change

This information has been reported to Monroe Products and The Monroe Institute by individuals and/or by professional practitioners about the use of Hemi-Sync.

I cannot remember a time when I didn't bite or rip my fingernails. More often than not I would have a fingernail half off before I consciously realized what I was doing. If, with great effort, I managed to grow nails at all, it would not last long. After listening to *De-Hab* once I began to use the verbal cue every time I felt I was going to bite my nails. I saw immediate results: the desire to bite or rip my nails would go away. I continued to use the verbal cue for two or three weeks and, to my amazement, the desire to bite my finger nails went away. At the time of this writing, it has been about three and a half months since I used the verbal cue. I just don't feel the desire to bite my nails any more.

***

I gave *Remembrance* to friends who weren't dealing very well with the sudden, totally unanticipated need for them to raise their two grandchildren. The qualitative difference in their attitudes is remarkable. The glass is now half full instead of half empty, they are less fearful, they have been able to resolve some longstanding issues, and the grandparent with congestive heart failure has been experiencing fewer heart spasms since listening to *Hemi-Sync*.

***

H+ *Off-Loading* is a very versatile tape to "off load" just about anything. One forty-year old used it to help herself overcome a strong irritation with her husband's behavior and to lose twenty pounds. It worked so well that three weeks later she started using it to stop drinking and then to stop smoking. She achieved all of these desired goals in six weeks. She said that the H+ tape helped her to overcome inertia and fear associated with these personal problems.

***

I have long been terrified of public speaking. A major event occurred when my pastor at church asked me to give the homily and to sing a favorite song of mine for the congregation. I used the H+ *Speak Up* Function Command and was able to continue speaking smoothly, evenly, and easily. In the past, I wouldn't have had the courage or the words to accomplish this.

***

Throughout my life I avoided public speaking at all costs. The few times I had to speak, my voice would either crack noticeably or disappear altogether. *Hemi-Sync* helped me overcome this incapacitating fear in two ways. Musical meditation tapes enabled me to focus my attention on a lot of formerly unconscious material that was crippling me. I was eventually able to eliminate these self-defeating concepts. H+ *Speak Up* helped me re-program myself mentally so that I was not only able to speak clearly and smoothly but could also relax enough to do so from an expanded level of awareness. Most important is that I began to enjoy speaking to groups.

***

Changes seem to be subtle and tend to come in waves since I have been listening to *Hemi-Sync* tapes. I have noticed more emotional spontaneity. What I seem to be going through is a peeling away of encrusted patterns, some of which require that I view myself with a level of objectivity I haven't had before. It is no longer impossible for me to ignore emotional messages and just swallow my anger. I must express it, and this comes as a big surprise to me. I am surprised at all the emotions which have been buried underneath encrusted patterns for years.

***

My relative found herself in yet another abusive relationship. During the last few days as the relationship was coming to an end, she would wake to find her cassette player unplugged. She had been listening to *Deep 10 Relaxation* before going to sleep for several months, and he evidently felt threatened by the changes in her. A subtle "alignment" seemed to be taking place within her, and she was becoming clearer about herself and her goals for the first time in many years.

***

Since I started listening to the *Concentration* tape, I've been able to focus better on tasks and follow through with them, instead of procrastinating. Paperwork, writing, and finishing a project on time have become easier for me. What a great feeling! This change helps to keep the days from just passing by, and that gives me pleasure and a sense of accomplishment.

***

An orphanage in Rumania was home for our daughter's first 2 1/2 years. When we first saw her she was in a "cage," penned up with other children who were never held, never bathed, only given bottles. In the five years since we adopted her, we've made the rounds of every possible treatment and facility from sensory training to neuropsychiatric wards. Her behavior constantly shifted between super passive and super aggressive and back again. After learning about *Hemi-Sync* through a support group for parents of post- institutional children we bought *Surf, Midsummer Night, Sandman Suites (no longer available),* and *Remembrance* and kept one of the tapes playing all the time. We saw immediate results and, over time, her behavior has evened out. It feels like a miracle.

***

A consulting firm for financial industries features *Hemi-Sync* in a workshop on the psychology of successful trading in the stock and futures markets. With the help of *Hemi-Sync,* traders learn mental techniques to monitor their thoughts to determine if they are in states that are most conducive to giving themselves money. Traders learn to use H-PLUS *De-Hab* to neutralize dysfunctional thoughts.

***

In addition to the effects produced by the low-frequency binaural beat stimulation, the high level of participation required—mental focus, personal choice, and willingness to use the Function Command—makes the H-PLUS system so effective in helping people create desired change. Interestingly, most people who take the workshop have had very little exposure to information or concepts related to self-awareness or learning to change oneself through directed conscious effort. Despite this, virtually everyone's initial reaction to the H-PLUS tapes is overwhelmingly positive, regardless of how skeptical or uncomfortable they may have been at the first listening. It is clear that the tapes resonate with people at a very deep and fundamental level, regardless of whether they understand the dynamics at work.

***

I decided a long time ago that my distressing habit of procrastination was unbreakable. However I tried to counteract it, I continued to sabotage my life with postponing and delaying and avoiding things that were important for me to do. Then I heard about your *De-Hab* tape from a friend. The end of the story is that I've cleared up four months' worth of mail. Thanks for this invaluable tool.

***

When I started a new job that was going to have me giving presentations to upwards of 300 people, I was terrified. I had never before had to face up to my old fear of public speaking. I started using the H+ *Speak Up* tape while taking a presentations class that my company was giving. At that point it felt like a comfortable, helping hand, nothing dramatic. I did my first presentation to the class without collapsing in terror, but it was still VERY stressful. I continued listening to the tape, and then it was time for my second class presentation. My heart was racing, my palms were sweaty, and my mind said, "Tilt!" I began to repeat the Function Command over and over mentally. I felt a physical sensation in my brain that I could identify as the source of the fear. I mentally grabbed it with my "hand" and threw it out. Serenity. All systems returned to normal. I did my presentation with just a trace of nervousness, but it was very manageable.

***

I have always experienced a lag in my energy level in the afternoon. There's been a big change in this since I began using the *Recharge* tape to give myself a boost whenever I need to. My late afternoon productivity is much better than it used to be.

***

I am the type of person who likes to "ease" into the morning. That sometimes causes a struggle since I also have to be at work on time! Listening to *Remembrance* while I get ready for work has helped me to become more focused and prepared for the day ahead, and I no longer need that caffeine jolt to get moving.

***

I heard my colleague in the next office grumbling about the amount of paperwork to be done. I offered my cassette player and the *Remembrance* tape to see if it would make a difference. After about 45 minutes, I heard her exclaiming, but with more energy. She returned the player with the comment, "Better take this back. I began feeling more energetic, and actually found myself looking for more to do!"

***

I've been listening to the *Concentration* tape for a few weeks, and find I am able to focus more on tasks and follow through with them. These have included paperwork, writing an important letter and having the words flow, and finishing a project that has been dragging on for months. What a great feeling! It gives me pleasure and a sense of accomplishment.

***

The *Think Fast* function works more subtly than some of the other H+ functions. Using it is like giving extra spin to a wheel that is already spinning. I notice that I think now in a more organized way.

***

The counselor loaned *Cloudscapes* and *Remembrance* to a mother and daughter whose prolonged difficulties included the child's lying, stealing, bedtime tears, and other attention getting behavior. At their next appointment, two weeks later, the mother returned the tapes, saying "They didn't do any good." To the therapist's questions about the previously reported problems Mom responded that the crying, lying and stealing had stopped; her daughter had no problems at bedtime and was sleeping through the night. Midway through this litany the mother began to smile and said, "Oh, I see what you mean." Several months passed before there was a repetition of complaints about the child's behavior. After the counselor's probing uncovered that they'd discontinued the tapes for several weeks. *Portraits (no longer available)* for sleep and *Remembrance* for starting out each morning were recommended. Things smoothed out within a week after tape use resumed.

***

The first time I listened to *De-Hab* it felt as if I were floating, gently swaying back and forth, like on a water bed. I felt tranquil, peaceful, and more relaxed than I have been in several years. After listening four times the happiness, peace and relaxation is even deeper. I find myself more assertive, and yet even more in harmony with those around me. Also, my smoking habit is way down.

***

I've been listening to the *Concentration* tape for a few weeks, and find I am able to focus more on tasks and follow through with them. These have included paperwork, writing an important letter and having the words flow, and finishing a project that has been dragging on for months. What a great feeling! It gives me pleasure and a sense of accomplishment.

Hemi-Sync Exercises Related to Behavior Change

Hemi-Sync Series
Opening the Heart Series
Positively Ageless

Heart-Sync Titles
Partners Meditation
Transforming Life's Challenges
Your Heart's Song

Human Plus Titles
Attention
De-Hab
Do This Now
Eat/No Eat
Eight-Great
Let-Go
Möbius West

Nutricia
Off-Loading
Option Relax
Restorative Sleep
Sex Drive
Speak Up
Think Fast

Metamusic Titles
Cloudscapes
Concentration
Einstein's Dream
Energy Walk
Midsummer Night
Morning Exercise
Opening the Heart
Portraits
Remembrance

Mind Food Titles

Deep 10 Relaxation
Emerging from Depression and Anxiety
Energy Walk
Freedom from Smoking

Breaking Free from Addictions
Claiming Your Self
Creating Success

Guide to Serenity
Manifesting
Morning Exercise
Partners Meditation

Resonant Tuning
Surf
Total Relaxation
Weight Loss

Blood Pressure

Experiences Related to Blood Pressure

This information has been reported to Monroe Products and The Monroe Institute by individuals and/or by professional practitioners about the use of Hemi-Sync.

I have worked tapes since the mid-eighties, and have benefited in a number of ways. I have successfully controlled stress and flare-ups of hypertension so successfully that I have been taken off medication to control blood pressure.

***

I suffer from a heart condition which brings about sudden changes of blood pressure. There's been a distinct difference since I started listening to H+ *Circulation* and *Heart: Support & Maintenance*—markedly fewer changes in pressure, and when there is a change, it's more moderate.

Hemi-Sync Exercises Related to Blood Pressure

Human Plus Titles
Circulation
Heart: Support & Maintenance
Hypertension

Relax
Tune-Up

Heart-Sync Titles
Transforming Life's Challenges

Mind Food Titles
Deep 10 Relaxation
Restorative Sleep
Total Relaxation

Brain Injury

Experiences Related to Brain Injury (Closed Head Trauma)

This information has been reported to Monroe Products and The Monroe Institute by individuals and/or by professional practitioners about the use of Hemi-Sync.

Travis, born with severe brain abnormalities, was expected to live in a vegetative state if he survived at all. By age four, receiving every kind of support the medical profession had to give including physical, occupational and speech therapy, he was unable to walk, talk, feed himself, or communicate his needs or wants. His mother began to play *Remembrance* at his bedside throughout the night. After a few days, his father noticed how much more alert and active Travis was becoming. Within two weeks of consistent playing of the tape, Travis began to feed himself.

Shortly after, the therapists at the day center Travis attends asked his parents what they were doing differently to account for the marked improvement they were noticing. When the physical therapist learned about the tape, she said she had long known about *Hemi-Sync* technology. She had repeatedly recommended that parents use *Hemi-Sync* with their brain injured children but stopped trying after countless failed efforts to convince the families that something so simple could have so much potential value.

Within weeks Travis' mother told me, "He's talking, and I don't mean baby talk! He's telling us what he wants to eat. He stayed with his grandparents while my husband and I went on vacation and when we returned could clearly call their names. A woman at the mall held the door for me as I maneuvered Travis inside in his stroller. I thanked her and then Travis echoed my words and said to the woman, "Thank you." Now when I tell him we're going to day care, he replies, "Yeah, OK."

Further breakthroughs come often now for Travis. He sings his favorite songs, can pull himself up to a standing position and holds onto furniture, much like a child who is about the gain the skill of balance and walking. *Hemi-Sync* has facilitated a life rich in communication with family and friends and the pride of doing more for himself than anyone thought would ever be possible.

***

After a fall which resulted in brain injury, I was physically weak, emotionally demoralized, out of balance, and mentally insecure. After some difficult years I learned about *Hemi-Sync* and began to notice results after listening to H+ *Brain: Support & Maintenance* about four times. They were very subtle, but concrete. The more I used the Function Command, the easier it became to express myself both orally and in writing, and the more my vision improved. I use the Function Command several times each day, beginning in the shower each morning and ending as I go to sleep at night. As I use it, I feel as if a veil is being slowly but gently lifted from my mind. I also use H+ *Synchronizing* and *Circulation*, and the *Resonant Tuning* tape. They seem to have a cumulative effect.

***

For some years I have had a jerk-like tremor in my head due to a "minor" head injury. I could feel it at the top of the brain stem just below the skull. Sometimes at night it would keep me awake because of the feeling of tension which would build up and then release in a jerk. After several months of using the tape *Brain: Support & Maintenance*, and later adding the tape called *Energy Walk*, the tremor is almost non-existent.

***

They were doing patterning for a small child whose central nervous system had been affected from a brain injury. I told the mother that *Metamusic* tapes might be helpful. She called to let us know that the tapes were helping her child to relax and enjoy the physical patterning exercises. She indicated that when the tape stopped, the child would tense up and stop making any sounds. As soon as they started the tape again, the child would relax and make happy sounds.

***

In January 1984, I was involved in an automobile accident. Although the car was "totaled," I was released from the hospital after only a quick examination. There were no broken bones, lacerations, or loss of consciousness. My symptoms of concussion were dismissed.

During the next six years I experienced different kinds of mental dysfunction and disability, and then started using *Hemi-Sync* tapes from the *Human Plus* series. My support group began noticing changes. They said, "In the last two or three weeks, you've been so much brighter. You've had more energy. You've been so much quicker. Why, you're making jokes left and right." When I told a joke at work one day, a co-worker said, "Don't tell me you're brain damaged if you can make a remark that fast." Back at my desk, I realized that I'd been using the *Human Plus* tape *Brain: Support & Maintenance*, and obviously it was working. At that point, I contacted The Monroe Institute to tell them how effective their tapes were in my healing process.

The people who had noticed the difference in me didn't know about the tapes. They were remarking on my brightness and quickness. Until others noticed the changes, I hadn't realized that I was improving. When it was brought to my attention, I asked myself, "What's different?" The only difference was listening to the tape every night. I was sleeping better, things were going more smoothly, and I experienced various breakthroughs. At times I'd think, "Oh, I'm handling this much better now. I'm doing this easier now." It wasn't a case of listening to the tape one day and the next day saying, "Oh, I listened to the tape last night and now look how good I am." It was an ongoing process rather than a dramatic, overnight change.

The *Hemi-Sync* tapes have definitely helped in retraining my brain and recovering lost abilities to concentrate and think clearly. By practicing intensely, I've recovered my gift of music, lost at the time of the accident. Like others in recovery, I work on healing each day, one day at a time.

***

After an auto accident left me with brain injury, I stopped reading because I could no longer follow a train of thought. I discovered *Hemi-Sync*, have gone back to school, and am doing very well. *Remembrance* helps me with my studies, and *Sleeping Through the Rain* helps me rest at night.

***

He was having memory loss and anxiety after being beaten over the head during a robbery. I was amazed at the changes over a two-month period of listening to *Hemi-Sync Metamusic* tapes. His attitude became more positive and less anxious, his writing skills became more lucid, and his nonverbal communication normalized.

Hemi-Sync Exercises Related to Brain Injury

Human Plus Titles	**Metamusic Titles**	**Mind Food Titles**
Brain: Support & Maintenance	Remembrance	Energy Walk
Circulation	Sleeping Through the Rain	Resonant Tuning
Synchronizing		

Breathing

Experiences Related to Breathing

This information has been reported to Monroe Products and The Monroe Institute by individuals and/or by professional practitioners about the use of Hemi-Sync.

(See also: Experiences Relating to Cancer, Dental Pain, Pain Management, and Stress.)

Although nervousness and restlessness were her frequent complaints, she lay quietly after listening to the *Surf* tape, finally opening her eyes and saying, "I'm too relaxed to move." She also was delighted with the tape *Energy Walk* and said, "I played the tape twice today and it quieted my nerves. Not only does it help and relax me, I feel that something is happening in my body, and I know it is doing something for me. I played it again today and counted my breathing with my hand over the cancer. It makes me feel all over better and relaxed. I went off to sleep."

***

Some form of stress management was indicated. I persuaded the patient to use headphones and listen to the *Hemi-Sync* tape *Sleeping Through the Rain.* I told him that the latest research from major hospitals and universities finds that hypnosis, certain relaxation techniques, and even special types of musical tapes greatly help people relax and regulate breathing and blood pressure. He seemed fascinated and very receptive to this. Apparently the idea of hypnosis and relaxation techniques was all new to him.

Within just a few minutes of listening to the tape, the patient's breathing slowed and became clearer. His face relaxed and the familiar wheezing and gurgling sounds stopped. He also quit coughing, which made treatment much easier.

***

Three of the seven children in this group showed minimal gains in improving their attentional focus and reducing hyperactivity. Each of these children had a history of severe respiratory disorder. This varied from structural lung disorders related to prematurity to severe respiratory incoordination with irregular breathing and breath-holding. One child was on a portable oxygen unit. As a group, these children were unresponsive to Hemi-Sync. On days when the breathing was less stressful two children were able to respond with greater attention and less hyperactivity.

One child who eventually showed major gains in focusing attention was initially highly inconsistent in his initial response to *Hemi-Sync.* Because there was no negative reaction and the music assisted the therapist in meeting his needs in a more creative fashion, *Hemi-Sync* music was continued as a background to therapy.

Over a three-month period (24 sessions) a change was observed in his breathing patterns. As the breathing became more regular and breath-holding incidents reduced, his attentional response to *Hemi-Sync* improved and he showed a consistently positive response to his therapy sessions. This was particularly significant since the no measurable gains had been seen in therapy for 9 months. It is possible that the other children with respiratory problems would also have profited from a longer trial. (Open Ear, 2, pp. 14-17, 1996 *Music and Hemi-Sync in The Treatment of Children with Developmental Disabilities.*)

Hemi-Sync Exercises Related to Breathing

Human Plus Titles
Lungs: Support & Maintenance
(Digital Download only)

Restorative Sleep
Tune-Up

Mind Food Titles
Resonant Tuning

Cancer Support

Experiences Related to Cancer Support

This information has been reported to Monroe Products and The Monroe Institute by individuals and/or by professional practitioners about the use of Hemi-Sync.

(See also: Experiences Relating to Pain Management.)

The scheduled doses of morphine were no longer controlling the pain of his terminal cancer. When the doctor started continual morphine drips, it was hard to know if he was sleeping or not because even when awake, he wasn't really here. His wife played the *Pain Management* tape and he very soon fell into a deep sleep with his abdomen breathing rhythmically. In the morning he was much more alert and asked for more tapes. *Energy Walk* was his favorite. The following day he was even more alert and asked the doctor to remove the morphine drips. He passed away peacefully this morning.

***

Report from psychologist. The patient's cancer continues to spread and he has been in considerable pain. He had been taking large amounts of medication:125 mg of Tegretol three times a day, 12-15 cc a day of Dilantin, Darvocet every four hours, and Zantec. He had also been taking 11cc of Methadone four times a day and this was recently changed to morphine. Despite all the medication, his pain was poorly controlled.

I introduced him to the *Hemi-Sync Pain Management* tape to use at home, and he finds it helps reduce pain between medications. After only four sessions, he is now seeing me on an "as needed" basis. The *Pain Management* tape has furnished the backbone of his treatment program.

***

My husband was diagnosed as being in Stage III of testicle cancer. Surgery would kill him, we were told. Chemo was the only hope and, even with that, his chances of survival would be 30%. Throughout four months of chemotherapy I watched him lose his hair, lose weight, be violently ill from the side effects.

The mass was reduced in size, though still huge in terms of medical safety. His doctors advised surgery even though there was very high risk that his lungs were now too weakened by chemotherapy drugs to withstand anesthesia for a ten-hour operation. We started using the *Surgical Support Series* days before the surgery, and consulted (and educated) the anesthesiologist about using the tapes during the operation.

The ten-hour operation took four hours. The surgeons were able to remove the tumor mass intact and no live cancer cells were found.

***

Report from a social worker. A 72-year-old widow with cancer was admitted to Hospice, and asked for a relaxation tape because, "I've never been a nervous person, but I've been climbing the walls since the chemotherapy." The *Hemi-Sync* tape *Deep 10 Relaxation* was left with her. The following week she reported, "I haven't been taking as many pills since I began listening to the tape. I had been taking one pill every four hours or less. Yesterday, I only took one pill all day. I know the tape is helping me." She also reported improved sleep.

***

Although nervousness and restlessness were her frequent complaints, she lay quietly after listening to the *Surf* tape, finally opening her eyes and saying, "I'm too relaxed to move." She also was delighted with the tape *Energy Walk* and said, "I played the tape twice today and it quieted my nerves. Not only does it help and relax me, I feel that something is happening in my body, and I know it is doing something for me. I played it again today and counted my breathing with my and over the cancer. It makes me feel all over better and relaxed. I went off to sleep."

***

My friend's whole body system had broken down in the last days of his terminal cancer. The continual morphine drips were not keeping him comfortable and he was "gone," not really with us even when he was awake. Very soon after we started playing the *Pain Management* tape in his hospital room, he fell into very deep sleep with his abdomen breathing rhythmically. He didn't wake till morning, was much more alert than the day before, and asked to listen to the tape again.

***

Her doctors said she would be in the hospital for at least two weeks after her surgery for cancer. She was released in three days. Doctors were shocked at how quickly she had recovered. The tapes she had with her were *Energy Walk*, *Deep 10 Relaxation*, *Surf*, and *Pain Management*.

***

My brother was diagnosed with esophageal cancer. In a desperate effort to save his life, I called upon the *Hemi-Sync* process. As he listened to the taped exercises I saw how he welcomed this intensive exposure to mind expansion. Although the final battle was lost, there were triumphs on the way. After more than 300 hours of highly toxic chemotherapy, my brother did not lose his hair, as the doctors predicted he would. He maintained his mental and physical stamina through 18 sessions of radiation. Six weeks before he died his physical strength began to wane, and he was virtually pain-free until three days before his death. It was only during his final hours, when his body chemistry was out of balance, that his mental power was unable to overcome the pain.

***

The tapes (*Surgical Support Series*) have been used with a number of gastrointestinal oncology patients at The Cancer Institute, and we've found them to be enormously helpful in the preparation of these patients prior to surgery (frequently 12-18 hours in the operating room) and in the follow-up period during the extended hospital stay (sometimes 4-6 weeks). Patients often experience a significant reduction in intra-operative blood loss, fewer post-surgical complications, greater sense of mastery over pain and discomfort, and frequently a reduced length of stay.

***

A therapist reports on her experience with cancer patients: "The *Surgical Support Series* is quite good. The *Pre-Op* and *Intra-Op* tapes are very helpful to use during infusion and right after chemo treatments, as they reduce the ill feeling and aid in the normalization process. *Metamusic* tapes are also very helpful for creating a sense of well-being, especially the tape called *Inner Journey*."

***

Recently a friend was diagnosed with breast cancer and I ordered your *Surgical Support Series* for her use. She was very impressed by the help the tapes provided in the areas of pain and stress reduction.

***

An M.D. reports on the experience of a fifty-six-year-old, terminally ill woman with metastatic breast cancer. She was aware of having only a short time to live and chose to be at home with hospice support and her family. She was having more and more frequent "foggy periods" and was barely arousable when the doctor played *Touring the Interstate* from the *Going Home Package* at her bedside. She became very relaxed and slack as the Focus levels increased to 27. Returning, she stirred actively at *Focus 15*, then fully awoke back at *C-1*, smiled, and drifted off to sleep. She died several days later after listening to both exercises on the tape more times. Her husband had played the *Relocation Theme* at her death. As he sat holding her hand during this, he clearly and deeply felt her lift off—and his sense of burden go at the same time. A month later he feels very much at peace, with a sense of completion.

***

About a patient whose cancer had recurred and metastasized, the doctor said, "She listened to *Hemi-Sync* tapes (*Metamusic*, *Gateway Experience*, and *Going Home*) while undergoing five courses of chemotherapy. Everyone who knows her, including myself, has been impressed with her level of inner peace, her ability to be "in the moment" and take delight in small pleasures. Other feelings are there too—anger and fear—but they don't overshadow the joy and peace."

Hemi-Sync Exercises Related to Cancer Support

Gateway
Gateway Experience

Heart-Sync Titles
Transforming Life's Challenges

Hemi-Sync Series
Cancer Support Series
Going Home
Positive Immunity Program
Surgical Support Series

Human Plus Titles
De-Discomfort
Immunizing
Relax
Restorative Sleep
Tune-Up

Metamusic Titles
Dreamland
Hemi-Sync Support for Healing
Inner Journey
Seaside Slumber
Sleeping Through the Rain
The Music of Graceful Passages

Mind Food Titles
Chemotherapy Companion
Deep 10 Relaxation
Energy Walk
Healing Journeys Support
Journey Through The T-Cells
Pain Management
Radiation Companion
Surf
Total Relaxation

Children

Experiences Related to Children

This information has been reported to Monroe Products and The Monroe Institute by individuals and/or by professional practitioners about the use of Hemi-Sync.

After my child spent a period of weeks listening to *Metamusic* tapes while falling asleep, her preschool teacher said to me, "I am amazed at her attention span, her ability to listen to and follow directions, her desire to do what pleases, and the effort she is willing to expend to master activities that are hard or challenging for her."

***

I give piano lessons to a seven-year-old girl and was training her to play scales with a metronome. For several weeks she was able to play at 126 beats per minute (bpm). This week I played the *Concentration* tape through speakers during the lesson. We started the metronome at 126 bpm and speeded it up gradually. She was able to play at 160 bpm. Hey, that's great!

***

Your children's sleep tapes have changed bedtime from an ordeal that used to last all evening long to a peaceful, happy routine.

***

My 2 1/2-year-old granddaughter asks that I keep playing *Cloudscapes* over and over throughout her visits. She listens for the 'ting, ting, ting' near the end of the piece and we imagine together that our fairy godmother is touching us with her magic wand and drenching us with love.

***

A three-year-old boy I'd been treating in play therapy for several months had finally been asked to leave his daycare because of his sporadic, violent behavior. In our regular session, after asking him if he'd like to hear some special music, I gave him headphones and played *Remembrance*. While listening, he became very calm, his eyes widened, and he smiled vibrantly. He turned to his mother and said, "Listen, Mommy—it's the angels!"

Hemi-Sync Exercises Related to Children

Metamusic Titles
Baroque Garden
Breakthrough
Cloudscapes
Dreamland
Einstein's Dream
Guitarra Clásica
Illumination

Lullaby
Seaside Slumber
Seasons at Roberts
Mountain
Sleeping Through the
Rain

Mind Food Titles
A Unicorn Named
Georgia
Angels, Fairies and
Wizards
Concentration
Healing the Inner Child
Indigo
Joy Jumper
Lightfall
Milton's Secret

Remembrance
Robbie The Rabbit
Sleep Deeply
Sleepy Locust
Soft & Still
Super Sleep
Surf
Turtle Island

Circulation

Experiences Related to Circulation

This information has been reported to Monroe Products and The Monroe Institute by individuals and/or by professional practitioners about the use of Hemi-Sync.

For five years, I suffered with edema in my left foot, which failed to respond to treatment. When I first started using the *HUMAN PLUS* (H+) Program *Circulation* tape, the swelling reduced almost immediately and now, after frequent use over the past three years, it seldom swells at all.

***

H+ *Circulation* relieved a lifetime problem of unnaturally cold hands and feet, which meant that I had to sleep under a heavy weight of blankets. Within two months of using the tape this condition ceased to trouble me.

***

A patient whose hands always felt cold due to poor circulation used the H+ *Circulation* tape. A bioExperiences machine indicated a very quick raise in temperature at a fingertip sensor from 32 to 37 degrees centigrade.

***

Because of poor circulation, I always felt colder than anybody else, and was especially bothered by icy hands and feet. *Resonant Tuning* gives me an increase in heat throughout my body, as well as a tremendous rush of energy.

Hemi-Sync Exercises Related to Circulation

Human Plus Titles
Circulation

The Classroom

Experiences Related to The Classroom

This information has been reported to Monroe Products and The Monroe Institute by individuals and/or by professional practitioners about the use of Hemi-Sync.

Several of my colleagues and I keep *Concentration* and *Remembrance* playing constantly all day long in the classroom. We've found a definite improvement in the students' ability to stay on task. The difference is especially noticeable in those who have poor impulse control, which often gets them in trouble. It's rewarding to see the rise in their self-esteem that accompanies better performance.

***

Since I began playing nonverbal *Hemi-Sync* tapes in my classroom (*Concentration* and *Metamusic*) I've observed significant improvement in my attitude as well as in that of my students. The work climate is calmer and more conducive to learning, which has allowed me to pick up the pace of lessons.

***

A 4th grade teacher reported at the end of the first day of using *Hemi-Sync* in the classroom. "This day went quite well and at 2:30, my usual time to feel 'done in,' I didn't feel so tired. In fact, I felt great when the day ended. Several days later a student came up to me and said, "Can you turn that stuff on again while we do our math? It makes me feel good!" Another said, "When I came in I felt uptight, nothing had gone right. But I feel better now."

***

A teacher with grade 6, 7, 8 special education students describes her experiences playing as background. "All the students sat down in their seats and began the assigned work much sooner than usual. They were very involved in their assignment. When talking did occur, it concerned the math assignment. Whenever a disruption occurred, they immediately returned to being on task. The students behaved and responded in a more relaxed manner than usual; there was much greater involvement with the academic work. Cooperativeness prevailed!" Of the last class of the day, which is usually rowdy and restless, she said, "The atmosphere was more mellow; the behavior-disordered students were more quiet and calm."

***

A 3rd grade teacher reports after playing *Hemi-Sync* in the classroom, "Nine out of 22 students handed in spelling tests with zero or one error and all others accomplished As or Bs. This is the best performance of the year!"

***

A high school physical education teacher reports on the use of *Metamusic*, "Some of the students were closing their eyes and getting into their weight lifting. At the same time, their technique while lifting was superb. Generally they tend to get sloppy while lifting, and I believe the music helped them concentrate and perform better. Their overall attentiveness greatly improved and the actual rotating went more smoothly than ever before. Students behaved with confidence and didn't need to ask where the next station was."

***

A college teacher reports on the use of *Hemi-Sync* in a variety of courses to enhance cognitive learning and mental imagery, to promote creativity, and to allay anxiety. All of these uses, he says, depend upon focusing attention. This is accomplished by *Hemi-Sync*'s auditory stimuli at frequencies which induce the brain into an appropriate state while simultaneously synchronizing the hemispheres to eliminate hemispheric rivalry. Results of a carefully controlled assessment of cognitive learning indicated that students using *Hemi-Sync* consistently scored an average of 10 points higher on six different tests. Additionally, students volunteered such statements as, "My whole day seems brighter," "I feel good about myself and my studies," "For the first time in my life I really enjoy school," "My mind seems to be clearer and I understand things better."

***

A teacher of creative writing used *Metamusic* in a classroom experiment. "Listening to the music helped some who did not normally feel comfortable writing to get going with considerable enthusiasm. There was a great range of images and a keen sense of involvement which expressed itself in metaphor."

***

During lecture and discussion in an evening college class, the *Concentration* tape was played over stereo speakers separated by approximately 16 feet. Results: marked attention to the subject, excellent rapport between speaker and class and among class members, minimal body movements, good eye contact, relaxed postures and voice tones, warm interactions as class members lingered excessively (30 minutes) after class. Several class members first noticed art works which had been in the room for more than a year.

***

I have been teaching perception and the ability to draw realistically for five years. A year ago I began using *Metamusic* tapes and the *Surf* tape to help my students achieve a right hemisphere shift. I use two speakers on opposite sides of the art room.

Students report that they 'feel' a difference when the *Hemi-Sync* tapes are played. I hear fewer 'sighs' caused by left hemisphere resistance, and I see the children able to focus more easily on their task. They seem to prefer *Surf*, and ask for it if I neglect to put it on right away. Many students have said, 'I draw better with *Surf*,' and a few actually ordered tapes for their use at home.

The culmination of the drawing classes is realistic portraits which use shadow and value. Last year, the first year I used *Hemi-Sync,* the portraits were more sensitively and accurately rendered than those of previous years. Many faculty members told me, `This year's portraits are better than ever.' Was it *Hemi-Sync* that made the difference? I'm sure of it!"

***

Metamusic tapes were used in a creative writing experiment with children from 11 - 16 as follows: a) 15 minutes of listening without writing, during which the students were invited to let their minds range freely; b) 15 minutes of discussion and sharing of ideas and images from the preceding listening period; c) a 30-minute writing session, with the tape playing throughout.
The experiment was well-received by the students, and some who did not normally feel comfortable with creative writing got going with considerable enthusiasm. There was a great range of images with certain recurring themes: sea, flying, falling without fear.

All students described a detachment from the perceived experience, e.g., falling endlessly without anxiety. This detachment was contrasted sharply with a sense of keen involvement in the writing, a sense of involvement which came out in metaphor and transitions built upon each other to a higher degree than usual in creative writing lessons.

***

The Department of Instructional Resources gave a recommended rating to the *PAL Student Package (Progressive Accelerated Learning)* for use in its school system. It was deemed suitable for grade levels 9 through 13 and continuing education.

***

I am an art therapist in a school for children with severe learning disabilities, and have been using the *Metamusic* tapes. Most students work contentedly and don't comment on the music. An 11-year-old autistic child at first sat with his hand in front of his face. Then his hand gradually came down and he became attentive, with much more eye contact than usual. After 30 minutes he didn't want to leave, and pointed at the tape player. A 15-year-old brain-damaged girl with little speech listened for a few minutes, then said, "What's that?" I turned off the tape player. She said, "More." I turned it back on and she sat quietly and painted for 15 minutes—a long time for her.

***

My students are learning disabled, socially and emotionally maladjusted, including multiple impairments (speech and sight), inner-city Latino with very limited use of English. In spite of these conditions, they responded very well to the *Hemi-Sync* tapes *Relax* and *Attention* through an entire school year. I alternated between the tapes, playing them first thing in the morning on a daily basis, listening to both the *Prep* and *Function* sides initially, then using only the function reinforcement. We had a designated listening area with the children laying on the floor on an area rug. They positioned themselves between the detachable speakers of my portable tape player to facilitate the hemispheric synchronization process. As the children became familiar with the tapes, they had the option of requesting individual listening time using headphones. Although this was not a controlled experimental environment, the results have been noticeable.

a) The children acquired a marked increase in self-control, initiating the necessary Functions with the situation so required, most of the time on their own initiative. This became more and more firmly established as the year progressed.
b) They gravitated to self-initiated reinforcements, requesting individual use of the tapes, whenever they perceived the need in order to avoid disruptions and/or to release tensions or stress.
c) Their learning capabilities were enhanced in as much as they could progressively engage more of their attention in a more focused way to the tasks at hand.
d) The social interactions markedly improved simply because they now had an available mechanism to deactivate hostile or reactive behavior. It seems that the tapes gave them that critical time or gap, an instant of suspension of the previously learned reaction to a given situation that under other circumstances would have created disruption. Instead, they would take a deep breath, trigger the relaxation response, and more on to more productive activity. In summary, the learning environment improved dramatically and the children now own a skill that will be theirs for life.

***

The results of introducing *Hemi-Sync* to children in a special education setting were incredible. *Hemi-Sync* seemed to stimulate cortical integration and whole-brain learning. One autistic child was able to sleep at night for the first time, with the *Surf* tape, which also improved the ability of an emotionally-impaired six-year-old to relate interpersonally.

***

A teacher reports: I began using *Hemi-Sync* played through stereo speakers for my split level first/second grade class, and was soon enjoying the benefits of a highly functional and creative classroom. The following year, *Hemi-Sync* was introduced into three other classrooms. All the teachers experienced immediate benefits of a quieter environment, increased productivity, and fewer disruptions.

***

My colleague who teaches learning disabled kids was delighted with the calming effect of *Sleeping Through the Rain* and *Inner Journey* on her class. She said that they didn't seem to be noticing it at all until it ended, when they looked a bit surprised and not sure what had happened.

***

A preschool teacher says, "School hours were especially trying with a difficult group of hyperactive children. The classroom was always chaotic, and I hadn't been able to get the children down for a nap all year. I was totally frustrated, unable to do what I was trained to do. The first time I played a tape from *Sandman Suites (no longer available)* at nap-time the children settled down almost immediately. It was like a miracle. I play different *Metamusic* tapes now as background for various activities, and find a completely different level of comfort in the room. Obviously, it's good for the children. And I know it's great for me."

Hemi-Sync Exercises Related to The Classroom

Hemi-Sync Series
PAL Student Package

Human Plus Titles
Attention
Relax

Metamusic Titles
Inner Journey
Portraits
Remembrance
Sleeping Through the Rain

Mind Food Titles
Concentration
Surf

Creativity

Experiences Related to Creativity

This information has been reported to Monroe Products and The Monroe Institute by individuals and/or by professional practitioners about the use of Hemi-Sync.

A pilot study to investigate the impact of *Hemi-Sync* on creative responses and divergent thinking used two tapes. *Deep 10 Relaxation* was played for the *Hemi-Sync* group to induce deep physical and mental relaxation, followed by *Surf* (ocean sounds with no verbal instructions). The control group listened to the same tapes, but without the *Hemi-Sync* tones. According to the *Guilford and Doodles Tests of Creativity*, the *Hemi-Sync* group demonstrated significantly increased creativity and divergent thinking.

***

An artist reports. Before I pick up my paint brush, I sit quietly for a few moments with my eyes closed and listen to Higher, *Cloudscapes*, or *Sleeping Through the Rain*. I begin to paint with the *Metamusic* still playing, allowing the sounds to flow through me. With no preconceived ideas about what I'm going to put on paper, my paintings are full of movement with vibrant colors and shapes. It feels as if the *Hemi-Sync* enables me to tap into deeper than usual sources of creativity and energy that comes through me and is expressed on paper. When other people look at paintings I've done with and without *Hemi-Sync,* they easily identify the qualitative difference that *Metamusic* makes.

***

A teacher of creative writing used *Metamusic* in a classroom experiment. "Listening to the music helped some who did not normally feel comfortable writing to get going with considerable enthusiasm. There was a great range of images and a keen sense of involvement which expressed itself in metaphor."

***

I write music and have been very successfully using *Contemplation* to tap into higher levels of creativity. It's so easy, when I'm working out something new on the piano, to just say the Function Command. It feels like I'm being lifted into a different space where I can think of new approaches to what I'm doing.

***

I'm been giving workshops on developing creativity for many years and just recently started playing your musical *Hemi-Sync* tapes as background to the various exercises I give my students. I'm noticing a difference in responsiveness, in spontaneity, and in results, and the workshop participants really enjoy the music. If I forget to start the music when people are ready to begin the next exercise, they miss it and remind me.

***

Part way through the book I've been writing, a friend did me the big favor of introducing me to Hemi-Sync. I start a work session with the function commands for *Relax* and *Attention* to help me get into the mood. *Remembrance* is my favorite tape to play when I'm sitting at the computer. Ideas flow quickly and words come easily. Less re-writing is necessary now, because I'm more often pleased with the first way I say things. It's as if *Hemi-Sync* helps my brain operate in high gear.

Hemi-Sync Exercises Related to Creativity

Hemi-Sync Series
The Creative Way

Human Plus Titles
Attention
Contemplation
Eight-Great
Options
Relax
Think Fast

LightSOURCE Arts
Blossoming Lotus

Metamusic Titles
Baroque Garden
Breakthrough for Peak-Performance
Cloudscapes
Egyptian Sun
Einstein's Dream
Emergence
Gaia
Guitarra Clásica
Illumination

Indigo
Midsummer Night
Oasis
Prisms
Remembrance
Revelations
Sacred Realms
Seasons at Roberts
Mountain
Streamhaven
The Maze

Mind Food Titles
Concentration
Creating Success
Deep 10 Relaxation
Exploring Our
Future
Morning Exercise
Soft & Still
Surf
The Visit
Total Relaxation

Cystic Fibrosis

Experiences Related to Cystic Fibrosis

This information has been reported to Monroe Products and The Monroe Institute by individuals and/or by professional practitioners about the use of Hemi-Sync.

(See also: Experiences Relating to The Immune System.)

The drug for cystic fibrosis that seven-year-old Danny has been taking since birth brings on diabetic symptoms and cysts on the lung. During one of his frequent hospital stays, unable to get enough air, he started gasping. The nurse played *Lungs: Support & Maintenance*, left at the bedside by Danny's mother. Her young patient began to breath more and more normally, settled back, and relaxed.

***

At home, Danny likes to have musical *Hemi-Sync* playing when he's in bed. His mother keeps the volume very low, almost inaudible, and when Danny falls asleep, she turns off the sound. More often than not, Danny drowsily tells her, "Don't turn it off, it helps me breathe."

Hemi-Sync Exercises Related to Cystic Fibrosis

Human Plus Titles
Lungs: Support & Maintenance *(Digital Download only)*

Death and Dying

Experiences Related to Death and Dying

This information has been reported to Monroe Products and The Monroe Institute by individuals and/or by professional practitioners about the use of Hemi-Sync.

An M.D. reports on the experience of a fifty-six-year-old, terminally ill woman with metastatic breast cancer. She was aware of having only a short time to live and chose to be at home with hospice support and her family. She was having more and more frequent "foggy periods" and was barely arousable when the doctor played Touring the Interstate from the *Going Home Package* at her bedside. She became very relaxed and slack as the Focus levels increased to 27. Returning, she stirred actively at *Focus 15*, then fully awoke back at *C-1*, smiled, and drifted off to sleep. She died several days later after listening to both exercises on the tape more times. Her husband had played the Relocation Theme at her death. As he sat holding her hand during this, he clearly and deeply felt her lift off—and his sense of burden go at the same time. A month later he feels very much at peace, with a sense of completion.

***

The scheduled doses of morphine were no longer controlling the pain of his terminal cancer. When the doctor started continual morphine drips, it was hard to know if he was sleeping or not because even when awake, he wasn't really here. His wife played the *Pain Management* tape and he very soon fell into a deep sleep with his abdomen breathing rhythmically. In the morning he was much more alert and asked for more tapes. *Energy Walk* was his favorite. The following day he was even more alert and asked the doctor to remove the morphine drips. He passed away peacefully this morning.

***

A clinical psychologist, who incorporated the concepts and images of the *Going Home Package* in working with a patient in the final process of dying, found especially helpful "the image of the metamorphosis of the caterpillar into a butterfly, specifically the inability of the caterpillar to know ahead of time the beauty and freedom it would enjoy at its transition."

***

The brain tumor was inoperable. His wife had accepted the fact that these were his last weeks but was terribly distressed by the growing frequency of the seizures that wracked his entire body. "I want him to go peacefully, not from a seizure," she said. She had been the helpless witness of enough of these episodes that she recognized the increase in physical restlessness that marked the onset of a seizure. After being given *Hemi-Sync* tapes by a friend, she turned on the cassette player as soon as she saw the beginning of the twisting and turning. Her husband had no further seizures, and when it was time to go, he did so peacefully.

***

While visiting a terminally ill friend, I asked about the tape that was playing in the room while he was asleep and the hospice nurse told me about *Going Home*. The next day another *Going Home* tape was just starting and I decided to relax in the chair, close my eyes, and follow the instructions on the tape. It was a wonderful experience—peaceful, reassuring, and inspiring. I bought my own set of tapes and find them a very rewarding and guide for living as well as for dying.

***

At first I was very disappointed that I couldn't use the *Going Home* tapes for my mother because she didn't understand English. Then I translated the English words and played the tapes for her while I read the translation. In her last weeks we had many important talks about her experiences with *Going Home*. In some ways, we became closer than we had ever been. I'm very grateful for this help in living my mother's death.

Hemi-Sync Exercises Related to Death and Dying

Hemi-Sync Series	**Metamusic Titles**	**Mind Food Titles**
Going Home Package	The Music of Graceful Passages	Destination: Higher Self!
	Seaside Slumber	Deep 10 Relaxation
	Sleeping Through the Rain	Energy Walk
		Into the Light
		Pain Management
		Surf
		Total Relaxation

Dental Pain

Experiences Related to Dental Pain

This information has been reported to Monroe Products and The Monroe Institute by individuals and/or by professional practitioners about the use of Hemi-Sync.

I've always been phobic about dental treatment, usually taking three or four days to recover emotionally from a visit to the dentist. After my husband had three fillings without Novocain while listening to *Cloudscapes*, I decided to give *Hemi-Sync* a chance—but I wasn't brave enough to do without the Novocain. I didn't feel the needle going in and remained comfortable and relaxed during the entire treatment. When the Novocain wore off later in the day, some slight soreness of the jaw reminded me "Oh, yes, I went to the dentist this morning.

***

Report from an MD who operates a pain-control clinic: A local dentist refers patients to me for assistance with dental analgesia. It consists of giving the patient the *Pre-Op* tape from the *Surgical Support Series* to listen to daily for one week prior to the procedure. During the dental procedure, the *Intra-Op* tape is played. I have treated three patients to date using this procedure.

The first had tremendous fear of dental pain and didn't want injectable analgesia. She needed both an inlay and a crown, both considered to be extremely uncomfortable procedures. She experienced no pain and felt totally relaxed and happy during and afterwards.

The second patient had a previous negative experience in the dental chair with an acute hypertensive episode accompanied by agitation requiring paramedic assistance. It was unclear whether the episode stemmed from extreme fear and anxiety, or was a reaction to the local anesthetic. Regardless, it was evident an alternative was needed. She was to have some very extensive work. A three-unit bridge and inlay, and a four-unit bridge were all to be accomplished during two separate visits. During both visits, the same treatment was used. The patient had one area in her right anterior mandible which remained a bit sensitive, but she endured on both visits with minimal discomfort and no agitation. She noted that the tape helped her to feel at ease and detached from discomfort.

The third patient was a very environmentally sensitive woman who could not tolerate drugs or anesthesia of any kind and needed several fillings. She, too, did well and had minimal to no discomfort during her procedure.

***

Report from a dentist. Patient A requested a local anesthetic in conjunction with the treatment. I played the *Pre-Op* tape from the *Surgical Support Series* for him. He commented, "That's pretty good, Doc. I only felt a little pain, not bad, mind you. I'll be back."

At a second visit, the patient again requested local anesthetic. After the procedure he stated, "Didn't feel a thing, Doc. That stuff's really good." At his third visit, he did not mention local anesthetic and none was used. Four teeth were prepared for crowns. He told me, "Didn't feel a thing, Doc. If I knew about this, I would have been here much sooner. I'll never wait this long again."

For Patient B, several large restorations were completed using the *Pre-Op* tape. The patient reported, "I didn't feel a thing. That's really great." On his next visit, a single tooth was prepared for a crown. He reported, "The pinched nerve in my neck has quit hurting. I feel good all over." (No mention of the dental procedure.) He concluded with, "There's just nothing to be afraid of. We'll be in touch more often."

***

I needed to have three new cavities filled and ten mercury fillings removed and replaced. The night before the procedure I played the *Pain Management* tape continuously while I slept, and again on awakening. The dentist was curious and supportive of my decision; not to have gas or injection, and made it possible for me to play the tape while he worked. It had been well over 15 years since I had allowed a dentist to look in my mouth, due to my fear of pain. There was no discomfort as he removed, redrilled, and cleaned out seven of the old fillings. The last three were deep, large cavities. He worked for 1 1/2 hours to complete all the drilling. We took a break. I rose from the chair with 13 gaping holes in my mouth, my body a little stiff from holding tension, but feeling great.

Thinking the worst was over, I switched to a favorite popular music tape to enjoy while he filled the cavities, and was caught totally unaware by unexpected pain. In need of immediate relief, I used the number sequence suggestion from *Pain Management* instead of taking time to switch tapes—and I was fine! What a pleasure to have completed the entire procedure in one visit, nearly free of pain, and feeling fine afterwards!

***

Report from a dentist. During a five-month period, I played *Sleeping Through the Rain* for 25 patients for procedures that are done with a local anesthetic. I selected this tape for its low bass tones which are excellent for drowning out the sound of dental equipment. The composition is particularly relaxing, and the *Hemi-Sync* frequencies integrated within the music are designed to lead the listener into a deeply relaxed state. It was rarely necessary to use any pharmacologic form of sedation, although occasionally nitrous oxide was used.

Twelve patients reported enjoying the tape because it allowed them to focus their attention elsewhere while their mouths were being worked on. Eight patients experienced deep relaxation, and two of these fell asleep during the procedure.

Five patients reported experiencing no apparent effect. Two of these stated that they thought the tape would be of more help to people who were nervous about coming to the dentist.

***

A dental practice decided to experiment with playing *Metamusic* on speakers heard throughout the entire treatment area. A new associate, who was not familiar with the experiment, came to the front and asked what kind of music was playing. After about fifteen minutes of listening she felt extremely relaxed. Patient comments range from "I can't believe I fell asleep in the dental chair," to "I feel more relaxed, but I can still hear the drill." Our conclusion is that both relaxation and pain control are benefited by *Hemi-Sync* and continue to use it in our dental office.

***

A cracked molar had to come out and the oral surgeon was going to have to drill to break it up before extracting the pieces. When I told my dentist how much I was dreading the appointment with the oral surgeon, he gave me his *Hemi-Sync* tapes and encouraged me to try them. I listened to the *Pre-Op* tape from the *Surgical Support Series* at home and then again in the surgeon's waiting room. While in the chair I listened to *Intra-Op* and was aware that my short breaths turned into really deep breathing without effort. I felt calm and confident and comfortable. I went to bed when I got home afterwards, fell asleep listening to *Post-Op*, and went to work feeling fine the next morning.

***

All of my life I have been a very poor dental patient, and over the last few years have had major dental work done. Yesterday, I was more prepared, having listened several times to the *Pain Management* tape and mentally rehearsed the Quick Fix function. The procedure lasted two and a half hours, but during that time I felt calm and only needed one anesthetic injection. Since the injection wore off I have experienced no pain or discomfort.

Hemi-Sync Exercises Related to Dental Pain

Hemi-Sync Series
Surgical Support Series

Metamusic Titles
Cloudscapes
Sleeping Through the Rain

Mind Food Titles
Pain Management

Depression

Experiences Related to Depression

This information has been reported to Monroe Products and The Monroe Institute by individuals and/or by professional practitioners about the use of Hemi-Sync.

Now in her 40s and in a wheel chair, she had had the first of a series of strokes at age 25. I was treating her for depressive disorder, which included frequent, uncontrollable weeping. During one session I put on a *Metamusic* tape. The tears stopped and she became calmer almost immediately. After we talked about the experience, she asked for a tape of her own to play whenever she felt the need. She recognized that she had found a tool to use to help herself.

***

Report from a psychiatrist. I used the tape *Concentration* on patients with depressive syndrome, especially those with memory difficulties and whose ability to concentrate was diminished due to depression. They all had problems with concentration, attention-to-task deficit, lack of short-term memory, and felt unable to perform mental tasks as well as they had previously. These symptoms were present whether or not the patients were taking medication.

The patients liked this new approach, and reported improvement of their ability to concentrate during test preparation and other cognitive tasks, better short-term memory, greater interest in their studies, and an ability to sustain attention for longer periods than was previously possible.

***

Report from a psychologist. While an individual is clinically depressed, I provide *Metamusic* tapes. Many depressed clients report that this flowing, quiet music, with relaxing, balancing sound signals embedded in it provides them with strong temporary relief and consolation, and gradually helps in lifting their depression.

***

A minor stroke left me feeling very depressed about the reduction of my physical capacities. I sensed myself going into a downward spiral as I contemplated the limitations I now had to live with. I started using H+ *Off-Loading* and *Eight-Great* to focus on the positive, to reinforce my enjoyment of the things I was still able to do. The depression is gone and, an unanticipated bonus, I find myself able to do more and more.

***

After a life-long history of cyclical depression going back as far as I can remember, I've been free of depression for five years. Five years ago I discovered Hemi-Sync. Is the timing a coincidence? I can't say for sure. All I know is that I began working intensively with the H+ tapes *Let Go*, *Eight-Great*, *Off-Loading* and *Möbius West*. I listened to the tapes only for a short while and used the Function Commands regularly and often. After some months my use of the Function Commands tapered off. I just stopped remembering to "do something about my depressions" because the need was no longer there. It used to be that, between depressions, I lived in dread of the next one. After so many years, I had come to think a "next one" was inevitable. That dread is gone. I still use the Function Commands when I happen to think about it, which is only occasionally.

There's been no reason for me to see a psychiatrist, so I haven't had the opportunity to get a professional explanation for the dramatic relief. I have my own hunch, though; that the synchronizing of the two hemispheres brought about lasting physiological change in my brain. Maybe the *Hemi-Sync* sound frequencies "fixed" some neural connections that used to go haywire on a regular basis. Maybe it was the helpful verbal instructions on the tapes. But really, it doesn't matter. What matters is that I function like a normal person.

***

I have suffered with clinical depression on and off for over 15 years. Although medication does keep the most disabling symptoms in check, it always seemed to me that I could do something more for myself. Since I've been using your *Hemi-Sync* tapes, I feel like I have found that "missing link!" The *Morning Exercise* and *Eight-Great* tapes help to build and reinforce a positive attitude for me. I listen to the *Remembrance* tape whenever I need a boost either at work or when arriving home after a long day. It really nurtures my spirit! Whenever I have difficulty getting the sleep I need, *Sleeping Through the Rain* eases me into a peaceful frame of mind, and I always fall into a restful sleep with it.

Hemi-Sync Exercises Related to Depression

Human Plus Titles	**Metamusic Titles**	**Mind Food Titles**
Eight-Great	Remembrance	Concentration
Möbius West	Sleeping Through the Rain	Morning Exercise
Off-Loading		

Energy

Experiences Related to Energy

This information has been reported to Monroe Products and The Monroe Institute by individuals and/or by professional practitioners about the use of Hemi-Sync.

I offered my cassette player and *Remembrance* to my colleague who was grumbling about the amount of paperwork to be done. He later returned them with the comment, "Better take this back. I began feeling more energetic, and actually found myself looking for more to do!"

***

Epstein-Barr (chronic fatigue syndrome) has left me severely debilitated, very weak, and often in pain. I am finding the Pain Management tape very effective, and I feel tremendous energy surge through my body when I listen to *Energy Walk.*

***

I have always experienced a lag in my energy level in the afternoon. There's been a big change in this since I began using the *Recharge* tape to give myself a boost whenever I need to. My late afternoon productivity is much better than it used to be.

Hemi-Sync Exercises Related to Energy

Heart-Sync Titles
Transforming Life's Challenges

Hemi-Sync Series
Positively Ageless

Human Plus Titles
Access to Energy
Do This Now
Recharge
Reset
Restorative Sleep
Tune-Up

Metamusic Titles
Ecstatic
Hemi-Sync in Motion
Vision Quest

Mind Food Titles
Cable Car Ride
Energy Walk
Pain Management

Enhanced Well-Being

Experiences Related to Enhanced Well-Being

This information has been reported to Monroe Products and The Monroe Institute by individuals and/or by professional practitioners about the use of Hemi-Sync.

A retired Naval Officer states: Perhaps we get sick because we don't know how to stay well. My focus has been on seeking ways to stay well, and the Monroe Institute tapes have been a big part of my efforts.

The H+ tapes work for me as a direct mind-to-body experience. Initially I used one or two tapes every day at the same time, but now I listen when I feel the need. The tapes are a support mechanism, playing a dominant training role in the beginning and a less frequent, but important, refresher role when one becomes familiar with the techniques. They play a significant part in my continuing state of overall well-being.

***

H+ *Tune-Up* has become my all-purpose health helper. For example, using the Function Command stops insect bites from itching, ends the first throbs of headache in the early stages, eases the symptoms of indigestion, eliminates the stinging of paper cuts. I don't know why it works, but it sure does!

***

The *Circulation* tape helped a lot with diminishing deep bruising and reabsorbing the hematoma after a serious injury.

***

I have been using H+ *Immunizing* to combat nasty flu-bugs to which I was exposed and began coming down with. I experienced one particularly bad flu, which knocked people out for 3-4 weeks with multiple ear/sinus/throat/chest/intestinal symptoms, as a series of very mild symptoms for about a week.

***

I play the *Metamusic* Artist CDs for my brother-in-law who has Parkinson's Disease and dementia. They're wonderful. They relax him and also help him to speak a bit.

***

The patient was a 61-year-old woman admitted with severe emphysema, congestive heart failure, and depression, very anxious and struggling to breathe. Within 24 hours after I began using *Deep 10 Relaxation* with her the staff was reporting a significant reduction in her anxiety level.

***

My husband has been taking medication to control the symptoms of his Parkinson's disease for 15 years. As is usual with Parkinson's, there has been a constant, slow deterioration in his functioning, and his symptoms are sometimes more and sometimes less severe. I recently learned about *Hemi-Sync* and bought the tape *Brain: Support & Maintenance* for him. At this point, he is not able to use the verbal cue by himself to activate the desired brain-wave state, but I have been playing Side B in the bedroom at night. He looks forward to the tape, finds it very relaxing, and falls asleep quickly before the tape is finished. It seems to me that he is calmer and more aware since we've been using the tape.

***

While traveling abroad, I contracted the flu so severely that it was difficult to get out of bed. Luckily, I had several *Hemi-Sync* tapes and my Walkman with me. After listening only once to *Energy Walk*, I woke up feeling energized and stronger. The sore throat, muscle pain, fever, and other symptoms decreased steadily over the next 24 hours, and by the following day I was almost completely recovered.

***

For more than a year, I had much bladder discomfort due to tissue damage from previous infections. It is considered to be a medical "fact" that such damage does not repair, and people suffer the rest of their lives with irritation and pain, exacerbated by certain foods and liquids. In my case it was tomatoes, coffee, and chocolate, all containing serotonin which is excreted in the urine.

For about four months I faithfully used a combination of the tapes called *De-Discomfort*, *Energy Walk* and *Circulation*. At this writing, all symptoms have virtually disappeared except for relatively minor discomfort from coffee and chocolate.

***

Hemi-Sync Exercises Related to Enhanced Well-Being

Heart-Sync Titles
Transforming Life's Challenges
Your Heart's Song

Hemi-Sync Series
Network of Light Series
Positive Immunity Program
Positively Ageless
Surgical Support Series

Human Plus Titles
Access to Energy
Access to Information
Attention
Brain: Support & Maintenance
Circulation
De-Discomfort
De-Hab
De-Tox: Body

Do This Now
Eight-Great
Heart: Support & Maintenance
Hypertension
Immunizing
Let-Go
Lungs: Support & Maintenance
Nutricia
Off-Loading
Passages
Recharge
Relax
Reset
Restorative Sleep
Sensory: Hearing
Sensory: Seeing
Sleep
Think Fast
Tune-Up

LightSOURCE Arts
LightSOURCE 2nd Edition

Metamusic Titles
Chakra Journey
Chakra Journey DVD
The Dreaming Gate
Dreamland
Dreamseed
Hemi-Sync Relaxation
Hemi-Sync Support for Healing
Octaves of Light
Radiance
Reflections
Seaside Slumber
Serene Sleep
Sleeping Through the Rain
The Music of Graceful Passages
Touching Grace
Vision Quest

Angels, Fairies and Wizards
Breaking Free from Addictions
Catnapper
Chakra Meditation
Chemotherapy Companion
Connecting with Your Inner Guides
Deep 10 Relaxation
Emerging from Depression and Anxiety
Energy Walk

Mind Food Titles
Exploring Other Lives
Freedom from Smoking
Guide to Serenity
Healing Journeys Support
Healing the Inner Child
Healing Through Awareness
Hemi-Sync Nap
Hemi-Sync Relaxation
Into the Light: Near Death Meditations
Inner Healer
Journey Through the T-Cells

Manifesting
Pain Management
Resonant Tuning
Sleep Deeply
Sound Sleeper
Streamhaven
Super Sleep
Surf
The "SO" Chord
Timeless Peace
Total Relaxation
Weight Loss

Expanded Awareness

Experiences Related to Expanded Awareness

This information has been reported to Monroe Products and The Monroe Institute by individuals and/or by professional practitioners about the use of Hemi-Sync.

Each time I settle down to enjoy one of your *Metamusic* tapes, I know it will be rewarding, but I'm unable to predict how. Sometimes I achieve insight into situations that have been bothering me; sometimes I receive information that seems to come from some source outside of me. Occasionally, I drift into a lucid dream, or simply enjoy badly needed, profound relaxation. Thanks for the exciting adventures!

***

Listening to *Metamusic* makes it very easy for me to experience altered states of consciousness separate from my physical body.

"I spent eight years in a one on one apprenticeship with a Toltec shaman learning to shift awareness and perception. I was getting similar results in only a matter of days!" -Marcus Leader, Leader Research

Hemi-Sync Exercises Related to Expanded Awareness

Gateway
Gateway Experience

Heart-Sync Titles
Bridge to Paradise
Communicating with Animals
Your Heart's Song

Hemi-Sync Series
The Creative Way
Hemi-Sync Support for
Journeys Out of the Body
Lucid Dreaming Series
Opening the Heart Series
The Shaman's Heart Program
Inner States

LightSOURCE Arts
Hanta Yo
LightSOURCE 2nd
Edition Sacred Gaiametry
Yantra Mantra Sacred Light -
Sacred Sound

Mind Food Titles

Chakra Meditation
Connecting with Your Inner
Guides
Destination: Higher Self!
Into the Light
Exploring Other Lives
Exploring Our Future

Healing Journeys Support
Healing Through Awareness
Into the Light
Hemi-Sync Meditation
Inner Healer
Manifesting
Moment of Revelation

Resonant Tuning
The "SO" Chord
The Visit
Touching Earth
Transcendence
Wisdom In Essence

Metamusic Titles

Ascension
Between Worlds
Beneath the Moon
Beyond the Golden
Light
Celestial Meditation
Chakra Journey
Chakra Journey
DVD
Cloudscapes
Convergence
Cosmic
Consciousness
Cosmic Traveler
Crossing the Abyss
Cycles
Deep Journeys

Deep Time
Dreaming
Dimensions in Time
Dreamer's Journey
Dreamseed
Egyptian Sun
Emergence
Enchanted Forest
Eternal Now
Eternity Within
Flow
Gaia
Higher
Inner Journey
Into the Deep
It Dreams in Me
Land of Spirit
Maiden Voyage

Masterworks
Mayan Winds
Mystic Realms
Portraits
Prisms Radiance
Reflections
Sacred Realms
Sacred Space
Serenity
Spiral of Light
Spirit Gathering
Spirit's Journey
Strand
The Dreaming Gate
The Journey Home
The Lotus Mind
The Maze
Metamusic (Cont.)

The Music of Graceful
Passages
The Return
The Shaman's Heart
The Shaman's Heart II
The Visitation
Timeless
Touching Grace
Transformation
Tribal Journeys
Voyage to The Other
Side
Waves of Love
Where the Earth
Touches the Stars
Winds Over the World
Wisdom of the Heart

Fibromyalgia

Experiences Related to Fibromyalgia

This information has been reported to Monroe Products and The Monroe Institute by individuals and/or by professional practitioners about the use of Hemi-Sync.

The **Time Out for Sleep CD** has been very beneficial for me and others in my support group who have the physiological sleep problems that are inherent with Fibromyalgia. It enables one to get the deep sleep required for healthier functioning of the body. **De-Discomfort** and **Pain Management** are also favorites to help alleviate the all-over body pain.

***

I conduct *Hemi-Sync* workshops for those who suffer from the sleep disturbances associated with Fibromyalgia. One participant's sleep pattern was so disrupted that she could not sleep without drugs, ever. She could be so fatigued that her vision blurred and she stumbled while walking, yet when she tried, she could not sleep. During the first day of the workshop, she was awakened by another participant snoring (another success story), and started crying. It was the first time she had been asleep without drugs in 18 months. The following Monday morning, we received a call from her stating she'd had two full nights of undisturbed sleep while using *Hemi-Sync* sleep tapes. She and the other participants report similar experiences, and continue to benefit from the tapes.

***

Dysfunctional sleep had been one of my wife's most disturbing Fibromyalgia symptoms. During the week she spent at The Monroe Institute taking the Gateway Voyage program, she enjoyed quality sleep for the first time in a long while, and continues to benefit from improved sleep with the use of *Hemi-Sync* tapes at home.

***

I tried the Time Out for Sleep CD to see if it would help me overcome the sleep disorder that accompanies FMS. It really works, and my recovery has been rapid. It is now possible to walk upstairs without pain, and my body is pain free a lot of the time. One or two "Time Out" naps a day keep the chronic fatigue at bay. There are more comfortable times than painful ones, and I'm optimistic about full recovery.

Hemi-Sync Exercises Related to Fibromyalgia

(Note: Time Out for Sleep is no longer available. See the section on Hemi-Sync Exercises Related to Sleep and Dreaming for alternative suggestions.)

Gateway
Gateway Experience

Human Plus Titles
De-Discomfort

Mind Food Titles
Pain Management

Hemi-Sync Series
Positive Immunity

Financial Success

Experiences Related to Financial Success

This information has been reported to Monroe Products and The Monroe Institute by individuals and/or by professional practitioners about the use of Hemi-Sync.

A consulting firm for financial industries features *Hemi-Sync* in a workshop on the psychology of successful trading in the stock and futures markets. With the help of Hemi-Sync, traders learn mental techniques to monitor their thoughts to determine if they are in states that are most conducive to giving themselves money. Traders learn to use H-PLUS *De-Hab* to neutralize dysfunctional thoughts.

Hemi-Sync Exercises Related to Financial Success

Human Plus Titles
Buy the Numbers
De-Hab
Eight-Great

Imprint
Möbius West
Off-Loading

Metamusic Titles
Remembrance

Mind Food Titles
Manifesting
Morning Exercise

Fitness & Sports

Experiences Related to Fitness & Sport

This information has been reported to Monroe Products and The Monroe Institute by individuals and/or by professional practitioners about the use of Hemi-Sync.

A high school physical education teacher reports on the use of *Metamusic*, "Some of the students were closing their eyes and getting into their weight lifting. At the same time, their technique while lifting was superb. Generally they tend to get sloppy while lifting and I believe the music helped them concentrate and perform better. Their overall attentiveness greatly improved and the actual rotating went more smoothly than ever before. Students behaved with confidence and didn't need to ask where the next station was."

Hemi-Sync Exercises Related to Fitness & Sports

Human Plus Titles
Access to Energy
De-Discomfort
Eight-Great
Heart: Support & Maintenance
Lungs: Support & Maintenance

Reset
Restorative Sleep
Synchronizing
Tune-Up

Metamusic Titles
Hemi-Sync in Motion

Mind Food Titles
Energy Walk
Pain Management

Focused Attention

Experiences Related to Focused Attention

This information has been reported to Monroe Products and The Monroe Institute by individuals and/or by professional practitioners about the use of Hemi-Sync.

After my child spent a period of weeks listening to *Metamusic* tapes while falling asleep, her preschool teacher said to me, "I am amazed at her attention span, her ability to listen to and follow directions, her desire to do what pleases, and the effort she is willing to expend to master activities that are hard or challenging for her."

***

Super Sleep, played continually throughout the night with an auto-reverse player, was highly successful in modifying a 3-year- old's disturbed sleeping behavior and helping him sleep through the night. Additionally, the child worked harder and more persistently at tasks, spoke more clearly, and accepted correction of his speech more readily, listened better, and was less easily frustrated, started to enjoy books and to sit still for stories to be read to him.

Hemi-Sync Exercises Related to Focused Attention

Hemi-Sync Series
PAL Executive Package
PAL Student Package

Human Plus Titles
Attention
Imprint
Recall
Think Fast

LightSOURCE Arts
Blossoming Lotus

Metamusic Titles
Baroque Garden
Breakthrough
Einstein's Dream
Golden Mind
Guitarra Clásica

Illumination
Indigo
Lightfall
Remembrance
Seasons at Roberts Mountain

Mind Food Titles
Concentration
Retain-Recall-Release
Sleep Deeply
Super Sleep

Frustrations

Experiences Related to Frustrations

This information has been reported to Monroe Products and The Monroe Institute by individuals and/or by professional practitioners about the use of Hemi-Sync.

A teacher reported, "The classroom was always chaotic and I was totally frustrated. I now play different *Metamusic* tapes as background for various activities, and find a completely different level of comfort in the room. Obviously, it's good for the children. And I know it's great for me."

***

Super Sleep, played continually throughout the night with an auto-reverse player, was highly successful in modifying a 3-year-old's disturbed sleeping behavior and helping him sleep through the night. Additionally, the child worked harder and more persistently at tasks, spoke more clearly, and accepted correction of his speech more readily, listened better, and was less easily frustrated, started to enjoy books and to sit still for stories to be read to him.

Hemi-Sync Exercises Related to Frustrations

Heart-Sync Titles
Transforming Life's Challenges

Hemi-Sync Series
The Creative Way
Opening the Heart Series

Human Plus Titles
Access to Information
Buy the Numbers
De-Hab
Eight-Great
Let-Go
Off-Loading

Options
Relax
Reset
Sex Drive
Think Fast
Wake/Know

Metamusic Titles	**Mind Food Titles**	Sleep Deeply
Seaside Slumber	Deep 10 Relaxation	Super Sleep
Timeless	Guide to Serenity	Surf
	Retain-Recall-Release	Total Relaxation

The Gateway Experience

Experiences Related to The Gateway Experience

This information has been reported to Monroe Products and The Monroe Institute by individuals and/or by professional practitioners about the use of Hemi-Sync.

After listening to Wave l (Discovery) *Gateway Experience*, my meditation is much stronger and deeper than before. The tapes have been wonderful, and I'll be using them for much more than meditation.

***

I listen to the Discovery tapes 1 and 2 on a daily basis and find them to be well thought out, supportive, and gentle. You are potentially giving listeners the most valuable gift of all: self-knowledge.

***

Working with the Discovery tapes, I've been feeling generally more relaxed and more comfortable, as if I'm somehow "above" my usual bad feelings. There's a new sense of coming together with myself. Things can be going on all around me without my being disturbed. The first time I listened to the tapes, I was upset and angry at my partner. After the tape was over the anger just was no longer with me, and I was able to sincerely apologize for having been so snappy earlier.

***

Gateway Experience has brought me results that were totally unanticipated. In addition to my stress level dropping, I've been able to concentrate better and sleep more comfortably. I'm coming to know myself better, and I'm remembering dreams for the first time. There's been a marked improvement in my interactions with other people. My attitude is better. I smile more and feel more open and friendly.

***

So far I've completed Wave 1 and Threshold and have achieved the relaxation, awareness, and unusual vibrations. I feel as if I'm reaching for the stars.

***

Since working with *Gateway Experience*, things have evolved for the better in almost every part of my life. Life has not been treating me differently, but my outlook on the things that happen is different. It's clear that my life is my choice and I can make positive choices regardless of my environment. Other people see and respond to me in that light also, so generally life has been getting better from inside and out.

***

Over the year that I've been working with Wave 1, I've perceived a lot of loving help coming from the guides and teachers in *Focus 10 (Gateway)*. Now it's time to expand to *Focus 12 (Gateway)*!

***

Only 10 days after experiencing *Focus 10 (Gateway)* for the first time I notice improved thought retention and a longer attention span, better logic and problem solving ability, and better dexterity and eye-hand coordination. When I'm working on something, the job is done more easily without much conscious effort on my part. My mind and body seem to be more coordinated. I guess that's what hemispheric synchronization does.

***

When I listen to the *Gateway Experience* tapes I'm mostly in a very relaxed and calm state; just there, sensing and observing in a child/student-like manner without anything extraordinary going on. But a lot has been changing in my life when I'm not listening to tapes. I come away from a tape session with the insight that if I allow myself to feel and act as I would like to, I can be that. It's my choice, and not the choice of the world outside. My physical body has been feeling much better. My shoulder joints feel like they have more movement and l have more energy and strength. Before I couldn't walk a mile without my feet hurting. Now I'm jogging about two miles. My self-image is improving and people are responding to me more positively. I'm developing new habits that are reorganizing daily routines for the better. I'm becoming more focused, find myself planning better and saying no without feeling so guilty. Things don't seem so black and white and I have more respect for different opinions.

Headaches

Experiences Related to Headaches

This information has been reported to Monroe Products and The Monroe Institute by individuals and/or by professional practitioners about the use of Hemi-Sync.

A nine-year-old client had excruciating migraine headaches and needed occasional adjustments to relieve the pressure in his brain. As we began one counseling session, he was experiencing one of his headaches. I had my tape player with me and decided to see if the *Concentration* tape would help him through it while we continued the session. In less than five minutes he stopped in mid-sentence, looked at me in a combination of puzzlement, amazement, and relief, and said, "The headache is gone."

***

My wife suffered severe headaches (sometimes migraines) for two weeks at a time during her monthly cycle, along with breast pain. She has found that *De-Discomfort* reduced and often took away the constant pain. It made life manageable again. I've used the same tape to take care of headaches and other pain. It really works.

***

The H+ *Circulation* tape helped me with migraine headaches. My belief is that by redistributing blood throughout the body in a balanced manner, it enables the engorged blood in the head to dissipate.

***

For years I have had regular headaches as a result of a sinus problem caused by allergies. Since using *Tune-Up* I haven't had one. At worst, I have had some general discomfort in my sinuses, but this hasn't reached the level of pain. I have not used even an aspirin for pain since starting.

***

I had suffered all my life with bouts of headaches which lasted days or weeks. I was in the midst of a severe bout when I received the *Pain Management* tape. I used it and got immediate results, and the relief enabled me to continue with an important project. Doctors, medication, and relaxation techniques had failed to help me, but the tape worked.

***

Since I started listening to Brain: Support & Maintenance, my frequent headaches are history. I haven't had one!

Hemi-Sync Exercises Related to Headaches

Human Plus Titles
Brain: Support & Maintenance
Circulation
Lungs: Support & Maintenance
Tune-Up

Mind Food Titles
Concentration
Pain Control

Hearing and Vision

Experiences Related to Hearing and Vision

This information has been reported to Monroe Products and The Monroe Institute by individuals and/or by professional practitioners about the use of Hemi-Sync.

After years of congratulating myself on my good vision as more and more of my friends were getting glasses, it was really disappointing when, aged 46, I needed my first glasses. I was determined to work on eyesight with the help of Hemi-Sync. I consistently use the verbal cues from *Sensory: Seeing*, *Tune-Up*, *Circulation* and *Restorative Sleep*. Seven years have gone by and I haven't needed a stronger prescription.

***

A doctor explained that he recommends *Hemi-Sync* to patients with varying degrees of hearing loss ranging from mild to total. They benefit from the tapes because the sound vibrations that make up the *Hemi-Sync* patterns are carried to the brain by the bones in the ear canal. It is not necessary to consciously "hear" the Hemi-Sync.

***

I gave *Sensory: Hearing* to a colleague who suffered from episodes of ringing in his ear followed by intense headache. The diagnosis had been degenerative nerve disease. At his next episode, he listened to the tape five times over a three-day period-all the symptoms stopped and he hasn't had another episode for three months now. He's very grateful for the relief and also for the relaxation from *Hemi-Sync* tapes.

***

Several friends plagued by tinnitus (ringing or buzzing in the ears) commented that after using *Sensory: Hearing* several times their tinnitus disappeared for long periods. When it came back, they only had to listen to the tape again.

***

This 91-year-old patient has a profound hearing loss in the left ear, and almost profound in the right ear. He wears hearing aids in both. While wearing a set of earphones that went over his hearing aids without whistling, he listened to H+ *Circulation*. During the Prep side he listened very intently and said back to me out loud everything that was being said on the tape. During the second side, I suggested that he see if he could go to sleep. He nodded off very soon.

***

The doctors of an eighty-year-old nun who was due for a cataract operation feared that the herpes infection in her eyes might flare up and perhaps lead to blindness. She insisted on going through with the operation, given added confidence through using the tape H+ *Sensory: Seeing*. The operation was successful, with no complications. She continued with the tape afterwards and greatly surprised her doctor by the virtually total recovery of her vision.

***

A professional photographer told me that after moving into his 50s he found his vision becoming less and less sharp. I told him about *Sensory: Seeing*, and got a fancy dinner at a fancy restaurant as a Thank You. He now uses the function command before going out on assignment and during the assignment, and says that his sight is as good as it ever was.

Hemi-Sync Exercises Related to Hearing and Vision

Human Plus Titles
Circulation
Restorative Sleep
Sensory: Hearing
Sensory: Seeing
Synchronizing
Tune-Up

The Heart

Experiences Related to The Heart

This information has been reported to Monroe Products and The Monroe Institute by individuals and/or by professional practitioners about the use of Hemi-Sync.

I occasionally experience an unpleasant and sometimes frightening racing of my heartbeat. (My doctor has explained what this is and it is not something to worry about.) It feels as if a switch has been flipped. One minute, I'm fine; the next I feel a strong pounding in my chest and my heart seems to be racing top speed. It usually seems to occur when I've not gotten enough rest. Sometimes it is triggered by bending for something and coming up too fast. Other times, I can be reading for an hour—perfectly relaxed—and out of the blue the switch flips and I feel it.

This particular time, I'd bent down for something and came up fast. As I did, I felt the sudden hard, fast pounding and could hear it (blood pounding) in my ears. It was so strong, I felt that I might pass out. I got to a chair and sat down. My husband was six feet away from me around the corner in the dining room, but I could not call him; the pounding was too hard, my breath too short. The feeling of passing out was still strong. I immediately thought of HUMAN-PLUS but then my mind went blank. I couldn't remember the Heart Command. I knew I'd done other exercises that would help me (*Circulation, Tune-Up*) but could not even recall their names, let alone their Commands. Finally, the only one that came to mind was *Relax*. I tried to take a deep breath but was only able to inhale one half. I then started to say, Plus-*Relax, Relax*. The moment I said "Plus" in my mind, the pounding heartbeat stopped. I was so surprised I forgot to say the rest. What was so surprising was the utter stillness and quiet that I felt in my whole system and the absolute certainty that the word "Plus" had triggered this instant change. The stillness and quiet was incredibly beautiful; like the utter stillness of deep contemplation.

I was floating in this stillness and then, silly as this may sound, I mentally panicked and started checking my body for signs: couldn't hear my heart beating, no movement, no breathing. Rational thought came to the rescue. If I'd stopped my heart with the "Plus," would I still be sitting in the chair? I felt the cool glass of the table top under my arm; my eyes were definitely staring at the orange-brown tiles on the kitchen floor. And maybe I couldn't hear breathing because I was still holding my breath. With this realization, I started to breath out and finish the Function Command. As I released my breath slowly, I said "*Relax*."

The moment I said it, I felt a strong, single, pounding heartbeat in my chest and heard the beat `in' my ears. I felt an inner flutter of hesitation, Was the pounding, racing beat going to return? I finished the Command, letting out my breath slowly and saying the final "*Relax*." With that word, I felt the erratic, racing and pounding beat wash out of me in a single wave and felt this wave continue outward beyond me, out of the room, out of the house. I felt fine, as I had before this happened.

Why Relax?? My doctor has said people do faint when this happens if they get too panicky. Her advice—RELAX! Sit down or lie down. And just RELAX! This kind of experience is usually a frightening one; one which the body controls and turns on. Now I can mentally regain control with Plus and rebalance my system. It will be a great help to the many others who also experience this not uncommon phenomenon.

***

A 55-year old woman improved her heart function and her general physical condition with the following H+ tapes used three times daily: *Relax, Attention, Let Go, Off-Loading, De-Tox: Body, Circulation, Heart: Support & Maintenance*. The patient has been advised by her physician to keep up the *Hemi-Sync* and there is no need to return to medication. Patient is to have blood drawn in six months and monitor results. It is important to note here that this patient decided to forego any medication and used only *Hemi-Sync* technology to achieve excellent results under very stressful conditions.

***

I suffer from a heart condition which brings about sudden changes of blood pressure. There's been a distinct difference since I started listening to H+ *Circulation* and *Heart: Support & Maintenance*—markedly fewer changes in pressure and, when there is a change, it's more moderate.

***

Shortly after I started using *Hemi-Sync* tapes, I introduced them to my brother who has had two coronary bypass surgeries and a seriously dangerous aneurism repaired. He swears that he could not have made it through without the *Surgical Support Series*, and his recovery has been relatively easy.

***

I had been taking Beta blockers, 1 to 2 pills a day, for over 2 1/2 years for heart rhythm disorders. I listened to the tape *Heart: Support & Maintenance* one time, felt my heart go physically "thump" inside my rib cage, and then start off on a new rhythm. I decided to go off the Beta blockers the next day and have stayed off them ever since (about a year now). The cardiologist still doesn't know why my ECG is back to normal, but I do.

***

I have worked tapes since the mid-eighties, and have benefited in a number of ways. I have successfully controlled stress, and flare-ups of hypertension so successfully, that I have been taken off medication to control blood pressure. In a recent cardiac stress test, the attending nurse, who knows I use *Hemi-Sync* verbal commands, scolded me saying "Stop controlling your heart beat! We need to get it up to target faster!"

***

A man I knew from church went into the hospital for a radical five-bypass surgery. Two weeks later I was amazed to see him walking with his wife up the hill from the church parking lot. His wife was huffing and puffing, but he was not. He had enjoyed an amazingly fast recovery, and said that the *Surgical Support Series* was the reason. When I told him about my upcoming surgery he offered to lend me his album with the exception of *Energy Walk*. "I'm sorry," he explained, "but I won't be parted from that tape."

Hemi-Sync Exercises Related to The Heart

Hemi-Sync Series	**Human Plus Titles**	Let Go
Surgical Support Series	Attention	Off-Loading
	Circulation	Relax
Mind Food Titles	De-Tox: Body	Tune-Up
Energy Walk	Heart: Support & Maintenance	

The Immune System

Experiences Related to the Immune System

(Chronic Fatigue Immune Dysfunction Syndrome (CFIDS),   Epstein-Barr (EBV), Chronic-Viral Infections, Chrones)

This information has been reported to Monroe Products and The Monroe Institute by individuals and/or by professional practitioners about the use of Hemi-Sync.

Epstein-Barr and Chronic Fatigue Immune Dysfunction has left me severely debilitated, very weak, and often in pain. I am finding the *Pain Management* tape very effective, and I feel a tremendous amount of energy surge through my body when I listen to *Energy Walk*.

***

I have suffered from Chronic Fatigue Immune Dysfunction Syndrome (CFIDS) for years. The debilitating fatigue, chronic viral infections, and muscular pain kept me disabled for a long time. Although standard medical treatment did help with some of the symptoms, the healing effects of *Hemi-Sync* tapes made the greatest impact on my condition. In the beginning, I listened to a few of the nonverbal and musical tapes several times a day. The immediate effect was of release from discomfort to a feeling of well-being. Once I became aware of the other tapes the Institute offered, I added *Pain Management*, *Restorative Sleep*, and *Immunizing* to my collection, and experienced wonderful results. Within several months of using them, the aching in my body subsided and my overall energy increased quite substantially. *Hemi-Sync* tapes continue to give me relief.

***

My sister and I both have CFIDS, and a big part of the syndrome is the inability to get quality sleep. Usually I couldn't sleep without the aid of sleeping pills. Since I began using the *Hemi-Sync* tape *Deep 10 Relaxation*, I have been able to nap in the afternoon and have found a good night's sleep for the first time in many years. With the *Positive Immunity Program*, my sister and I have learned some very good techniques for managing other symptoms.

***

I battle with chronic Epstein Barr and cytomegalovirus infections, and this makes exposure to a cold or flu bug a real threat to my already fragile health. I have used the *Positive Immunity Program* to enhance the recuperative process when struck with a bug or even a bad cold. I now get well quickly from these things that previously took weeks to conquer.

***

The *Positive Immunity Program* is useful for building a better level of health and well-being for those who have a variety of Auto-Immune based illnesses. My family and I have had good results with using it for allergies, arthritis, and chronic herpes breakouts. Whenever symptoms begin to flare up, we use the tapes to help stabilize the conditions.

***

The loss of cognitive ability has been one of the most frustrating things to deal with in my journey through CFIDS. In addition to the physical disability, short-term memory loss has been a problem for me. The *Imprint* and *Remembrance* tapes have been helpful in this area. I have improved recall and clarity, and feel more confident about myself.

***

About a year after I was diagnosed with CFIDS, a friend gave me a few *Metamusic* tapes to try. He said the tapes might be soothing to listen to, but did not explain anything about *Hemi-Sync* to me. After a week of listening daily, much to my amazement, I noticed an improvement in the way I felt physically and emotionally. That was 7 years ago. In the years since then, I have incorporated several types of *Hemi-Sync* tapes into my daily routine, and I have gained control of my symptoms. *Surf*, *Energy Walk* and *De-Discomfort* are some which are very effective for me. I have been able to resume a 6 hour a day work schedule for the past four years, and when I return home, all I need do is rest for an hour or so, listen to one of my tapes, and I'm replenished again for several hours in the evening. This is quite an accomplishment for someone who was totally debilitated. *Hemi-Sync* has greatly enhanced the quality of my life.

***

A therapist reports: "On the first visit the client complained of tiredness after physical exercise of any sort, inability to concentrate, and general depression, all classic symptoms of ME (CFIDS)." After using *Hemi-Sync* tapes for a while, the client reported, "The tapes provide a safe environment in which to get to know myself. I'm feeling in control again after a long period of feeling controlled by illness and doctors. *Hemi-Sync* gives me the freedom and encouragement to recognize my own needs and to use the appropriate tapes as a solution." *Tune Up*, De-Tox: Body, *Circulation*, *Relax*, and *Off-Loading* are among the tapes she uses.

***

A therapist reports on two clients who use *Hemi-Sync* to deal with post viral fatigue syndrome: "While neither client is completely "cured," both have gone a very long way to being able to cope effectively with their symptoms. Both women still have days when they become extremely fatigued and need periods of rest, but mentally they are now attuned to handling these symptoms and they soon recover from them."

***

A physician who suffers from Chrones disease reports: "I am very impressed and excited with the *Positive Immunity Program*. Although I hadn't expected any improvement to occur so quickly, I have already experienced a reduction in cramping, diarrhea, and stress, and I feel in control of my illness for the first time. I have completed listening to the program twice, and during a long hospital stay, used it for reinforcement. The amount of pain medication needed was significantly reduced and I was able to maintain a remarkably positive attitude."

Hemi-Sync Exercises Related to the Immune System

Heart-Sync Titles	**Hemi-Sync Series**	**Metamusic Titles**
Transforming Life's Challenges	Positive Immunity Program	Remembrance

Human Plus Titles

Circulation	Imprint
De-Discomfort	Off-Loading
Deep 10 Relaxation	Relax
De-Tox: Body	Restorative Sleep
Immunizing	Tune-Up

Mind Food Titles

Deep 10 Relaxation
Energy Walk
Healing Journeys Support
Journey Through The T-Cells
Pain Management
Surf
Total Relaxation

Learning and Memory/ Learning Disabilities

Experiences Related to Learning and Memory

This information has been reported to Monroe Products and The Monroe Institute by individuals and/or by professional practitioners about the use of Hemi-Sync.

Research on *Hemi-Sync* has reported that teachers who have used it in their classrooms noticed a decrease in student distractibility and an increase in academic performance. A study conducted with an introductory psychology class found significantly higher scores in the experimental group on five out of six tests. A study conducted at a government training center found a 30% increase in scores for Morse code students and a 75% increase on mental-motor skills. The U.S. Army reported positive results in using *Hemi-Sync* to improve acquisition of a second language.

***

Hemi-Sync tapes were used in a study of memory. The subjects carried out four different learning tasks while listening to an instrumental music tape played at low volume via headphones and a stereo tape player. The tape played for the experimental group included *Hemi-Sync* binaural beat signals while the control group was exposed to the same music without binaural beats. *Hemi-Sync* was found to be an effective method of facilitating memory for three of the four dependent variables studied. The researcher concludes that *Hemi-Sync* tapes "provide a portable, inexpensive method of assisting . . . in memory tasks [and] . . . a cost-effective, non-drug alternative to those individuals and educational systems seeking to augment standard techniques. . . Mainstream education could benefit from making widely available a form of brainwave training which makes the learning environment more enjoyable and productive."

***

A college instructor, who had been lecturing for a decade on the importance of bilateral synchronized brain waves for super learning (or a super performance state) recognized that hemispheric synchronization in a slow alpha/theta rhythm was a key factor. She had experimented with a variety of audiotapes, none of which aided learning or truly facilitated the desired response. When she first came across Monroe Institute information, she decided to give the HUMAN-PLUS tapes a "test drive" with an advanced undergraduate class. In her words, "having tried many other tapes that looked promising but did not pan out, I was pleasantly surprised by the positive impact of the tapes, as reported by the students, within two weeks. The tapes truly seemed to help in the self-change for the students."

***

At 9:00 p.m. I settled down to study on the bed between my small speakers with *Remembrance* playing softly. Time flew as I read faster and faster. I read even more pages than we had been assigned, got a lot out of it, and the reading was pleasant rather than the chore I thought it would be. The tape energized me and got me in the mood for studying eagerly and with enthusiasm. I really didn't want to stop because I was on a roll. By 10:15, with no breaks in between, I stopped, having accomplished twice what I normally would have. It was great!

***

For help with study habits, concentration, and test anxiety, two especially helpful tapes are *Imprint* and *Think Fast*. I use *Imprint* to imprint information the first time I read it. *Think Fast* is great as an all-around tonic for creative thinking and reading comprehension, and has provided a positive panacea for the mental slowdown I experienced after turning forty.

***

Retain-Recall-Release has given me spectacular results. Previously, I had real problems with memory and concentration, and was unable to recreate a picture, color or shape from memory. Using the cues from this tape, I now can easily create colored pictures under my eyelids to help me remember words in foreign languages, or things I need to do. It works!

***

I give piano lessons to a seven-year-old girl and was training her to play scales with a metronome. For several weeks she was able to play at 126 beats per minute (bpm). This week I played the *Concentration* tape through speakers during the lesson. We started the metronome at 126 bpm and speeded it up gradually. She was able to play at 160 bpm. Hey, that's great!

***

A proud mother said, "My sixteen-year-old son had been getting only 40s and 50s on written tests. He used *Remembrance* while studying for final exams, made no score below 84, and was ecstatic."

***

Buy the Numbers is a marvel! I'm studying physics and finding that *Hemi-Sync* helps enormously with complex mathematical computations.
My ten-year-old grandson had been tested with an IQ of 70. That's borderline retarded. Since working with the *Concentration* tape, which he loves to listen to, he's getting straight As. Isn't that miraculous? He said to me, "Grandma, if I could take my magic tape to school, all my friends could get As, too."

***

The high school students reported that *Concentration* and *Remembrance* helped them to be more focused and improved their ability to concentrate. They were able to sit for hours without a break, they remember more, and they find studying more enjoyable. *Catnapper* helps them have a refreshing short nap after school, without sleeping for hours.

***

I always had trouble in school while I was growing up, and dropped out before high school, grade eight, to be exact. All my life this bothered me. I felt like a big failure. I decided to go back to school around the time someone told me about your tapes. I truly believe that if it weren't for *Hemi-Sync* I would never have done as well. I would use *Imprint* before I started to study. First thing in the morning I'd listen to *Concentration* and use either *Attention* or *Think Fast*. Then I'd go to school and write the test or exam. Not only did I do extremely well, but throughout the entire year I was the best student in all my classes, and never got more than one or two answers wrong. This to me has been a great accomplishment. I also use *Synchronizing*, *De-Hab*, *Möbius West*, *Wake/Know* and *Deep 10 Relaxation*. Thank you for the great help these tapes have been for me.

***

Buy the Numbers is a favorite among students. Many who have difficulty with math requirements in pursuit of their degrees successfully use *Buy the Numbers* to help them pass math and to understand its principles better. The *Attention* tape has helped students enhance their focus while studying. *Options* helps with creativity. *Speak Up* helps rather dramatically with nervousness about speaking out in class or giving public speeches.

***

Responses from a questionnaire on the use of *Remembrance*:
I felt total clarity of thought, energetic, calm without sleepiness...

By 10:00, two hours into a busy Monday at the office while playing *Remembrance*, I realized I had completed three tasks and seven phone calls without missing a beat . . .

I was able to think about numerous topics/tasks/jobs at one time . . .
Listening to *Remembrance* gave me a profound feeling of openness, joy and release. A few problems I had been working on suddenly became clear. . .

The tape gives me a tug back to the subject at hand . . .
When reading, I listen with headphones and find my concentration much deeper. For doing creative work I sit between speakers . . .

The tape produced a feeling of balance, sustained energy, and the ability to zero in on the tasks at hand . . .

I experienced heightened awareness, absence of distractions, greater absorption and depth of focus.

***

Intuitive skills can be taught successfully and enhanced when *Hemi-Sync* is used as a tool for rapid learning. I developed more respect and response to the gut level feelings. I am now less likely to dismiss such feelings before noting them and considering them in decision-making. Accuracy of my impressions has improved dramatically. Over time my perceptions have become quite refined and precise, and I am able to use intuition more easily in therapy and classroom settings.

***

Never having enjoyed mathematics, I knew one of the greatest challenges in getting my pilot's license would be the calculations needed to pass the written and practical exams. I decided to play *Buy the Numbers* for some quick help. After listening twice I began the calculations—still I was stiff and unable to get down to work. Then I remembered that I get the best results when I start by chaining *Relax/ Attention* and then adding other H-Plus Function Commands as needed.

***

I began my study sessions with *Concentration* playing over headphones and immediately activated the following H-PLUS Functions: *Relax/ Attention/ Imprint/ Let-Go/ Off-Loading/ Buy the Numbers*. (The reason I used the *Let Go/Off-Loading* Function Commands was because of old patterns, limiting patterns that I was unable to perform mathematical calculations easily). Much to my amazement, I was able to easily, confidently, and cheerfully perform the calculations and continue studying for the written examination. I used *Concentration* each time I studied. The morning of the exam, I reviewed all the material (using *Concentration*) and then took a nap before going into the exam room completely calm and anxiety free. I chained together the following Function Commands: *Relax/ Attention/* Recall/ *Let-Go/ Off-Loading/ Think Fast/ Buy the Numbers*. I passed the written exam with flying colors, and with most of the mathematical calculations correct.

***

I knew the next part of the studying was going to be a bit more complicated. Each time I flew with my instructor and he presented me with a skill to learn or a new challenge to overcome, I simply chained together the following Function Commands: *Relax/ Attention/ Imprint/ Think Fast/ Synchronizing*. As H+ helped me encode each new learning, I became more relaxed, more confident, and a better pilot. When my instructor noticed I was able to assimilate more information quicker and more completely, he asked how I was able to do this, and received a brief overview of *Hemi-Sync* and H-Plus. When the day came for the FAA Examiner to test me in the air, I moved confidently and easily from one skill to the next, and received my license.

***

While attending a professional conference, I stuck my Walkman in my suit jacket, put on the headphones and listened to the *Concentration* tape during all lecture sessions. This provided the narrow focus of attention that was conducive to learning. I also used the *Metamusic* tape, *Midsummer Night*, which created a more open focus for my awareness. I was immediately aware of the increase in my ability to concentrate and remember what I learned in the various lectures and courses I attended.

***

When needing to read some highly technical papers, I experimented with and without *Remembrance*. The difference really impressed me. With the tape I was much more able to attend to the content, stay focused, not have to re-read sentences for comprehension, etc.

***

With only one day to study for the state insurance licensing exam, I thought it was hopeless. I'd never be able to remember a manual of 190 pages. Although I wasn't confident, I decided to give it a shot. I began studying at 9 a.m. and by 1 p.m. was losing my ability to concentrate. I put the *Concentration* tape into my continuous tape player and finished the book at 3:05 a.m. the next morning. I passed with an 86, thanks to *Concentration* which enabled me to maintain my concentration for 18 straight hours.

***

As I listened to *Remembrance* more and more, I noticed that I started to hear it less. I actually didn't even notice that it was playing. This is when the benefits really started showing. I was studying for a major test which required lots of formulas and memorization. The concepts came easily to me. I got a perfect score on the test and I know the tape helped me study more efficiently and with fewer interruptions.

***

Report from a psychiatrist. I used the tape *Concentration* for patients with depressive syndrome, especially those with memory difficulties and whose ability to concentrate was diminished due to depression. They all had problems with concentration, attention-to-task deficit, lack of short-term memory, and felt unable to perform mental tasks as well as they had previously. The patients liked the effectiveness of the tape, and reported improvement of their ability to concentrate during test preparation and other cognitive tasks, better short-term memory, greater interest in their studies, and an ability to sustain attention for longer periods than was previously possible.

When I used the Function Command for H+ *Attention*, it was as if someone opened the top of my head and breathed fresh air into it. All of my senses snapped open!

***

A British race car driver credits the *Concentration* tape for reducing his lap time by a full two seconds. He remarked that he made fewer mistakes and that it just felt easy (189 mph easy?), and he had been a lot more consistent in braking and cornering. His wife said she had never seen him so relaxed while under pressure, with no sweating or hyper-speech symptoms.

***

320 professionals attended five-day workshops that incorporated *Hemi-Sync* signals in background music to enhance participant learning. Following the workshop 96% stated that they were both more relaxed and more attentive than usual during the workshop.

***

A law student, desperate about the overload of material he needed to learn, heard about *Remembrance*. "It's terrific," he reported, "helps me feel relaxed and geared up to study effectively, all at the same time."

***

On the first day of a workshop for learning to play the dulcimer, I had a lot of difficulty. The next day I wore my headphones and listened to the *Concentration* tape softly throughout the day. I listened to the new musical patterns with greater ease. I was aware that even though I could not play the pattern smoothly, or even remember the tune with ease, there was not the emotional overlay I had experienced before. Rather than feeling that I would never be able to do this, I simply knew that I was learning and would be able to produce what I had learned at a later time. I don't know whether the *Hemi-Sync* increased my ability to learn, but I know that it prevented me from unconsciously interfering with my own learning by eliminating negative messages and scenarios. The most noticeable difference was my ability to hear my own instrument and to concentrate during the group practice times. Even when I did not wear the headphones, there was a carryover, and the sound of my own dulcimer came to the foreground of my awareness.

***

The Retain-Recall-Release tape helped me retain the information to pass a rather detailed five-item essay exam. Before these tapes, essay exams and I never got along!

***

Mr. and Mrs. G. had their first contact with the *Hemi-Sync* technology of The Monroe Institute in November 1992, and started playing the tape *Surf* over open speakers during television and play time for their son, Marcel. They also used *Surf* as background while Marcel was studying. In February 1993, Marcel began writing his first readable sentences. He knew and recognized with certainty every letter. At about the same time, he complained that playing *Surf* during study time distracted him. The tape *Concentration* was substituted.

***

Marcel's ten-year-old sister also had a history of reading and writing problems and was working on both skills with a therapist. It was observed that while she was experiencing the *Hemi-Sync* patterns of the *Surf* tape, she reduced her average of twenty-two spelling errors per dictation to seven.

***

Brain: Support & Maintenance should be titled Brain Enhancement. The title doesn't do it justice. When I use the verbal command I feel more aware of things in an interested, excited way, without being overwhelmed. I used the command yesterday while worrying about my finances and I immediately became less anxious and started to think more clearly. I'm discovering how well this function works in combination with other H+ functions for even better results.

***

The work load in my class on the human brain was very heavy, especially for someone working full time with family commitments as well. The *Think Fast*, *Imprint*, and Recall tapes helped me process and retain the material, also the concepts expressed in the tapes directly relate to what is taught in the class. This kept me very interested in the biological working of the brain, and in turn, helped me to understand both the class material and how your tapes work.

***

My sixteen-year-old son was having difficulty in school. He got A's and B's in regular class work, but did poorly on written tests, scoring in the 40's and 50's. A family therapist gave him the *Remembrance* tape to use while he studied for final exams. I am so pleased to report that he made no test score below an 84 on his finals, and was ecstatic.

***

The loss of cognitive function has been one of the most frustrating things I've had to deal with in my journey through Chronic Fatigue Syndrome. I experience the sensation of my mind being in a fog, especially in the afternoon and evening. At times, my ability to access short term memory or recall fades from my grasp. This had caused me to feel inadequate in many circumstances. A short while after I began listening to *Remembrance* as background music in the office, my capacity to retain information and focus my attention has improved dramatically. I have also worked with *Imprint* and *Attention*, and whenever I begin to feel that I am "fading," the verbal cues are most helpful to restore and enhance a more productive state of mind."

A thirty-year-old dyslexic called to say that *Hemi-Sync* is like a "shot in the arm." After only a month of using the *PAL Executive Package*, *Attention*, *Synchronizing*, and *Think Fast*, he's aware of a noticeable improvement in cognitive ability. This has made a big difference in on-the-job effectiveness, and has changed his self-image from someone with a handicapping condition to that of a self-directed achiever.

***

I was worried about passing the test I would soon have to take to become a court reporter. I had been studying hard, but my speed wasn't what it needed to be. After I started using the *PAL Student Package* for practice sessions, my speed picked up. I knew I'd pass, and I did so in a relaxed and confident manner.

Experiences Related to Learning Disabilities

This information has been reported to Monroe Products and The Monroe Institute by individuals and/or by professional practitioners about the use of Hemi-Sync.

Dyslexia: Mr. and Mrs. G. had their first contact with the *Hemi-Sync* technology of The Monroe Institute in November 1992, and played the tape *Surf* over open speakers during television and play time for their son, Marcel. They also used *Surf* as background while Marcel was studying. By February 1993, Marcel began writing his first readable sentences. He knew and recognized with certainty every letter. At about the same time, he complained that playing *Surf* during study time distracted him. The tape *Concentration* was substituted.

***

My ten-year-old grandson had been tested with an IQ of 70. That's borderline retarded. Since working with the *Concentration* tape, which he loves to listen to, he's getting straight As. Isn't that miraculous? He said to me, "Grandma, if I could take my magic tape to school, all my friends could get As, too."

***

A psychologist reports excellent results from using *Super Sleep* for children with learning disabilities and/or attention deficits. With *Super Sleep* playing all night, parents and teachers observe better concentration and less irritability during the day.

***

My students are learning disabled, socially and emotionally maladjusted, including multiple impairments of speech and sight. They responded very well to the H+ *Relax* and *Attention* tapes, self-initiating the cues they learned. The results include a marked increase in self-control and decidedly improved social interactions. The tapes have given these children a mechanism to deactivate their previously learned hostile and disruptive responses. The classroom environment has dramatically improved and—most important -the children now have a skill that will be theirs for life.

***

Report from a speech-language pathologist. Parents have reported changes in their own reactions to their children when *Hemi-Sync* tapes are used at home. One mother stated she felt very relaxed, and less angry and impatient with her son's feeding problems. Another mother was initially quiet and withdrawn and often left the room during therapy sessions I conducted with her son. She was interested in using *Hemi-Sync* tapes at home because she knew her son was happier with the music [*Metamusic* tapes]. Within a month of regular *Hemi-Sync* use at home she was more outgoing, wanted to be present during therapy sessions, and offered more spontaneous comments about his progress and needs. Changes have also been observed in brothers and sisters. This was particularly evident when tapes were played for 45 minutes as children who shared a room were going to sleep. One sibling showed a reduction in bed-wetting and another showed major improvements in school work.

Hemi-Sync Exercises Related to Learning and Memory/Learning Disabilities

Hemi-Sync Series
PAL Executive Package
PAL Student Package
LEK: Learning Enhancement Kit

Human Plus Titles
Access to Information
Attention
Brain: Support & Maintenance
Buy the Numbers
De-Hab
Imprint
Let-Go
Möbius West
Options

Recall
Relax
Speak Up
Synchronizing
Think Fast
Wake/Know

LightSOURCE Arts
Blossoming Lotus

Metamusic Titles
Baroque Garden
Breakthrough
Einstein's Dream
Elation
Golden Mind

Guitarra Clásica
Illumination
Indigo
Lightfall
Midsummer Night
Remembrance
Seasons at Roberts Mountain

Mind Food Titles
Concentration
Deep 10 Relaxation
Retain-Recall-Release
Sleep Deeply
Super Sleep
Surf
Total Relaxation

Massage and Bodywork

Experiences Related to Massage and Bodywork

This information has been reported to Monroe Products and The Monroe Institute by individuals and/or by professional practitioners about the use of Hemi-Sync.

A remedial therapist reports, "I have been using *Metamusic* tapes with patients with conditions including stroke, Parkinson's, arthritis, asthma, and neurological states, using an auto-reverse player so I don't have to stop treatment to turn the tape over. *Midsummer Night* is especially popular. All patients relaxed more easily and quickly. There was a very marked reduction in the more obvious types of stress, chatter quickly stopped, and the tranquil, relaxed state enabled a deeper level to emerge.

***

As a practitioner, I believe that *Hemi-Sync* is a great aid to massage from the patient's point of view, giving a greater sense of relaxation and well-being. The first, almost immediate effect—relaxation of the body. Then a quieting of the mind that leads to inner stillness, so the overall effect becomes a generalized serenity.

***

From a massage therapist: *Hemi-Sync* tapes are especially helpful with clients who are trying to get in touch with emotional trauma stored in their bodies, particularly those who have had difficulty doing so in the past. *Hemi-Sync* also supports those who are using Swedish massage as a medium to reach a transcendent or altered state to do personal work or just to be with themselves. Their experience seems to be deeper and more rewarding. For stressed-out corporate types the tranquil, relaxed state enabled a deeper level to emerge (specifically, the personnel manager of a large company laying off significant numbers of employees). *Hemi-Sync* calms them.

***

Hemi-Sync makes a difference with those who have trouble accessing their feelings due to fear around the original trauma or because they are just uncomfortable in that part of their brain. The *Metamusic* selection, *Sleeping Through the Rain*, works nicely in this application.

***

Faster and more complete releases occurred week after week; I attribute this, more than anything else, to the addition of Hemi-Sync. It supported increased abilities for the client and allowed us to interact at a more intuitive, and effective level.

My massage therapist began a series of deep tissue massages after an evaluation of "scar marbles" resulting from tissue and bone re-knitting in a bulky, awkward fashion. The area of the nodules was extremely sensitive to pressure and difficult to palpate deeply. During the first deep tissue session, I used the *Pain Management* command successfully to distance from the discomfort so that the area could be worked in a controlled manner. During the second massage, I used *Sleeping Through the Rain* to attain a deeper state of muscle relaxation, and was able to tolerate her working more deeply on the injured area. By the third massage, she was able to work at the level of the bone and gently manipulate the scar nodules directly. They began to shrink and flatten very quickly, the entire shoulder girdle became more flexible, and I experienced an unusual (for me) level of relaxation in my neck and scalp. I believe that *Hemi-Sync* has uniquely supported and speeded my healing, and my overall energy level has measurably increased.

***

Working with Swedish massage (light pressure which is more pleasurable and relaxing than the deep work) produced some interesting reactions in combination with *Super Sleep*. It was possible to induce a very deep state, in which the person was just "not there" whatsoever, and experienced intense dreaming and processing.

***

A remedial therapist in England plays *Hemi-Sync* in the background when working with clients. She reports about Bob who has a chronic illness that diminishes his energy. *Super Sleep* enhances his rest periods very beneficially, and he's a great fan of H+ *Relax*. He says it helps him lie and relax for nine hours at a time, and he also uses it every evening to get a good rest before the exertion of his nightly bath.

***

Relaxation and receptiveness are the mindsets we are trying to achieve to help clients let go and accept healing energy, and *Metamusic* is ideal for setting the mood at our Reiki clinic. When I received your *Metamusic* CDs, I couldn't wait to bring them to work. *Inner Journey* and *Sleeping Through the Rain* are particular favorites, and are being used by our massage therapist as well. The CDs are wonderful because no one has to hurry and turn the tape over. To do so would disrupt the flow and concentration of the practitioners.

Hemi-Sync Exercises Related to Massage and Bodywork

Hemi-Sync Series
Massage Therapy Collection
The Shaman's Heart Program

Human Plus Titles
Relax

Metamusic Titles
Angel Paradise
Breath of Creation Solo Huaca
Chakra Journey
Chakra Journey DVD
Dreamcatcher Dreamland
Dreamseed
Enchanted Forest
Eternal Now

Hemi-Sync Support for Healing
Inner Journey
It Dreams in Me
Maiden Voyage
Midsummer Night
Octaves of Light
Path to Peace
Pearl Moon
Radiance
Reflections
Sacred Realms
Seaside Slumber
Serenity
Sleeping Through the Rain
Star Spirits
The Dreaming Gate

The Lotus Mind
The Music of Graceful Passages
The Return
The Shaman's Heart
The Shaman's Heart II
Timeless
Touching Grace
Wisdom of the Heart

Mind Food Titles
Pain Management
Sleep Deeply
Soft & Still
Super Sleep
Surf

Meditation & Spiritual Growth

Experiences Related to Meditation & Spiritual Growth

This information has been reported to Monroe Products and The Monroe Institute by individuals and/or by professional practitioners about the use of Hemi-Sync.

Probably the best thing for me about your *Gateway Experience* (Wave I) course has been my new ability to meditate, to relax, to calm down. I hadn't been able to meditate properly before, though I had been trying for a long time.

***

I have listened to *Metamusic* as a deliberate meditative aid, or just as background to relax with. Each time, it has brought out a strong emotional response, often to the point of tears streaming down my face, either over something specific which had been brought into the conscious mind, or for no obvious reason. My state of mind prior to each listening was not particularly emotional. Often I was anticipating no value other than relaxing background music. Sometimes I spent the first quarter of the tape restlessly thinking that I should get up and do something else—only to succumb the next minute to profound absorption in the tape.

***

I have found a quantum leap in my meditations since using your tapes. As far as inducing the bliss state, your nonverbal tapes are fantastic in that regard.

***

A long-time meditator reported, "When I play *Metamusic*, not only do I achieve a meditative state much more quickly, but I feel as if my meditation is more profound than it is when I don't have this soft, unobtrusive yet supportive background. Without *Hemi-Sync* it generally takes me about seven minutes to get into a meditative state. *Hemi-Sync* it takes about two minutes for me to get markedly deeper than I otherwise go."

***

Listening to musical *Hemi-Sync* tapes makes it very easy for me to experience altered states of consciousness separate from my physical body.

***

Lama Saddhatissa wrote, "Our weekly meditation group, which focuses on transforming the mind, played Transformation as background for the first time last night. The beautifully expansive and awakening energy it generated was amazing. Instead of remaining for the usual hour or so, people didn't want to go home."

***

After listening to *Gateway Experience* (Wave1), my meditation is much stronger and deeper than before. The tapes have been wonderful, and I'll be using them for much more than meditation.

***

"These tapes/CDs (*Gateway Experience*) represent a splendid tool for hiking the spiritual path. If you're serious about going for the OOBE, these tapes/CDs are the ones to use for repeated practice." –Steve Graf, Ph.D., Professor of Psychology

***

I cannot tell you what it means to me to be able to go inside with the cassettes and slowly find my way; to ask my Higher Power for direction and help and find it through inner guidance.

When I ordered the *Gateway Experience* program, I had high hopes of increasing my psychic development and overcoming fear blocks about astral travel. I never dreamed that within a month of beginning the series and using the CDs every day, I would not only astral travel without fear, but would increase my clairaudience and clairvoyance triple fold. Since I use the senses every day in my work, this has been a priceless investment, and an invaluable opportunity to boost my spiritual level as well. —Josie Galante

Hemi-Sync Exercises Related to Meditation & Spiritual Growth

Gateway
Gateway Experience

Hemi-Sync Series
Hemi-Sync Support for Journeys
Out of the Body
Journeys Out of the Body
Going Home
Inner States
Opening the Heart Series
Out of Body Techniques
The Shaman's Heart Program

LightSOURCE Arts
Blossoming Lotus
Hanta Yo
LightSOURCE 2nd Edition
Sacred Gaiametry
Yantra Mantra

Heart-Sync Titles
Bridge to Paradise
Partners Meditation

Human Plus Titles
Contemplation

Metamusic Titles

Angel Paradise
Ascension
Awakening
Consciousness
Beneath the Moon
Between Worlds
Beyond the Golden Light
Breath of Creation Solo
Huaca
Celestial Meditation
Chakra Journey
Chakra Journey DVD
Cloudscapes
Convergence
Cosmic Consciousness
Cosmic Traveler
Crossing the Abyss
Cycles
Deep Journeys

Deep Time Dreaming
Desert Moon Song
Dimensions in Time
Dreamcatcher
Dreamer's Journey
Egyptian Sun
mergence
Enchanted Forest
Eternal Now
Eternity Within
Flow
Gaia
Higher
Himalayan Soul
Inner Journey
Into the Deep
It Dreams in Me
Land of Spirit
Maiden Voyage

Masterworks
Mayan Winds
Medicine Work
Mystic Realms
Pearl Moon
Portal to Eternity
Quest of the Mystic
Radiance
Reflections
River Dawn
Sacred Realms
Sacred Space
Spiral of Light
Spirit Gathering
Spirit's Journey
Strand
The Dreaming Gate
The Journey Home

The Lotus Mind
The Return
The Shaman's Heart
The Shaman's Heart II
The Visitation
Timeless
Touching Grace
Tranquility
Transformation
Tribal Journeys
Vision Quest
Voyage to The Other Side
Waves of Love
Winds Over the World
Wisdom of the Heart

Mind Food Titles

Blue Moon Journey
Chakra Meditation
Connecting with Your Inner Guides
Destination: Higher Self!
Exploring Other Lives
Exploring Our Future

Healing Through Awareness
Hemi-Sync Meditation
Inner Healer
Into the Light
Moment of Revelation
Resonant Tuning
Soft & Still
Surf

The "SO" Chord
The Visit
Timeless Peace
Touching Earth
Transcendence
Wisdom In Essence

Multiple Sclerosis

Experiences Related to Multiple Sclerosis

This information has been reported to Monroe Products and The Monroe Institute by individuals and/or by professional practitioners about the use of Hemi-Sync.

I have Multiple Sclerosis, so there's a lot of stuff going on with my body, unfortunately none of it good. I heard about your tapes on a TV program, how someone overcame all her pain with these tapes. I suffer chronic pain because of my M.S., among other symptoms.

The next day I went to my local bookstore and purchased *De-Discomfort*. I have to admit my attitude was bad, but I thought, what the heck, what do I have to lose? That night I went through the Prep side twice and was amazed that I was feeling happy and relaxed, then I went on with the exercise. The next morning when I got out of bed, I still had all my M.S. symptoms, minus pain. I thought I was dreaming. I didn't know how to act! For the first time in eight years I didn't have pain!

My next step was to get other tapes to help me with other symptoms. *Sensory: Seeing* for my sight, *Brain: Repair & Maintenance* for my short-circuited brain, *Recharge* for chronic fatigue, *Think Fast*, again for my short-circuited brain, and *Restorative Sleep* for the healing of my body while I am asleep. For the last three weeks I have been suffering from an exacerbation, so the real test is here. For the last two weeks I have been using the tapes and all I can say is: this is the best attack I have ever had! When I feel really crummy I listen to *Energy Walk*. I sleep like a baby, and wake up feeling good. No more daily pain medication or tranquilizers for anxiety and numbness, because I now have another way to deal with my life as a person who has M.S.

***

A Multiple Sclerosis patient reports: *Restorative Sleep* has been really helpful. Just giving the Function Command can start me yawning (usually I combine it with *Tune-Up*). *De-Tox: Body* is another favorite. I focus on body, mind, spirit, and aura while doing the Command and really feel a clearing effect. *Immunizing* and *De-Tox: Body* helped me through a couple of colds. Symptoms didn't seem as bad and they didn't seem to last as long. Using the Functions may have kept MS symptoms from getting worse then, too. I also keep *Contemplation* "on board"—it makes me aware of what I do all the time. Generally, I use the Commands several times a day and precede whatever else I'm using with *Relax*.

***

I have had debilitating Multiple Sclerosis since the 'eighties and had long been looking for something that would help relieve my symptoms. I am very enthusiastic about the results I've had tapes. In particular, the *De-Discomfort* tape has worked wonders in eliminating my pain.

Hemi-Sync Exercises Related to Multiple Sclerosis

Human Plus Titles
Brain: Support & Maintenance
Contemplation
De-Discomfort
De-Tox: Body

Immunizing
Recharge
Relax
Restorative Sleep
Sensory: Seeing

Think Fast
Tune-Up

Mind Food Titles
Energy Walk

Pain Management

Experiences Related to Pain Management

This information has been reported to Monroe Products and The Monroe Institute by individuals and/or by professional practitioners about the use of Hemi-Sync.

(Note: See also Experiences Related to Dental Pain)

One patient at my pain control clinic was very resistant to the concept of Hemi-Sync tapes, but agreed to listen to them as directed. She admitted that, although she thought it sounded like "crazy stuff," the tapes helped her to get pain relief and to relax. After her treatment was over, she purchased several tapes for herself. At follow-up visits she told me that at the end of a stressful day, she listens to a tape and has been able to prevent her back from hurting.

***

The Department of Surgery at Columbia Presbyterian Hospital uses *Hemi-Sync* tapes in conjunction with other therapies to help patients heal more quickly and with less anxiety and pain. They recommend the *Surgical Support Series* tapes for use prior to and during a medical procedure and while in recovery. They recommend a variety of other *Hemi-Sync* tapes to foster healing and maintain optimal wellness in the hospital and at home.

***

The scheduled doses of morphine were no longer controlling the pain of his terminal cancer. When the doctor started continual morphine drips, it was hard to know if he was sleeping or not because even when awake, he wasn't really here. His wife played the *Pain Management* tape and he very soon fell into a deep sleep with his abdomen breathing rhythmically. In the morning he was much more alert and asked for more tapes. *Energy Walk* was his favorite. The following day he was even more alert and asked the doctor to remove the morphine drips. He passed away peacefully this morning.

***

A patient with myofascial pain and dysfunction was able to lower tension in a band across her forehead almost instantaneously after learning the Function Command for H+ *De-Discomfort* by listening to the tape twice. With electrodes placed on her forehead and connected to an ORION bioExperiences system, the reading immediately dropped from 6 mv to 3 mv when using the Plus-55515 command.

***

Report from psychologist. The patient's cancer continues to spread and he has been in considerable pain. He had been taking large amounts of medication:125 mg of Tegretol three times a day, 12-15 cc a day of Dilantin, Darvocet every four hours, and Zantec. He had also been taking 11cc of Methadone four times a day and this was recently changed to morphine. Despite all the medication, his pain was poorly controlled.

I introduced him to the *Hemi-Sync Pain Management* tape to use at home, and he finds it helps reduce pain between medications. After only four sessions, he is now seeing me on an "as needed" basis. The *Pain Management* tape has furnished the backbone of his treatment program.

***

Report from an MD who operates a pain-control clinic: A local dentist refers patients to me for assistance with dental analgesia. It consists of giving the patient the *Pre-Op* tape from the *Surgical Support Series* to listen to daily for one week prior to the procedure. During the dental procedure, the *Intra-Op* tape is played. I have treated three patients to date using this procedure.

The first had tremendous fear of dental pain and didn't want injectable analgesia. She needed both an inlay and a crown, both considered to be extremely uncomfortable procedures. She experienced no pain and felt totally relaxed and happy during and afterwards.

The second patient had a previous negative experience in the dental chair with an acute hypertensive episode accompanied by agitation requiring paramedic assistance. It was unclear whether the episode stemmed from extreme fear and anxiety, or was a reaction to the local anesthetic. Regardless, it was evident an alternative was needed. She was to have some very extensive work. A three-unit bridge and inlay, and a four-unit bridge were all to be accomplished during two separate visits. During both visits, the same treatment was used. The patient had one area in her right anterior mandible which remained a bit sensitive, but she endured on both visits with minimal discomfort and no agitation. She noted that the tape helped her to feel at ease and detached from discomfort.

The third patient was a very environmentally sensitive woman who could not tolerate drugs or anesthesia of any kind and needed several fillings. She, too, did well and had minimal to no discomfort during her procedure.

***

My friend had a severe allergic reaction to morphine while she was in the hospital and was suddenly aware that her heart was pounding to the point of bursting; her whole body was a mass of pain and was convulsing uncontrollably. She felt total terror and knew she was dying. She heard someone say, "We've sent for her family." Then the function command 55515 (the cue learned on the *Pain Management* tape) popped into her head, and the convulsions stopped and the pain and fear disappeared. After her second mental repetition, she heard someone say, "We have a pulse." Her next awareness was that all the people who had been hovering over her were gone and she was alone and in total peace. Within an hour of the reaction, she was fully awake, pain free, and able to talk to her children. She says that since that experience she feels totally accepting of death, and even more remarkably, she's able to be in the midst of family turmoil and, for the most part, remain serene. She continues to listen to tapes several hours a day, and although her medical prognosis is not good, she's actually enjoying her life.

***

A patient with chronic pain from a neck injury and nerve root entrapment listened to *De-Discomfort* and *Circulation* two times each. The bioExperiences system showed electrical activity in the forehead dropping from 3.4 mv to 1.2 mv using the *Pain Management* command.

***

My massage therapist began a series of deep tissue massages after an evaluation of "scar marbles" resulting from tissue and bone re-knitting in a bulky, awkward fashion. The area of the nodules was extremely sensitive to pressure and difficult to palpate deeply. During the first deep tissue session, I used the *Pain Management* command successfully to distance from the discomfort so that the area could be worked in a controlled manner. During the second massage, I used *Sleeping Through the Rain* to attain a deeper state of muscle relaxation, and was able to tolerate her working more deeply on the injured area. By the third massage, she was able to work at the level of the bone and gently manipulate the scar nodules directly. They began to shrink and flatten very quickly, the entire shoulder girdle became more flexible, and I experienced an unusual (for me) level of relaxation in my neck and scalp. I believe that *Hemi-Sync* has uniquely supported and speeded my healing, and my overall energy level has measurably increased.

***

Report from a chronic pain clinic: To introduce the tapes, I offer a presentation on sleep, sleep cycles, sleep disorders and the importance of sleep as a restorative process. Then, each pain patient lies on a mat with a pillow and headphones to listen to just the Prep side of a H-PLUS tape. Sounds of snoring from two patients who said that they were usually unable to fall asleep were quite exciting. The simple procedure of listening to just Prep creates receptivity to the impact of the tapes. Patients cannot wait to hear the other side! Over the next few days, as we get acquainted, I recommend specific tapes for their individual problems.

From my personal observations—and from discussions with patients—the tapes are a hit! H-PLUS *De-Discomfort*, *Restorative Sleep*, *Circulation*, and *Off-Loading* had the biggest impact on reducing chronic pain. The **Mind Food** tapes *Sound Sleeper*, *Pain Management*, and Flying Free were also helpful.

***

The men were truck drivers, crane operators, or handlers of heavy equipment, all very sedentary occupations with most of the day spent seated. After using the *Pain Management* tape for several months they spoke of feeling the pain less, needing less medication, and improved morale. The clinical signs were still present, but they were responding more positively to their pain.

***

Muscular tightness often interfered with my getting a good night's sleep. Once I started listening to *Restorative Sleep*, the muscular pain and discomfort went away and hasn't come back.

***

Mrs. C. consulted me with severe migraines. Hypnotherapy gave her some relief but not as much as hoped. I suggested that she listen to *Brain: Support & Maintenance*, and she reported considerably more relief. She still gets migraines but far less frequently and less severe, and they pass quickly.

***

The *Circulation* tape has greatly reduced my constant ache from standing on cement floors all day at work. The bulging veins have reduced to fine "spider veins" around my knees and I feel comfortable using a stair climbing exercise machine again.

Your *Brain: Support & Maintenance* and *Lungs: Support & Maintenance* tapes have brought my headaches under control and have helped restore my endurance levels for the 3 mile walks I can now enjoy again without gasping for air.

***

A nine-year-old client had excruciating migraine headaches and needed occasional adjustments to relieve the pressure in his brain. As we began one counseling session, he was experiencing one of his headaches. I had my tape player with me and decided to see if the *Concentration* tape would help him through it while we continued the session. In less than five minutes he stopped in mid-sentence, looked at me in a combination of puzzlement, amazement, and relief, and said, "The headache is gone."

***

I use guided imagery as a mainstay in my practice at the *Pain Management* and Stress Management Clinic. My clients are much more receptive to imagery when I play *Hemi-Sync* musical tapes in the background. *Into the Deep*, *Inner Journey* and *Cloudscapes* are a few that I use often. The tapes are an extremely useful tool which accelerates the therapeutic benefits of guided imagery techniques.

***

I recently slipped and fell while getting into my car on a rainy day. As a result of the accident, I incurred broken bones in my left hand and foot, and both limbs were put in casts. Since the pain was quite intense, the orthopedic surgeon gave me prescription pain killers, and recommended that I remain immobilized for five weeks. Because I'd already worked tapes for many years, I knew my recovery would not be problematic. *Pain Management* eased the pain and reduced the swelling, so I needed to take medication for only two days. *Energy Walk* and *Restorative Sleep* lulled me into deep regenerative sleep states. I returned to work after only five days and my mobility and energy has been very impressive to the doctors and my colleagues throughout the ordeal.

***

My wife suffered severe headaches (sometimes migraines) for two weeks at a time during her monthly cycle, along with breast pain. She has found that *De-Discomfort* reduced and often took away the constant pain. It made life manageable again. I've used the same tape to take care of headaches and other pain. It really works.

Hemi-Sync Exercises Related to Pain Management

Heart-Sync Titles
Transforming Life's Challenges

Hemi-Sync Series
The Surgical Support Series

Human Plus Titles
Brain: Support & Maintenance
Circulation
De-Discomfort

Relax
Restorative Sleep
Tune-Up

Metamusic Titles
Cloudscapes
Inner Journey
Into the Deep
Seaside Slumber
Sleeping Through the Rain

Mind Food Titles
Energy Walk
Healing Journeys Support
Pain Management
Surf

Personal Growth / Self Improvement

Experiences Related to Personal Growth / Self Improvement

This information has been reported to Monroe Products and The Monroe Institute by individuals and/or by professional practitioners about the use of Hemi-Sync.

I'd been leading retreats for ex-addicts for a long time before I learned about *Hemi-Sync* and decided to play *Metamusic* for my participants. I was extremely impressed by the overall effect of the tape, calming and soothing the whole group. But what happened with one young woman, who had been addicted to heroin, was a revelation. During the first moments of the tape she sat holding her head with an expression on her face as if she was in pain. As I watched, the strained expression disappeared and she went through a total transformation right in front of my eyes. Needless to say, I'm going to continue using Hemi-Sync.

***

Each time I settle down to enjoy one of your musical *Hemi-Sync* tapes I know it will be rewarding but I'm unable to predict how. Sometimes I achieve insight into situations that have been bothering me. Sometimes I receive information that seems to come from some source outside of me. Occasionally I drift into a lucid dream, or simply enjoy badly needed, profound relaxation. Thanks for the exciting adventures!

***

That *Möbius West* tape is a great tool. I use the verbal cue to create just about anything and it really works. Often I create a mental picture that represents what I want to program for, and then I think of the picture while I say the cue. I like the whole Human Plus system in general, but this is one of my favorites.

***

Everyone in the workshop I gave loved Opening the Heart™. The tapes connected them to their higher selves/sources, and one person felt himself levitating—very powerful. I also use these tapes in teaching yoga. Students find it very relaxing and calming, and enjoy having a woman's voice on the tape.

***

My relative found herself in yet another abusive relationship. After hearing from me about Hemi-Sync, she began listening to *Remembrance* during the day as she worked, and liked it very much. When she asked for a tape to help her sleep better, I gave her *Deep 10 Relaxation*. She listened to it all night for several months and, as the relationship was coming to its inevitable end, she would wake to find her cassette player unplugged. He evidently felt threatened by the changes in her, which he attributed to Hemi-Sync. A subtle realignment seemed to be taking place within her, and she was becoming clearer about herself and her goals.

***

As a psychotherapist and Doctor of Clinical Hypnotherapy, I have spent the majority of my life studying the science of the mind and how best to help people. I have a number of hypnosis tapes, but they do not have your *Hemi-Sync* technology. I've found your tapes to be truly magnificent.

***

I cannot tell you what it means to me to be able to go inside with the cassettes and slowly find my way; to ask my Higher Power for direction and help and find it through inner guidance. I am learning more about balance. Huge bags of anger, revenge, hatred and resentments are slowly letting go. I am no longer afraid of getting stuck in a slow, downward spiral. All of this has happened in such a short while of using *Hemi-Sync* tapes; from no hope to hope. Each day I am making forward steps, while before the tapes I had given up. (Tapes used: *Going Home, Sleeping Through the Rain, Cloudscapes, Super Sleep*.)

***

As an artist and writer, I've found that your *Gateway Experience* series has enhanced my creativity enormously. I've been feeling more centered, have more energy for my work. Everything just flows, and I write much more easily.

***

At first I didn't know what to expect from *De-Hab* and *Eight-Great*. I thought I'd find ready-made solutions to all my problems. With passing time, as I learned to use the verbal cues, I understood that greater self-knowledge and improving access to intuition were what I had been looking for. For example, I had been asking myself whether to encourage my husband to take a certain action; the longer I went without an answer to the question, the more my anxiety about the situation increased. Immediately after using the verbal cue the first time, I felt calm and at ease. I gained some distance from the situation and understood that I could leave it alone to work itself out.

***

I've been listening to the *Concentration* tape for a few weeks, and find I am able to focus more on tasks and follow through with them. These have included paperwork, writing an important letter and having the words flow, and finishing a project that has been dragging on for months. What a great feeling! It gives me pleasure and a sense of accomplishment.

***

Wake/Know and *Let-Go* helped me deal with the issue of what kind of work I should be doing. My experiences with the tapes led me to realize how much I depended on appreciation from outside myself. Uncertainty about whether my job performance would satisfy others made me rush through tasks so I could end the stress of waiting for appreciation. I received no satisfaction from anything I did until awareness of this pattern led me to observe myself at work. I stopped rushing and began to enjoy even trivial occupations, like washing dishes. As a result, I knew I could consider doing the kind of jobs I had done before, but with interest and self-appreciation.

***

As I look back after working with *Gateway Experience* for a few months, I note that my professional efforts are achieving better results than ever before; there is more harmony and calm in my home life; I have greater self-control and better perspective on events; and I have realistic dreams in color and with full awareness.

***

In my search for self-knowledge, I've studied transcendental meditation, Zen Buddhism, Taoism, and just about every other means available. My experiences with *Focus 10* have been awesome! I'm certainly looking forward to the rest of the *Gateway Experience* course.

***

Since working with *Eight-Great* and *Sweet Dreams*, my mental processes have become clearer and brighter. I conduct business with clients with unusual calm and confidence, deal with conflict gently, and people seem far more friendly to me than ever before.

***

I always had trouble in school while I was growing up, and dropped out before high school, grade eight, to be exact. All my life this bothered me. I felt like a big failure. I decided to go back to school around the time someone told me about your tapes. I truly believe that if it weren't for *Hemi-Sync* I would never have done as well. I would use *Imprint* before I started to study. First thing in the morning I'd listen to *Concentration* and use either *Attention* or *Think Fast*. Then I'd go to school and write the test or exam. Not only did I do extremely well, but throughout the entire year I was the best student in all my classes, and never got more than one or two answers wrong. This to me has been a great accomplishment. I also use *Synchronizing*, *De-Hab*, *Möbius West*, *Wake/Know* and *Deep 10 Relaxation*. Thank you for the great help these tapes have been for me.

Hemi-Sync Exercises Related to Personal Growth / Self Improvement

Gateway	**Hemi-Sync Series**	**Human Plus Titles**	Möbius West
Gateway Experience	Going Home	Attention	Nutricia
	Lucid Dreaming	Contemplation	Off-Loading
Heart-Sync Titles	Opening the Heart	De-Hab	Options
Partners Meditation	Series	Do This Now	Sweet Dreams
Transforming Life's	Positively Ageless	Eight-Great	Synchronizing
Challenges	The Creative Way	Imprint	Think Fast
Your Heart's Song	The Shaman's Heart	Let-Go	Wake/Know
	Program		

Metamusic Titles
Cloudscapes
Chakra Journey
Egyptian Sun
Inner States
Sleeping Through the Rain
Transformation

Mind Food Titles
Breaking Free from Addictions
Claiming Your Self
Concentration
Creating Success
Deep 10 Relaxation
Emerging from Depression and
Anxiety
Exploring Other Lives
Guide to Serenity
Healing the Inner Child
Healing Through Awareness

Inner Healer
Manifesting with Hemi-Sync
Milton's Secret
Morning Exercise
Resonant Tuning
Retain-Recall-Release
Sleep Deeply
Super Sleep
The Gratitude Experience
Total Relaxation
Weight Loss
Wisdom In Essence

Pregnancy and Childbirth

Experiences Related to Pregnancy and Childbirth

This information has been reported to Monroe Products and The Monroe Institute by individuals and/or by professional practitioners about the use of Hemi-Sync.

Her previous pregnancy had ended in a miscarriage after seven months. This time, when the spotting and signs of premature labor began, the doctor ordered total bed rest. "Someone gave me *Opening the Way* and I was so bored in bed I listened to tape after tape for hours every day. I soaked myself in *Hemi-Sync*." In 10 days the doctor declared her out-of-the-woods and she went back to work part time. "I'm happy to be back at work except that it means I have less time to listen to *Hemi-Sync*."

***

I received *Opening the Way* only three weeks before my baby was born, and didn't have as much time to "practice" with the tapes as I would have liked. No drugs were necessary until I was fully dilated, and I believe that with more exposure to these tapes I may have a delivery without drugs next time. I have never felt so relaxed and rejuvenated as I do after listening to these tapes. I use the nursing/post-partum tapes frequently while breastfeeding my baby. Milk is plentiful, there's no pain or discomfort at all, no encouragement problems, no difficulties of any kind.

***

A pregnant friend was having an extremely rough time with nausea and vomiting. She was hospitalized five times for dehydration in the eighteen weeks of her pregnancy and spent one month in bed. After learning about this, I sent her *Surf* and *Tune-Up* by priority mail. She started using the tapes and began to be able to retain lunch and dinner. She's feeling much better, the nausea is minimal, she's able to enjoy food again, and has not been hospitalized since receiving the tapes. That may not sound like a big deal to most people, but to her it is definitely a miracle.

***

An RN and Senior Midwife reports on her use of *Hemi-Sync* in the delivery room. *Midsummer Night* and other *Metamusic* tapes have been very helpful in all cases, and at least two of my patients have been enraptured. With one patient, I had to stop playing the tapes because it put her husband to sleep!

Another patient said, as the sounds drifted over, "Oh, what beautiful music!" I played two tapes throughout her labor, which was fairly short, but turned the music off for the second stage as it didn't seem to blend with the activity of delivery. She needed an episiotomy and was dreading the suturing. I turned on a *Metamusic* tape, and she laid back, completely relaxed, while I did the stitching. I might add that I felt the benefits of the soothing sounds also!

***

During the second month I began to experience terrible nausea. I couldn't keep any food in my body and I lost a lot of weight. I listened often to the *Surf* and *Cloudscapes* tapes to assist my movement into a deep state of relaxation. The hours were often the only times I felt some peace and confidence. During those deep moments with the tapes I felt my connection with the baby to be very strong.

After about eight weeks the difficulties were over and I recovered very quickly. I then investigated and began using your verbally guided tapes. *Tune-Up* enhanced my physical well-being, and I added *Relax, Let Go, Immunizing,* and *Circulation.* I felt really wonderful during the last six months of my pregnancy, with no heaviness or slowness. Until the last moment I was very active, running around, working in our vegetable garden, just loving my big belly and never feeling handicapped by it.

After a marvelous Christmas dinner the contractions began and I started "*Resonant Tuning*" [a type of sustained vocalizing or chanting] during each wave. It was as if the tones were carrying me through the contractions, opening me up without tension or pain, and giving me energy. I was able to stay in the rhythm and the natural flow of my body. I listened to the *Surf* tape in the background over open speakers and felt just great until nearly the end. My body recovered immediately. Although I was nursing, three months after Raphael's birth I had all the energy I needed to function normally. I attribute this to the assistance of the *Hemi-Sync* process!

***

In the first three months of pregnancy, it is important that women be assisted in becoming accustomed to the physical changes taking place within their bodies. These changes can occur more smoothly and easily if the woman is able to relax into them, with little or no resistance. Later in the pregnancy, after the initial physical adjustments have been made, the mother can attempt to contact her child non-verbally, using deeper states of relaxation to facilitate the contact. Also, the patterning techniques in the *Gateway Experience* exercises can be used to visualize and affirm the best outcome for the pregnancy. The verbally guided tapes are excellent for overcoming physical problems, staying fit, and releasing emotional tensions.

***

It is best if, during the birth process, tapes can be played in the delivery room. If the mother chooses those *Hemi-Sync* tapes that she especially likes, the ones that really helped her to relax during the pregnancy, her body will remember when hearing the sounds and will allow her to let go more easily.

***

I'm so glad I took *Surf* and *Cloudscapes* to the hospital with me when I went in for the birth of my child. I couldn't have made it through such a trying labor without them. It was amazing how they set a mood of quiet and peacefulness in the room. Everyone who entered respected the very special atmosphere they created. The halls and other rooms were noisy and bustling, but the nurses and doctors tried extra hard to calm down when they came into my room. The tapes also helped my husband, mother, and sister relax enough to catch some sleep so they could be rested coaches for me. *Hemi-Sync* is great to keep a calm atmosphere now that we're home, too.

***

I love the tapes in *Opening the Way*, especially the labor tapes. I haven't gone into labor yet, but I listen to them anyway. I can't wait to use them in the delivery room.

***

My sister had a miscarriage last summer in the second trimester of her pregnancy. Although she and her husband were traumatized by this, they managed to get through the tough times and committed to try again.

Last week I received the wonderful news that she was able to become pregnant again, however, she is considered to be a "high-risk" case. Even though she has a very supportive family and medical doctor, she had been unable to sleep, and was full of anxiety and fear this time.

I really wanted to do something special for her, and decided to send her the series for pregnancy, *Opening the Way*. Within the last month, after using just the first and second tapes she has had remarkable results with reducing anxiety, and is now sleeping very well most nights. A sense of joy and confidence has replaced her fear. Since she shares her progress with me weekly, I am also gifted with the feeling of a greater connection to her during this special time in her life.

***

A good friend of mine is pregnant, and she was having an extremely rough time with nausea and vomiting. She had been hospitalized five times for dehydration in the eighteen weeks of her pregnancy, and had also been bedridden for one month. I consulted the TMI catalog, and found several tapes that I thought might help, and decided to send *Surf* and *Tune Up*. I was pleased to receive a note from her, telling me she had been using the tapes, and was feeling much better. She had been able to eat and retain lunch and dinner several times in that first week. I spoke to her recently, and she sounded wonderful. The nausea is minimal, she is able to enjoy food again, and has not been hospitalized since she began using the *Hemi-Sync* tapes.

***

I listened to the Labor and Pushing tapes from *Opening the Way* during the delivery of my child. They were an excellent source of support for relaxation and encouragement during the birthing process. I found it easier to handle my contractions, and I am pleased to say that I did not need to use any drugs until I was fully dilated. Since the birth, I've been using the *Postpartum Well-Being*, and *Nursing Baby* tapes while breast feeding my baby. I've had no difficulty with this at all, no pain or discomfort, have a plentiful supply of milk, and the tapes really enhance my enjoyment of this most precious time with my little one.

***

A Midwife who teaches homebirth classes introduces her clients to the *Opening the Way* pregnancy series. She reports that clients reaching a deeply relaxed state while listening to the tapes, and most are anxious to explore the further use of *Hemi-Sync* for additional benefits and most are anxious to explore the use of *Hemi-Sync* for benefits during the different stages of pregnancy.

***

One woman had experienced an elevation in blood pressure during the last part of her pregnancy and was put on strict bed rest. At her request, I sent several tapes home with her, and at the next class she stated that her blood pressure had remained at normal levels after she used the tapes. When it was time for the birth, she played the *Labor* tape, and after about three really strong contractions, pushed for five minutes and the baby was born! This couple has expressed deep gratitude for the extra support they received from *Opening the Way*.

***

I value the *Opening the Way* series very much, especially the Midwife's comments on the first tape. Her insights are interesting, eye opening, and comforting. I experienced a sense of being welcomed into a much deeper level of intimacy with a part of pregnancy that I had not thought of before. I also feel more confident, and empowered, and this has automatically enabled me to feel closer to my baby. My worry about being a good mother after birth has decreased and I am much more comfortable with the entire process.

Hemi-Sync Exercises Related to Pregnancy and Childbirth

Gateway
Gateway Experience

Hemi-Sync Series
Opening the Way
(cassette tapes only)

Human Plus Titles
Circulation
De-Discomfort

Immunizing
Let Go
Relax
Restorative Sleep
Tune-Up

Metamusic Titles
Cloudscapes
Dreamland
Hemi-Sync Support for Healing

Midsummer Night
Seaside Slumber
Sleeping Through the Rain

Mind Food Titles
Catnapper
Deep 10 Relaxation
Energy Walk
Healing Journeys Support
Hemi-Sync Nap
Pain Management
Surf
Total Relaxation

Problem Solving

Experiences Related to Problem Solving

This information has been reported to Monroe Products and The Monroe Institute by individuals and/or by professional practitioners about the use of Hemi-Sync.

The *Think Fast* function works more subtly than some of the other H+ functions. Using it is like giving extra spin to a wheel that is already spinning. I notice that I think now in a more organized way.

***

Only 10 days after experiencing *Focus 10 (Gateway)* for the first time I notice improved thought retention and a longer attention span, better logic and problem solving ability, and better dexterity and eye-hand coordination. When I'm working on something, the job is done more easily without much conscious effort on my part. My mind and body seem to be more coordinated. I guess that's what hemispheric synchronization does.

Hemi-Sync Exercises Related to Problem Solving

Heart-Sync Titles
Transforming Life's Challenges

Hemi-Sync Series
The Creative Way

Human Plus Titles
Access to Information
Attention
Eight-Great
Möbius West

Off-Loading
Options
Relax
Reset
Think Fast
Wake/Know

Metamusic Titles
Baroque Garden
Breakthrough

Einstein's Dream
Indigo
The Lotus Mind

Mind Food Titles
Concentration
Manifesting
Moment of Revelation
Surf
The Visit

Relaxation and Stress Management

Experiences Related to Relaxation and Stress Management

This information has been reported to Monroe Products and The Monroe Institute by individuals and/or by professional practitioners about the use of Hemi-Sync.

She returned to work two weeks after losing her son and grandson in an accident, needing to keep busy. Her stress level rose as she tried to handle the heavy demands of the job along with her grief. It soon became evident that her performance was severely affected. She was unable to bring the required focus to tasks needing attention and recognized that she was becoming a careless driver. After beginning to listen to the *Remembrance* tape, she functioned much better and was once again able to process information in her usual manner. She also used *Super Sleep* to help her sleep well again. "*Hemi-Sync* should be piped through the whole building 24 hours a day," she said.

***

My 83-year old father listened to his first *Hemi-Sync Metamusic* tape, *Cloudscapes*, and said, "I'm as loose as a goose. So relaxed. I never experienced anything like it!"

***

Reported by a social worker. A 72-year-old widow with cancer was admitted to Hospice, and asked for a relaxation tape because, "I've never been a nervous person, but I've been climbing the walls since the chemotherapy." The *Hemi-Sync* tape *Deep 10 Relaxation* was left with her. The following week she reported, "I haven't been taking as many pills since I began listening to the tape. I had been taking one pill every four hours or less. Yesterday, I only took one pill all day. I know the tape is helping me." She also reported improved sleep.

***

Although nervousness and restlessness were her frequent complaints, she lay quietly after listening to the *Surf* tape, finally opening her eyes and saying, "I'm too relaxed to move." She also was delighted with the tape *Energy Walk* and said, "I played the tape twice today and it quieted my nerves. Not only does it help and relax me, I feel that something is happening in my body, and I know it is doing something for me. I played it again today and counted my breathing with my hand over the cancer. It makes me feel all over better and relaxed. I went off to sleep."

***

I was working with a large group of foster parents, giving them information about addicted babies now coming into their homes. I treat children with cocaine addiction, and have been having some great effects on their nervous systems with the *Hemi-Sync* music. These exhausted, stressed, loving people had arrived at 7:30 PM for an hour session. I had *Metamusic* playing in the background and I just watched as they calmed, relaxed, and we worked together for one and one-half hours. I asked them if they would like the experience of really deep relaxation and, when they agreed, I gave them *Deep 10 Relaxation*. I've never seen those people so relaxed!

***

Some form of stress management was indicated. I persuaded the patient to use headphones and listen to the *Hemi-Sync* tape *Sleeping Through the Rain*. I told him that the latest research from major hospitals and universities finds that hypnosis, certain relaxation techniques, and even special types of musical tapes greatly help people relax and regulate breathing and blood pressure. He seemed fascinated and very receptive to this. Apparently the idea of hypnosis and relaxation techniques was all new to him.

Within just a few minutes of listening to the tape, the patient's breathing slowed and became clearer. His face relaxed and the familiar wheezing and gurgling sounds stopped. He also quit coughing, which made treatment much easier.

***

It is our belief that people operating from a relaxed state are more in touch with their "higher selves," enabling them to gain a perspective and become aware of greater choices in their lives. We have found that the use of *Hemi-Sync* facilitates relaxation and accelerates the healing process by accessing the client's deeper levels of awareness.

***

I had been under tremendous stress for two months. I thought I was handling it relatively well, but I wasn't able to take a deep breath. After listening to the *Relax* tape twice, I was finally able to take long, slow breaths again.

***

They were doing patterning for a small child whose central nervous system had been affected from a brain injury. I told the mother that *Metamusic* tapes might be helpful. She called to let us know that the tapes were helping her child to relax and enjoy the physical patterning exercises. She indicated that when the tape stopped, the child would tense up and stop making any sounds. As soon as they started the tape again, the child would relax and make happy sounds.

***

The responsibilities and pressure of my job were feeling heavier and heavier, and it felt like the last straw would be piled on any day. My only choices were to quit, which I couldn't afford to do, or go on to a nervous breakdown. At least, there would be insurance coverage for a nervous breakdown. I confessed to an old friend about the severity of my stress and my fears for the future. His response was to tell me about *Hemi-Sync* tapes and how they helped him. He loaned me H+ *Relax* and made me promise to listen to it, even though I had a hard time accepting that just saying "Plus *Relax*" would do anything.

I got into the habit of listening to the tape when I got home from work every day. Clearly it made me feel good at the time, and helped me keep the day's worries separate from the evening. Then one day at the office, when my boss shortened an already impossible deadline on a huge project, I was just about ready to blow. I said, "Plus, Relax" the way I learned on the tape, and the effect was instantaneous. I cooled down, spent some productive minutes organizing the reasons why the new deadline couldn't be met, presented them to my boss in a calm manner, and convinced her.

***

I've worked with teens for 23 years using many different modalities. Frankly, I'm highly impressed by the results I'm getting. At a drug prevention retreat weekend for teens, there were over 100 hyped-up kids in my session on the first night. I played *Deep 10 Relaxation* in a large room that had only one ceiling speaker, which meant I couldn't get a stereo effect. To my surprise, there was a 90% positive response— some kids asleep—almost all deeply relaxed. In contrast, a comparable group in another room with another presenter stayed silly and disruptive. The next day I played *Catnapper* for two different groups (in the same room with only one speaker) and got a 99% response. Only one person in each group did not fall asleep.

***

A new job and the move to a new city resulted in very heavy stress just when I wanted to be able to perform at my best. When I felt myself getting tense, I would close my office door for half-an-hour and listen to *Hemi-Sync.* It does wonders for me.

***

The nurse's aide who visits me at home listens with me daily to *Metamusic*. She claims it relaxes her, makes her think, and is soothing.

***

Mrs. C., who consulted me for weight loss, either could not or would not allow herself to relax for a hypnotic induction. I asked her to listen to *Sleeping Through the Rain* as background music.

***

As a family, we listen to *Daybreak (no longer available)* or *Morning Exercise* while we get ready for the school and work day ahead. There seems to be less rush and confusion in our household as a result. In the evening we listen to either *Surf* or *Into the Deep* to help unwind before homework, dinner and family time. This a good activity for us to bond and make the transition into a family unit again. My husband plays *Remembrance* in his office to help relieve the stress and pressure of his hectic business.

***

I listen to your guided imagery tapes, *The Visit* and *Guide to Serenity* to unwind with and to just "get away" after a stressful day at the office. My energy and attitude is always much better after a tape session.

***

Your tapes have helped me learn to deal with stress and to relax more. Whenever I need a "time out" for myself, all I need to do is listen to *Surf* or *Soft and Still* and I am refreshed and centered again in no time at all.

Hemi-Sync Exercises Related to Relaxation and Stress Management

Gateway	**Heart-Sync Titles**	**Hemi-Sync Series**
Gateway Experience	Transforming Life's Challenges	Massage Therapy Collection
		Network of Light Series
		The Shaman's Heart Program

Human Plus Titles	Options	**LightSOURCE Arts**
Eight-Great	Recharge	Hanta Yo
Let-Go	Relax	LightSOURCE 2nd Edition
Off-Loading	Tune-Up	Sacred Gaiametry
		Yantra Mantra

Mind Food Titles		
Blue Moon Journey	Moment of Revelation	Surf
Catnapper	Resonant Tuning	The "SO" Chord
Chakra Meditation	Sleep Deeply	The Visit
Deep 10 Relaxation	Soft & Still	The Way of Hemi-Sync
Guide to Serenity	Sound Sleeper	Transcendence
Hemi-Sync Nap	Streamhaven	Timeless Peace
Hemi-Sync Relaxation	Super Sleep	Total Relaxation

Metamusic Titles

Angel Paradise
Ascension
Awakening Consciousness
Beneath the Moon
Beyond the Golden Light
Breath of Creation Solo Huaca
Celestial Meditation
Chakra Journey
Gaia
Heaven and Earth
Hemi-Sync Relaxation
Higher
Himalayan Soul
Chakra Journey DVD
Cloudscapes
Convergence
Cosmic Consciousness
Deep Journeys
Desert Moon Song
Dreamer's Journey
Dreamland
Enchanted Forest
Eternal Now

Inner Journey
Into the Deep
It Dreams in Me
Land of Spirit
Lullaby
Maiden Voyage
Masterworks
Midsummer Night
Mystic Realms
Oasis
Octaves of Light
Path to Peace
Pearl Moon
Portal to Eternity
Portraits
Prisms
Radiance
Revelations
River Dawn
Romantic Wonder
Sacred Realms
Sacred Space
Seaside Slumber

Serenity
Sleeping Through the Rain
Spiral of Light
Spirit's Journey
Star Spirits
Strand
The Journey Home
The Music of Graceful Passages
The Return
The Shaman's Heart
The Shaman's Heart II
The Visitation
Timeless
Touching Grace
Tranquility
Transformation
Voyage to The Other Side
Waves of Love
Where the Earth Touches the
Stars
Winds Over the World
Wisdom of the Heart

Self-Confidence

Experiences Related to Self-Confidence

This information has been reported to Monroe Products and The Monroe Institute by individuals and/or by professional practitioners about the use of Hemi-Sync.

I am less judgmental and attached to outcome. I trust myself and my intuition more, and am more confident and compassionate. Other people have noticed that I am more steady and unflappable—greater sense of purpose and fulfillment—more able to let go—released fear about what others think of me—more tolerant—my approach to life is consistently positive—greater acceptance of what is. I don't feel the need to be perfect to be ok.

***

I am enjoying a renewed sense of confidence, and tend to be less judgmental about myself.

***

A psychologist reports: "*Hemi-Sync* allows a smooth integration of technology with clinical skill. The tapes help many clients shorten the unpleasant and uncertain phases of therapy, leaving more time and resources for growth, discovery, and for celebration of their worth."

Hemi-Sync Exercises Related to Self-Confidence

Hemi-Sync Series	**Human Plus Titles**	Options	**Mind Food Titles**
The Creative Way	De-Hab Eight-Great	Relax	Claiming Your Self
Opening the Heart Series	Möbius West	Reset	Exploring Other Lives
The Shaman's Heart Program	Off-Loading	Speak Up Think Fast	Morning Exercise

Sensory Improvement

Experiences Related to Sensory Improvement

This information has been reported to Monroe Products and The Monroe Institute by individuals and/or by professional practitioners about the use of Hemi-Sync.

I gave *Sensory: Hearing* to a colleague who suffered from episodes of ringing in his ear followed by intense headaches. The diagnosis was degenerative nerve disease. During his next episode, he listened to the tape five times over a three-day period. All the symptoms stopped and he hasn't had another episode for three months now. He's very grateful for the relief and also for the relaxation from *Hemi-Sync* tapes.

***

The doctors of an 80-year-old nun scheduled for cataract operation feared that the herpes infection in her eyes might flare up and perhaps lead to blindness. She insisted on going through, using *Sensory: Seeing*. The operation was successful, with no complications. She continued with the tape afterwards and greatly surprised her doctor by the total recovery of her vision.

Hemi-Sync Exercises Related to Sensory Improvement

Human Plus Titles
Sensory: Hearing
Sensory: Seeing

Sensory Integration Difficulties

Experiences Related to Sensory Integration Disabilities

This information has been reported to Monroe Products and The Monroe Institute by individuals and/or by professional practitioners about the use of Hemi-Sync.

Since 1981 I have been using *Hemi-Sync* with young children who experience sensory motor and sensory integrative disabilities. Both clinical experience and preliminary research indicate that the addition of *Hemi-Sync* signals (containing frequencies which produce more theta patterns in the brain) to background music increases the child's focus of attention, calms the emotions, and creates a mental set of open receptivity. *Hemi-Sync* is an excellent example of the sensory integrative process of the brain. Two independent auditory signals are integrated in a way that produces a whole (i.e., *Hemi-Sync*) which is different from each of the separate parts. Initial processing and integration occurs in the brain stem. In addition, the tendency toward synchronization of the right and left hemispheres appears to enhance attention, sensory and extrasensory awareness, and intuitive processing, and to increase successful adaptation to personal experiences.

However, an unexpected response was seen in children who, prior to *Hemi-Sync* therapy, experienced severe difficulties with sensory organization and integration. These children showed major difficulties accepting touch to their bodies. Gentle hugs, light calming strokes or pats, or accidental touching usually elicited strong aversive reactions. The child would push the touching person away, screech or cry, hit the person, or withdraw and begin a series of stereotyped self-stimulatory behaviors. They did not like to get their hands messy, have their hair washed or combed, or sit outside in the wind and grass. Many of the children became frightened and disoriented with movement or changes of position. They tended to increase these behaviors in complex sensory environments. A busy household, a school classroom or cafeteria, or a trip to the grocery store would reduce the child's ability to function and would increase the frequency and strength of the behaviors used to cope. Because of the intensity of their reactions to their environment, most of these children were labeled autistic, profoundly retarded, or emotionally disturbed.

When *Hemi-Sync* was added to therapy and classroom environments, these children responded in a totally different way. Eye contact increased. They accepted touch and became curious and interested in the sensory input. They were no longer startling and putting their hands over their ears to sounds that were previously upsetting. The amount of frustrated screeching and crying was reduced, and more functional communication emerged. There was a reduction in behaviors previously used by the child to cope with sensory overload. The children stopped rocking, spinning, and flapping and began to pay attention.

It appeared that the *Hemi-Sync* signals enhanced the child's ability to organize and integrate sensory information. This resulted in an increase in the ability to focus attention, to discriminate specific sensory properties, and to filter unwanted sensory input. What were these children telling us about the use of *Hemi-Sync* in our own lives?

Hemi-Sync Exercises Related to Sensory Integration Difficulties

Human Plus Titles
Brain: Support & Maintenance
Circulation
Sensory: Hearing

Sensory: Seeing
Synchronizing
Tune-Up

Heart-Sync Titles
Transforming Life's Challenges
Mind Food Titles
Healing Journeys Support

Shamanic Programs

Experiences Related to Shamanic Programs

This information has been reported to Monroe Products and The Monroe Institute by individuals and/or by professional practitioners about the use of Hemi-Sync.

"True shamans see through their hearts, live a life of honor and respect, and have a light and joy shining through their eyes that Westerners long for. *The Shaman's Heart Program* by Byron Metcalf (in collaboration with Monroe Products) teaches us how to embrace all these gifts. His work is brilliant and accessible to all. Those new to shamanism as well as experienced shamanic practitioners will receive great benefit from this program. I know I did!" –Sandra Ingerman, author of *Soul Retrieval* and *The Shamanic Journey: A Beginner's Guide.*

***

"I have used Byron Metcalf's [*Spirit Gathering*] in shamanic divination journey work of various kinds, and have found it to be extremely valuable in taking one to the deep, at times frightening inner spaces that one often encounters in self-exploration. The deep resonant bass pulls and driving rhythms keep one moving through the changes, and provide a safe container for this kind of work." –Ralph Metzner, Ph. D

Hemi-Sync Exercises Related to Shamanism

Hemi-Sync Series
The Shaman's Heart Program
Out of Body Techniques by
William Buhlman

LightSOURCE Arts
Hanta Yo
LightSOURCE 2nd Edition

Metamusic Titles
Between Worlds
Deep Time Dreaming
Dreamcatcher
Dimensions in Time
Egyptian Sun
Flow
Mayan Winds

Medicine Work
The Dreaming Gate
The Shaman's Heart
The Shaman's Heart II
Spirit Gathering
Vision Quest

Sleep and Dreams

Experiences Related to Sleep and Dreams

This information has been reported to Monroe Products and The Monroe Institute by individuals and/or by professional practitioners about the use of Hemi-Sync.

After listening to a *Hemi-Sync* tape (no matter which one) before sleep, I wake up in the morning at 7:00 a.m., fresh and energetic, without help from my alarm clock. During my daily activities I am much more balanced and rarely get angry over trifles as I did before.

***

My father has been able to sleep only with the aid of pills for the last several years. One evening he listened to *Sound Sleeper* and never returned from his bedroom to watch the TV program he had wanted to see. He was fast asleep. He listened to it another night, again sleeping. Since then he's slept even without listening to the tape.

***

Listening to *Hemi-Sync* has had a strong influence on my sleep. It no longer includes echoes of strain and worry related to my job, and seems to be deeper, fuller, more restful. I'm remembering my dreams now, which are in color and very real.

***

An M.D. reports about an obese man in his 50s who wanted help in improving his sleep. He had some degree of sleep apnea and had to sleep on his side. He felt chronically tired and "fuzzy." I loaned him the sleep tape from the *Positive Immunity Program* album for overnight use. He reported feeling restless all night," but it had a "spectacular effect," resulting in greatly improved clarity the next day.

***

Not once have I managed to stay awake for the whole of *Guide to Serenity*, even when I have tried. No matter what has happened during the day, all I need do is play that tape and breathe deeply, and before I know it, the morning is here.

***

Twelve flight attendants on international flights participated in a survey about the use of the *Hemi-Sync Catnapper* tape in combating fatigue and jet lag. All reported, "I experience less fatigue on duty after listening to the tape," and recommend its use by flight attendants. Other comments include, "I sleep much better when I'm on layovers now." "I used to find myself too wired and too tired to sleep, I was able to relax, and I also used it to nap before my all-night flight." "Each time I listened to the tape I felt more relaxed and rested. Before, I tossed and turned and was waking up every hour." "When I was having problems overseas due to over-exhaustion, the tape released the tensed-up state that prohibits relaxing sleep."

***

The doctor, in addition to using tapes for patients with sleep disturbances, reported that, "When I use *Hemi-Sync* at the end of a long day, the effect is one of feeling greatly rested and refreshed, and allows me to experience much increased efficiency and alertness for extended evenings of work."

***

One of my best results was with a client who is vice president of a nation-wide chain, who reported a severe case of insomnia. This has gone on most of his life. He was extremely high strung, restless, etc. I had him use H+ *Relax*, *Restorative Sleep*, and *Options*. After 3 weeks he reported that for the first time in his life he is sleeping very well. When I saw him, he was much more relaxed, calm, and not so restless.

***

For the past four months, few days have passed without my calling on H+ *Recharge* for a "boost in operating voltage." For me it works best to sit in a comfortable chair, arrange not to be disturbed for about

20 minutes, close my eyes, and activate the *Recharge* Function. Usually I think of the length of charging period I think I need. This might be from 5 - 15 minutes for the catnap period plus about 5 minutes at the beginning and at the end. I drift into sleep and wake up feeling refreshed and ready to go. It is entirely different from the groggy feeling I can associate so clearly with the aftermath of an old man's nap.

***

I am a devoted fan of *Catnapper*. I'm a person who is on the move and most often don't get the sleep I need at night. I use *Catnapper* almost daily between my running around, and it helps me keep my senses sharp.

***

The *Metamusic* tapes have virtually the same effect. Upon listening I become deeply relaxed and sleep very soundly, which seems unusual as I have always suffered from insomnia. Further, my recall of dreams improved tenfold and the actual dreams seem longer and more frequent.

***

From the moment I used *Sound Sleeper* and other *Hemi-Sync* sleep tapes, I have recovered normal sleep after years of white nights.

***

A hospice worker reported her hesitance to recommend *Restorative Sleep* to her client, an extremely macho policeman whose heart condition and gall bladder disease left him unable to sleep. Only after his distressed wife confided that the patient's increasing irritability was becoming impossible for her to cope with did the hospice visitor overcome her reluctance and leave the *Hemi-Sync* tape with them. The wife answered her phone call three days later. "He loves it!" she said. "He'd tell you himself, except he's asleep now. And I love it too!"

***

Catnapper is great to bring along on business trips. I use it after a long day, before dinner, and I'm rejuvenated for the evening. It's especially good to have with me when I go to conventions and conferences. The depth of relaxation it brings about in a short time is astounding.

***

A prisoner in a state penitentiary reports. I thought it would take far longer than it has to see any results from these tapes. My sleep problems have been a nightmare for so long, it's hard to believe that something so simple can be so helpful. *Catnapper* was a real blessing. I'm not really sure if I actually nap or not, but at the end of the tape I do feel rested and refreshed. In a place like this, it's like a miracle. To get the effect of *Super Sleep* I had to reset the equalizer a little bit. Now only on my worst nights am I sleepless.

***

My psychologist husband and I have listened to *Inner Journey* several times before we go to sleep. He experiences pleasant visualizations and notices a difference in the soundness of his sleep. *Metamusic* tapes have affected my well-being in a subtle and positive way. I notice that the images in my dreams seem to be more vivid and clear. Colors stand out, even if I don't recall the dream. Since listening to *Hemi-Sync*, two messages in my dreams were clear to me on a conscious level, whereas before, the messages may have been more obscure, requiring interpretation.

***

I was telling a friend about how *Hemi-Sync* sleep tapes have seemed to stop the bad dreams that often woke me and help me sleep through the night. They calm me down and enable me to get badly needed rest. To my friend's question, "What's on the other side of the tape?" I answered, "What other side? I'm asleep before the first side is finished."

***

Report from an MD: "I'd been treating an obese patient for sleep apnea. My first suggestion was that he try sleeping on his side, but after a few nights, he complained that he awoke feeling tired and fuzzy. Then, I loaned him the *Restorative Sleep* tape. This seems to work very well for him, as he reported it had a spectacular effect, and he felt much clarity the next day."

***

I've been a chronic insomniac for many years, but since using *Sound Sleeper* and other *Hemi-Sync* tapes, that problem has become a thing of the past!

***

Our nine-year-old developed bronchitis and a touch of pneumonia. She was so uncomfortable and restless that she couldn't sleep. As I played *Energy Walk* for her, she went from being restless and frustrated to lying perfectly still, eyes closed, smiling, relaxed. "This is wonderful, mom. It's so beautiful. I feel so good," Then she drifted off into sleep.

***

Super Sleep, played continually throughout the night with an auto-reverse player, was highly successful in modifying a 3-year-old's disturbed sleeping behavior and helping him sleep through the night. Additionally, the child worked harder and more persistently at tasks, spoke more clearly, and accepted correction of his speech more readily, listened better, and was less easily frustrated, started to enjoy books and to sit still for stories to be read to him.

Hemi-Sync Exercises Related to Sleep and Dreams

Hemi-Sync Series
Lucid Dreaming Series

Human Plus Titles
Recharge
Restorative Sleep
Sleep
Sweet Dreams
Wake/Know

Metamusic Titles
Dreamcatcher
Dreamland
Lullaby
Seaside Slumber
Serene Sleep
Sleeping Through the Rain
The Return

Mind Food Titles
A Unicorn Named Georgia
Attention / At Ease

Catnapper
Deep 10 Relaxation
Hemi-Sync Nap
Joy Jumper
Robbie The Rabbit
Sleep Deeply
Sleepy Locust
Sound Sleeper
Super Sleep
Total Relaxation
Turtle Island

Stroke Recovery

Experiences Related to Stroke Recovery

This information has been reported to Monroe Products and The Monroe Institute by individuals and/or by professional practitioners about the use of Hemi-Sync.

Now in her 40s and in a wheel chair, she had had the first of a series of strokes at age 25. I was treating her for depressive disorder, which included frequent, uncontrollable weeping. During one session I put on a *Metamusic* tape. The tears stopped and she became calmer almost immediately. After we talked about the experience, she asked for a tape of her own to play whenever she felt the need. She recognized that she had found a tool to use to help herself.

***

My mother has been in what the chronic care hospital calls a vegetative state since her stroke, and her caretakers had "given up" on her. I wasn't ready to give up, and continued to believe that she was aware, even if she couldn't speak or move. Since I've been playing *Hemi-Sync* tapes for her (from the *Surgical Support Series*), she seems more relaxed, calm, and peaceful. Now when I ask her a question, I tell her to blink twice to mean "yes", and she is able to do it. The nurses are intrigued and will be trying *Hemi-Sync* with other patients.

***

The physical therapist who has been working regularly with my mother since her stroke was astounded by the effect of the *Remembrance* tape. Because this tape has been so useful in helping me to concentrate, I had decided to experiment with playing it softly as background in the bedroom during a therapy session, hoping it would increase mother's responsiveness to the therapist's directions. Within the first few moments of the tape, the expression on mother's face changed dramatically from tight and negative to relaxed and positive, and her cooperation with the therapist was at a higher level than had been possible before. After the tape ended, the therapist and I spoke together about the remarkable transformation we had witnessed. When our attention returned to mother, we saw that the pinched, strained expression had replaced the earlier *Hemi-Sync* expression.

***

I loaned the stroke patient *Brain: Support and Maintenance* and my own cassette player and headphones. That afternoon she was sleeping soundly, her whole body relaxed and her mouth open, snoring away. By evening she was sitting up, more alert and smiling for the first time. During our meeting the next day she said of the tapes, "They're wonderful. I feel so relaxed." Her recovery progressed nicely, and I spoke to her as she was preparing to return home. She cried when she told me how much she thought *Hemi-Sync* had helped her, saying she was deeply moved.

***

Joan is a badly disabled stroke patient, confined to a wheelchair, with no use of her left arm and leg. Some months after listening to a selection of *Human Plus* tapes and tapes from the Discovery album of *Gateway Experience*, she reported, "I looked at my outstretched and spasmed fingers; then, with closed eyes, I gently curved them down." Several months later: "I am aware of a sort of "pre-movement," a definite impulse in the affected side, especially in fingers, toes and forearm. The ankle is slightly moving. I'm gradually starting to work with the *Hemi-Sync* sound patterns by working them down the body and into the extremities. I am aware of an interlacing between right and left hand sides." Later still: "Since I've been working with the tapes I'm less and less aware of my disability. In fact, if I hold an image of myself it's not one of a disabled person. Neither is it the person I used to be. Rather, the Joan that is. This has given me the freedom to explore, to take risks, to be curious about my possibilities, and to push back the boundaries and limits."

***

He had a stroke in '87 and made little progress until two years ago. Since he began listening to *Hemi-Sync* he is now driving his car again on short runs, is recovering speech function, can now be understood when talking on the phone, and lives an active retirement.

***

My father had severe back pain following his CVI and has encountered many difficulties involving pain control. Medications intended to be relaxing and pain-easing have had the opposite effect, leaving him restless and unable to sleep while, at the same time, doing little to alleviate the constant pain. To make matters worse, he didn't like the way the medications left him. As he put it, "They make me feel bad." *Energy Walk* and *Pain Management* have given him tools that relieve the pain so well he rarely takes any pain medication. The tapes also help him relax (which in itself helps with the pain) and to sleep at night. These good results have come with listening through speakers placed on his right and left sides.

***

A minor stroke left me feeling very depressed about the reduction of my physical capacities. I sensed myself going into a downward spiral as I contemplated the limitations I now had to live with. I started using *Off-Loading* and *Eight-Great* to focus on the positive, to reinforce my enjoyment of the things I was still able to do. The depression is gone and—an unanticipated bonus—I find myself able to do more and more.

Hemi-Sync Exercises Related to Stroke Recovery

Heart-Sync Titles
Transforming Life's Challenges

Hemi-Sync Series
Support for Stroke Recovery
The Surgical Support Series

Human Plus Titles
Brain: Support & Maintenance

Circulation
Eight-Great
Hypertension
Off-Loading
Restorative Sleep
Tune-Up

Metamusic Titles
Dreamland

Hemi-Sync Support for Healing
Remembrance
Seaside Slumber

Mind Food Titles
Energy Walk
Healing Journeys Support
Pain Management
Surf

Surgery

Experiences Related to Surgery

This information has been reported to Monroe Products and The Monroe Institute by individuals and/or by professional practitioners about the use of Hemi-Sync.

I recently used your *Surgical Support Series* with incredible results. When I checked in to the hospital for abdominal surgery I gave the floor nurses the Caregiver booklet, since they were going to be taking care of me. During my two days there they saw the results with their own eyes and became interested in testing the tapes with other patients. The anesthesiologist was skeptical, but humored me and changed the tapes as I went into surgery and later came out. I was awake as they wheeled me into the recovery room, talked with the nurses in there, and even spoke to friends by phone that afternoon. It was a total surprise to me and to them that I was awake, alert, and feeling up to it so soon after surgery. My nurses were amazed at how coherent I was and how little pain I experienced. After 36 hours I was completely off pain meds and had had no need to use any PCA (patient controlled analgesia). I used the post-surgery tapes for two weeks afterwards and believe they helped speed my recovery. The tapes helped me to feel comfortable without masking the pain.

***

Report from an MD on the use of the *Surgical Support Series* tapes: A hysterectomy patient required minimal self-administered analgesia the first day and virtually no medication on the second day. The nursing staff encouraged the patient not to be stoic and to use medication when she felt pain. However, the patient insisted she had little or no discomfort. She was discharged on the third day.

Another patient, diagnosed with a ruptured disc, underwent a lumbar laminectomy. She reported very little need for pain medication after the procedure and was released from the hospital much sooner than expected. She was very pleased, as was the hospital staff, at her fast recovery rate.

***

The Department of Surgery at Columbia Presbyterian Hospital uses *Hemi-Sync* tapes in conjunction with other therapies to help patients heal more quickly and with less anxiety and pain. They recommend the *Surgical Support Series* tapes for use prior to and during a medical procedure and while in recovery. They recommend a variety of other *Hemi-Sync* tapes to foster healing and maintain optimal wellness in the hospital and at home.

***

My husband was diagnosed as being in Stage III of testicle
cancer. Surgery would kill him, we were told. Chemo was the only hope and, even with that, his chances of survival would be 30%. Throughout four months of chemotherapy I watched him lose his hair, lose weight, be violently ill from the side effects.

The mass was reduced in size, though still huge in terms of medical safety. His doctors advised surgery even though there was very high risk that his lungs were now too weakened by chemotherapy drugs to withstand anesthesia for a ten-hour operation. We started using the *Surgical Support Series* days before the surgery, and consulted (and educated) the anesthesiologist about using the tapes during the operation.

The ten-hour operation took four hours. The surgeons were able to remove the tumor mass intact and no live cancer cells were found.

***

I was back home 48 hours after surgery (three days early!), active and energetic. I'd needed no pain medications, slept wonderfully, and was up and around as soon as the anesthesia wore off. Within a month I was back to full activity with the scar as the only physical reminder.

***

A Clinical Psychologist reported on a patient whose extreme anxiety was causing her to resist the surgery that would relieve her extensive pain from cervical nerve damage. After following his recommendations to listen to *Metamusic* tapes continuously at home, she agreed to undergo the surgery on condition that the neurosurgeon permit her to listen to *Hemi-Sync* throughout the operation. The doctor complied, and she underwent the procedure without difficulty.

***

I introduced *Hemi-Sync* to my brother, who has had two coronary bypass surgeries and a very serious aneurism repaired. He swears he could not have made it through without *Human Plus* functions and the *Surgical Support Series* tapes.

***

My use of the first three tapes in the *Surgical Support Series* before, during, and immediately after my surgery enveloped me in a kind of "comfort cocoon." *Pre-Op* helped me relax and get in the right mood. I woke up briefly in the midst of the procedure and the *Intra-Op* tape helped me re-enter my secure, sheltered, pain-free space easily. I could hear the doctors and nurses talking without moving out of that wonderful *Hemi-Sync* state.

***

In the days before I went into the hospital, the *Surgical Support Series* tapes helped me relax and get in the right mood. During the operation I was in a beautiful *Hemi-Sync* awake state, could hear the doctors and nurses talking but felt wonderful—no pain.

***

I listened to the *Pre-Op* tape for a week before the removal of a fifteen-pound abdominal tumor, and used other *Hemi-Sync* tapes instead of pain medication after the surgery. My recovery was remarkably quick. I went home two days later, instead of the week that had been expected, and was excited about getting up to walk again.

***

For the first surgery I wanted to use the *Surgical Support Series* tapes, but the hospital staff didn't take me seriously. I was in the hospital for six days with numerous infections and it was eight weeks before I was without pain.

Prior to the second surgery, my doctor agreed to listen to the tapes, and began to understand what I was trying to accomplish. This time everyone was on my side. The difference was drastic. When I woke up in recovery, I was completely awake and alert. I felt fine, they were able to remove the IV and give medication by mouth. I had a great appetite and no infections, and was able to go home in three days.

***

I was told that only a minimal amount of anesthetic was required to keep me sedated during the surgery. My vital signs were strong and I was relaxed and calm throughout the entire operation. The following day I was alert and energetic. Much to the consternation of the nursing staff I did not require anything for pain, because I had no pain. I resumed normal activity within three weeks, which is months sooner that with my two previous surgeries.

***

I sent the *Surgical Support Series* air express to a friend who needed emergency spinal surgery. She used the tapes as recommended, and is going on a 33-day tour of Australia, Fiji, and New Zealand just fourteen days after the spinal surgery. I should tell you she will be seventy this year. She was absolutely thrilled with her recovery, as she had to be hospitalized for months at a time for several prior spinal surgeries.

***

On the morning after my surgery the nurse said, "This room is different from all the other rooms in my care. There is such calm and peacefulness here. This room is a sanctuary." I was plugged into one of my *Surgical Support Series* tapes. Not only were the tapes a splendid support system throughout, but they also obliterated intrusive sounds of hospital clatter.

***

I found the *Pre-Op* tape unbelievably soothing. The night before surgery I found it hard to sleep—I was anxious and the persistent, intermittent sound of the foghorn on Lake Michigan bothered me. "I hope the tape will knock out the foghorn sound," I thought as I put the Walkman on. It didn't, but it made me feel so good and so relaxed that I wasn't bothered by the foghorn anymore. After the surgery I realized that the tape did the same thing with pain and discomfort—it was still there but it didn't bother me, just as the tape said."

***

Thanks to the *Surgical Support Series*, the patient was very calm before entering the OR for gall bladder surgery, and needed less muscle relaxant than normal during the procedure. In the recovery room she was the only quiet one: she awoke as if from a nap, very calm with no agitation or nausea. She had less than average pain medication in the recovery room and required none for the rest of her hospitalization. Her stay was reduced to 3 days (national average 7-10 days).

***

Two previous surgeries had caused weight loss, hypoglycemic episodes, and had added to her feelings of losing inner control. She decided to use the *Surgical Support Series*, gained the support of her surgeon, anesthesiologist, and nursing team, and negotiated to have a local surgical intervention rather than general anesthesia. After the procedure she experienced significantly less pain and used no pain medication for the first six hours. In the recovery room she ate heartily without experiencing nausea or vomiting, did not have cyclic constipation during her post-op days, and experienced no weight loss. At the first dressing change, her surgeon remarked about how clean and clear her suture line looked.

***

Report from a surgeon. The patient was scheduled for a second stage reconstruction after a right modified radical mastectomy. She was given the *Surgical Support Series* and used them according to instructions. Except for 50cc of Xylocaine with epinephrine for local anesthesia, she required no intravenous sedation or pain medications pre-, intra-, or postoperatively. The patient reported that she needed no pain medications during her recovery at home.

***

An anesthesiologist who uses the *Surgical Support Series* tapes with patients reported on two radical mastectomies in which the tapes were "supportive in allaying the patients' anxieties before surgery to the point where both went to sleep without medication only minutes before surgery.

***

I have found the use of the *Surgical Support Series* very helpful to patients undergoing major surgery, such as bilateral knee replacement. There has been a significant reduction in the use of anesthesia and narcotic medications for pain, as well as a more rapid, uncomplicated, and less painful recovery phase.

***

My experience with the tapes was kind of strange. I did all the preparation with them, and the Doctor and recovery room nurse agreed to help. I came to in the recovery room wide awake and was back in my room very shortly entertaining a guest who didn't realize I had just come back from surgery because I was so wide awake. My recovery was uneventful and fairly pain-free and I am doing beautifully.

***

I tell everyone about the *Surgical Support Series*, and keep the tapes as a lending library. My best friend's delivery was much easier and more comfortable, my father was back in his room "in record time" after quintuple heart bypass surgery, and Michael's hip replacement was significantly less painful and his recovery almost twice as fast as the first time he'd had it done. In all cases, recovery has been rapid and relatively comfortable.

***

Because of my preparation prior to entering the hospital, I was particularly serene and did not suffer any anxiety at all. During the 3 1/2 hour of surgery no blood transfusion was required and Hematocrit the next day was normal. The lab re-performed the blood test and rechecked the results to confirm this excellent reading. I changed the Function Command for the H+ *Tune-Up* tape to "Plus, balance, heal blood pressure" to bring my blood pressure down quickly. My body has an absolutely lovely response to it.

***

I was particularly serene anticipating the surgery, and did not experience any anxiety. There was absolutely no surgical pain at any time, a fact which I attribute to the *Hemi-Sync* tapes with which I had prepared myself in advance, and which were used prior and after surgery. (*Surgical Support Series* and a number of Human Plus tapes: *Restorative Sleep, Circulation, De-Discomfort*).

***

Initially, I did not trust the quality of the *Surgical Support Series*, despite what I had read and heard. I told the doctors and nurses to observe me using the tapes. If they worked, fine, but if not, I wanted my codeine immediately. Though the surgery lasted four and a half hours, I never needed any pain medication afterwards and had minimal bruising and swelling. The *Pre-Op* tape gave me intense calmness, with lowered blood pressure and temperature before surgery, instead of my former experiences of queasiness and uncontrollable shaking. By the next surgery [five hours] I used the tapes and sailed through. I was nervous about pain, but repeated "55515" and erased all pain signals. For my final surgery, the confusion of getting ready for the operating room washed over me without effect due to the strong inner calm from the *Pre-Op* tape. The surgery seemed to last a fraction of a minute, although I later found it had been five hours.

The H+ series enriched my recovery. I found less need for the *Pain Management* tape if I went to sleep with H+ *Restorative Sleep.* I alternated H+ *Circulation*, and *Tune-Up* for naps.

***

Report from an anesthesiologist. In preparation for a second back surgery, the patient discussed the *Surgical Support Series* tapes with me, and told me he wanted to use as little medication as possible. He seemed quite relaxed about the upcoming surgery, and we agreed that I would not order any premedication for him. He arrived in the "holding area" calm and listening to his tape. I started his intravenous and gave him a small amount of Valium (5mg) and Fentanyl (1cc). The surgery was uneventful. He required less than the usual amount of anesthesia, and lost minimal blood. He awakened immediately in the recovery room, used the Recovery tape, and required no pain medication. He required no post-operative pain medication during his hospital stay and was discharged on the fourth post-operative day.

In contrast, the hospital records of his first back surgery showed he was medicated twice in the recovery room, required more narcotic after he returned to his room, and continued to need this for the next four days. He had significant blood loss in surgery, developed a post-operative hematoma accompanied by a fever of several days duration, and was not discharged until the ninth post-operative day.

While it is not necessarily valid to compare the two experiences, the patient and surgeon were the same, the operations were similar and for the same problem, and the basic anesthetic techniques and agents were the same. Even on a non-comparative basis, the patient's entire perioperative course the second time was exemplary.

***

A patient who had hip replacement surgery reports: I started listening to the tapes two days before my surgery, and the had a very calming influence. The doctor had taken me off pain medication and I was having trouble sleeping. *Energy Walk* enabled me to get a good night's sleep. I listened to *Pre-Op* in the hospital before surgery and I felt very good about the whole thing. I remember someone saying, "It didn't take much to put her to sleep." As soon as I came out of recovery I started listening to *Post-Op*, continued every day, and really felt wonderful. My first time up I had no pain and I did exercises without discomfort.

I went from the hospital to a rehab facility where, after a few days of doing fine, I ran out of batteries. While waiting for someone to bring me new batteries I started having severe cramps in my leg. The cramps stopped when I got new batteries and started listening to the tapes again.

Preparing to go home after a week of rehab, I was told that a nurse, a physical therapist, and an occupational therapist would visit me at home to evaluate my condition and provide help. Each one told me on their first visit that I was doing so well on my own I would need no further help from them.

***

A friend recently had a mastectomy of the left breast following a diagnosis of breast cancer. She had been very anxious about the surgery, with only a week to prepare herself for the operation. During that week she used the *Pre-Op* tape numerous times and reported that it reduced her anxiety level significantly. She told me that it was unbelievable that she could actually sleep the night before the surgery. The operation was on Monday morning, and she was released from the hospital on Tuesday. Two weeks later, her chest began filling with fluid and a new drain had to be inserted. The drain clogged up, and she was in considerable pain. She used the *Energy Walk* tape and reported that one half hour following the tape, the drain "unclogged itself," and remained open. If pain awakened her in the middle of the night, she reported going quickly back to sleep while playing *Sleeping Through the Rain*.

***

Summaries from reports of patients who have used the *Surgical Support Series* and *Metamusic* tapes for recovery from surgery:

a) Male, age 73: prostate surgery: This client was in good health at time of his surgery, which was performed at UCLA Medical Center. The head anesthesiologist agreed to allow the *Intra-Op* tape from the *Surgical Support Series* to be listened to with headphones during the operation. The patient was walking and alert the morning after surgery. He reported that the physicians and nurses expressed amazement with the pace of his recovery. He was released on the third day postoperatively and continued to enjoy a rapid recuperation. His most significant comment was "I never experienced pain . . . not once!"

b) Female, age 39: abdominal hysterectomy: This patient was a diabetic weighing approximately 250 pounds. She did not use *Hemi-Sync* intraoperatively but did use other tapes frequently pre- and postoperatively. The patient reported that the *Hemi-Sync* tapes were far more effective than Percodan® for pain management. Although the surgery was difficult, the patient said she knew intuitively that she was healing quickly, and stated that she felt so good the day after she returned home from the hospital that she actually walked through the park while listening to *Energy Walk* from the *Surgical Support Series*.

c) Female, age 45: hysterectomy: The anesthesiologist assisted with the use of *Intra-Op* by turning the tape over at the end of each side. The patient began using the *Pre-Op* tape seven days before her surgery. She had not been exposed to *Hemi-Sync* before this occasion and mentioned that she "had to get used to it." Adjusting to the new experience, she soon reported that the tapes became her "security blanket." After being transported to the recovery room following surgery, the Recovery tape was placed in her cassette player. She reported that she woke up quickly in the recovery room feeling very alert and was pleased, once again, to be aware of the calm, soothing voice on the tape. She reached the point where simply thinking of the voice stimulated instant relaxation. The patient's most significant comment was "I have no doubt that the tapes have helped speed my recovery. When I need rest, it is easy to fall asleep. I feel very positive about getting well and about the whole healing process."

An orthopedic surgeon reports that he uses *Hemi-Sync* tapes in his surgical practice and at an institute for pain and stress management. He recommends that patients use the *Surgical Support Series* to encourage relaxation in the operating room, and to promote healing in the recovery room afterward. He finds the tapes valuable during surgery because he believes patients are aware of what is going on even under anesthesia.

***

At the pain and stress management institute, *Hemi-Sync* tapes are broadcast over the public-address system throughout the center and in the waiting room. Different tapes are used to achieve desired effects from encouraging relaxation to enhancing concentration and cognitive function.

***

The doctor reports: "Anyone who has undergone major surgery, [with] the tapes found a significant reduction in the pain experienced afterward. The audio signals helped reduce the constant psychological turmoil that people go through."

***

A large mass was discovered in my breast. Surgery was scheduled and general anesthesia was ordered. During the surgery, I used the verbal cue of the *Relax* tape and my feelings of panic were immediately washed away. After the surgery was completed, I went to the recovery room awake, alert, and feeling great. After only twenty minutes, I was moved to a unit for two hours of observation. Thirty minutes later I was told I could go home. Using my *Metamusic* CD at work and my DEC tape at home, I never needed to take a pain pill. The 2 ½ inch incision healed in record time. I feel so lucky to be a registered nurse who understands physical needs, and to know that *Hemi-Sync* is available to complement traditional medicine for those who seek it.

***

I took *Sleeping Through the Rain* with me to the hospital when I had an operation. I have always found it to be very soothing and relaxing and it stood me in good stead during hospital nights when I would wake up. It kept me relaxed and rested and I breezed through with no problems. *Recuperation*, *Energy Walk*, and *Restorative Sleep* are also favorites. The doctor said I healed so fast he couldn't believe it. In fact, whenever I get a cold or am not feeling up to par, I get out these same tapes and put them to use.

***

I recently slipped and fell while getting into my car on a rainy day. As a result of the accident, I incurred broken bones in my left hand and foot, and both were put in casts. Since the pain was quite intense, the orthopedic surgeon gave me prescriptions for pain killers, and recommended that I remain immobilized for up to five weeks. Because I had been a long-time user of *Hemi-Sync* tapes, I knew my recovery would not be a problem. I listened to *De-Discomfort* and *Pain Management* to ease the pain and swelling, and only needed to take medication for two days. *Energy Walk* and *Restorative Sleep* lulled me into deep regenerative sleep states. I returned to work after only five days and my mobility and energy has been very good throughout the ordeal.

Hemi-Sync Exercises Related to Surgery

Books
Focusing the Whole Brain

Heart-Sync Titles
Transforming Life's Challenges

Hemi-Sync Series
The Surgical Support Series

Human Plus Titles
Circulation
De-Discomfort
Relax
Restorative Sleep
Tune-Up

Metamusic Titles
Dreamland
Hemi-Sync Support for Healing

Seaside Slumber
Sleeping Through the Rain

Mind Food Titles
Deep 10 Relaxation
Energy Walk
Healing Journeys Support
Pain Management
Surf
Total Relaxation

Therapy

Experiences Related to Therapy

This information has been reported to Monroe Products and The Monroe Institute by individuals and/or by professional practitioners about the use of Hemi-Sync.

As a psychotherapist and Doctor of Clinical Hypnotherapy, I have spent the majority of my life studying the science of the mind and how best to help people. I have a number of hypnosis tapes, but they do not have your *Hemi-Sync* technology. I've found your tapes to be truly magnificent.

***

Report from a psychiatrist. I used the tape *Concentration* for patients with depressive syndrome, especially those with memory difficulties and whose ability to concentrate was diminished due to depression. They all had problems with concentration, attention-to-task deficit, lack of short-term memory, and felt unable to perform mental tasks as well as they had previously. These symptoms were present whether or not the patients were taking medication.

The patients liked this new approach, and reported improvement of their ability to concentrate during test preparation and other cognitive tasks, better short-term memory, greater interest in their studies, and an ability to sustain attention for longer periods than was previously possible.

***

Report from a psychologist. The patient was experiencing intense anxiety about an upcoming MRI test, which involves the person remaining motionless inside a very cramped tube for hours as the machine takes pictures of the brain. Anesthesia cannot be used for this procedure. The medical team reported that no one who was even moderately claustrophobic had ever completed the MRI test. After three weeks of working with the H+ tapes *Relax*, *Let Go* and *Off-Loading* and the **Mind Food** tapes *Energy Walk* and *Morning Exercise*, the day for the MRI test came. She was successful and entered into a very relaxed state and eventually went to sleep during the three-hour procedure.

***

Report from a clinical psychologist. In general, *Hemi-Sync* increases:
- the all-important rapport with the client
- a client's dream content and recall, and
- a client's memory, especially repressed memories.

Concentration is generally useful for "pulling people together," and *Catnapper* is great for PMS, general anxiety, and individuals suffering from jet lag.

***

As a psychotherapist and Doctor of Clinical Hypnotherapy, I have spent the majority of my life studying the science of the mind and how best to help people. I have a number of hypnosis tapes, but they do not have your *Hemi-Sync* technology. I've found your tapes to be truly magnificent.

***

The patient, ready for release from the hospital's psychiatric service, reported apprehension about his discharge. He was given H+ *Relax* to use at home. He reported that he was now able to relax and even sleep well for the first time in a number of years.

***

Previously, this patient had other forms of non-pharmaceutical intervention like bioExperiences, progressive relaxation, guided imagery, etc. Only *Hemi-Sync*, however, appeared to produce the desired results.

***

Report from a psychologist at an institution for the severely and profoundly retarded. S. is 35 years old, with frequent self-destructive outbursts requiring physical restraint. The use of the *Deep 10 Relaxation* tape in combination with therapy produced dramatic, positive changes after six or seven sessions. She went from disliking the staff to liking them and allowing them to help her. She progressed from a totally negative self-concept to saying things like, "I feel alive," and "I'm so happy." She reported better sleep and feeling more relaxed, and began to show a sense of humor. The tantrum behavior stopped except for one episode when another patient was, in fact, picking on her. Her thorazine medication was greatly reduced. She is now living in a group home, working in a sheltered workshop, continues to use the tape, and has not had a single outburst since she left the institution.

***

Report from a clinical hypnotist:
A 40-year-old woman had undergone two cancer operations, was in a very depressed state, weak, suffering from bad pain, had no desire to live. She was under medical and psychiatric care. I used the *Hemi-Sync Surf* tape [that reminded her of a nice holiday in Spain] to bring her into a hypnotic state, and let the pattern sink into her subconscious levels. After three weeks I had to go abroad and left her with a *Hemi-Sync* tape. On my return she had recovered nearly completely, went shopping again, and there was hardly any pain left.

***

A client reported to his psychiatrist, "The tapes have proved exceptionally useful in enabling me to attain and sustain a dreamlike state in which I have been able to visualize and verbalize images and thoughts I do not have contact with at the fully conscious level."

***

Report from a psychologist. While an individual is clinically depressed, I avoid the H+ tapes because they require active participation and concentration. Instead I provide patients with *Metamusic* tapes. Many depressed clients report that this flowing, quiet music, with relaxing, balancing sound signals embedded in it, provides them with strong temporary relief and consolation, and gradually helps in lifting their depression.

***

I regularly use *Hemi-Sync* tapes for training patients to achieve more easily the Alpha and Theta states which are useful in Behavioral Psychotherapy through the process of "reciprocal inhibition." These brain wave states inhibit the presence of anxiety. A variety of different *Metamusic* tapes are provided to the patient to avoid any boredom that might develop from listening to the very same tape on each and every occasion.

***

Hemi-Sync appeared to provide the high-energy coherent state that enabled the client to maintain a great degree of self-awareness, even while in the throes of releasing old thought forms and habits.

***

I find that, for clients, use of *Hemi-Sync*: a) reduces stress immediately, allowing the mind to focus on work to be done in the session; b) often provides a new experience for the client; c) begins to orient the mind to giving pleasure to the entire organism; d) provokes thinking of new means of relaxation; e) gives the mind a reference point for re-creating the whole-brain state; f) gives the mind permission to talk about inner, primary learning system behavior; g) evens out emotional highs and lows. As one client states, it brings him to a centeredness in which he can be more objective about himself. Without this centeredness, there seems to be a tendency to focus on negatives; h) begins the development of an effective attitude for problem solving and creative adventure.

***

Frequently I notice an interesting and surprising reaction to an introductory discussion with a client about *Hemi-Sync*. They often respond with what seems to be a newly found excitement, hope, or anticipation. In following conversations, they describe these initial responses as the point at which they consciously began to feel relief from the psycho-emotional pain they are experiencing, and the lessening of superfluous mental chatter.

***

My interest in the use of *Hemi-Sync* tapes with patients with severe personality disorders is connected to my efforts to find effective treatment modalities to add to our present armamentarium for severe personality and psychotic disorders. It has been my pleasure to find that the *Hemi-Sync* tape *Concentration* has been especially helpful with patients with schizoid personality tendencies, as well as, in a more general sense, individuals having difficulties with assertiveness and self-confidence. The tapes have been used in conjunction with psychodynamic psychotherapy and, if necessary, psychotropic medications to help maintain functioning in the community, and/or relieve excessive distress.

***

Patient with multiple anxiety related symptoms: Regular use of *Hemi-Sync* tapes for training the patient to achieve more easily the Alpha and Theta states which are useful in Behavioral Psychotherapy through the process of "Reciprocal Inhibition," wherein these brain-wave states inhibit the presence of anxiety. A variety of different *Metamusic* tapes are provided to the patient to avoid any boredom that might develop from listening to the very same tape on each and every occasion. The *Hemi-Sync* tapes reduced the patient's generalized anxiety level very quickly, and qualitatively better than did the psychotropic drugs he had been taking. The most logical interpretation is that these tapes very definitely and quickly help the mind-body unity to return much closer to homeostasis, the ideal state of mental and physical equilibrium.

Hemi-Sync Exercises Related to Therapy

Human Plus Titles	**Mind Food Titles**	
Let Go	Catnapper	Energy Walk
Off-Loading	Concentration	Morning Exercise
Relax	Deep 10 Relaxation	Surf
		Total Relaxation

Weight Control

Experiences Related to Weight Control

This information has been reported to Monroe Products and The Monroe Institute by individuals and/or by professional practitioners about the use of Hemi-Sync.

Many people I know have used H+ *Eat/No Eat* to help them control their eating habits and to lose weight successfully. Several have lost up to fifty pounds. I've personally used *Eat/No Eat* and Nutricia to help me lose twenty pounds and then to maintain my weight. These tapes complement any diet plan. They've been quite helpful with students suffering from anorexia and bulimia.

***

Report from a compulsive overeater. *Hemi-Sync* has been an invaluable resource in my struggle to keep some balance in my eating patterns. I knew I needed to let go of worries and upsetting emotions and calm down from general stress, but had been unable to do so on my own. Now that I have *Hemi-Sync* as a tool, I can use the encoded signal from the H+ *Let-Go* or *Relax* tapes to let go of an upsetting emotion or to relax. This has taken away much of my sense of powerlessness over my own responses.

***

From the first day I began using the tapes, about ten weeks ago, I noticed a calming effect. For the first week or so I played *Nutricia (no longer available)* once a day, usually falling asleep almost immediately upon starting the tape. During that period, I didn't consciously invoke the encoding signals, and I noticed I was calmer, more centered, more able to focus, much more able to make decisions about my life and daily events. The binges stopped for several weeks.

Since then I have had only two or three binge episodes, and have been able to come out of them quicker that I would have been able to before.

***

The sound frequencies on H+ *Eat/No Eat* induce me to relax so completely that I feel de-stressed and refreshed. That alone is valuable. In addition, when I use the Function Command, it gives pause to an otherwise compulsive action. A slight (though perceptible) physical change seems to take place. My throat responds by "shutting down"—I don't know of another way to describe this—and my sense of smell and taste are neutralized.

***

I use the *Eat/No Eat* Function Command when I walk into the kitchen on my way to the fridge for a snack. By the time I cross the room I find the desire to snack has passed. Diet and exercise have helped me lose weight, too, but *Eat/No Eat* provides the reinforcement and extra support I still need.

***

For a long time I had been successfully trying to deal with my weight problem through using will power. What got in the way was my habit of telling myself, "I'll just have this and then I'll stop tomorrow." Once

I discovered *De-Hab*, this changed. All I need to do is say, "plus - no more," and the pizza is no longer tempting. The tape helps me take action immediately instead of putting it off to another time.

***

The *De-Hab* tape has been very helpful in overcoming my compulsive eating.

***

I'm seeing some weight loss with the *Eat/No Eat* and *De-Hab* tapes, and for the first time in years am able to stick with the lifestyle changes which are necessary for weight reduction.

Hemi-Sync Exercises Related to Weight Control

Human Plus Titles	Eat/No Eat	**Mind Food Titles**
De-Hab	Möbius West	Breaking Free from Addictions
De-Tox: Body	Nutricia	Weight Loss

(TMI Focus, Vol. XII, No. 3, Summer 1990)

H-Plus® Potpourri

by Shirley Bliley, H-PLUS Coordinator

I'd like to take this opportunity to thank all of you who are using the H-PLUS Functions so diligently and taking the time to complete and return your Home Study Surveys. We want to hear about your successes and tribulations in order to develop H-PLUS in the way that best suits your needs.

In that vein, we'd like to share a selection of suggestions for additional Function exercises which have been gleaned from the survey forms submitted during the past year. They reflect great creativity and astute perception of the possibilities inherent in H-PLUS use.

Ready? Here are the most wanted H-PLUS Functions (by category). Listed with some of them are existing Exercises that can be used individually or in combination to achieve the desired results:

A tape directed to all portions of the Total Self for promoting inner confidence and bringing it into harmony and balance while generating and transforming energies into constructive, beneficial channels. Stated differently, an exercise for learning to erase poor self-image, fear of failure, and all other common deterrents to success and happiness and replace them with the desired attitudes and characteristics. [*Eight-Great, Contemplation, Wake/ Know, Mobius West, Speak Up*]

A Function for centering and grounding oneself. [Increased proficiency, through practice, with the H-PLUS exercises can contribute to a more centered life.]

An H-PLUS tape or series of tapes to support developing intuition and paranormal powers (i.e., psychokinesis, clairvoyance, telepathy, precognition, aura reading, channeling, psychometry); also, opening and developing the chakras and human subtle energy bodies, and achieving greater awareness of other realities. [Contemplation with any other meditative practices you favor]

A tape to enhance visualization ability. [*Think Fast, Contemplation*]

A Function Exercise to assist in recalling positive group energy and love; opening to greater experience of joy, humor, happiness. [*Recall, Empathizing, Make Your Day*]

One for learning to establish a "set point" in relation to weight and homeostasis (metabolism). [*Nutricia, Eat/No Eat, Mobius West*]

More specific physical Functions requested include: menopause symptoms; liver, kidney, and skin repair and maintenance; sinus conditions; improving night vision; and spinal adjustment. [*Tune-Up* by itself and with *Circulation, Heart: Repair & Maintenance, Sensory: Seeing, Detox: Body*]

Tapes geared to particular sports — golf, tennis, bowling, etc. [*See-Be, Light Foot, Synchronizing, Strong-Quick, Relax, Think Fast, Attention*]

Multiple Functions on one tape to play at night (like combining *Heart: Repairs & Maintenance* with *Tune-Up*, or *Sensory: Seeing* with *Sensory: Hearing*). [Try a dual-cassette tape player and create your own combinations.]

A tape to assist in learning foreign languages. [*Attention, Imprint, Recall, Think Fast, Speak Up, Relax*]

Modify *Buy the Numbers* to address the area of logical reasoning in symbols. [Focus your intention on that area while using the command.]

Financial success—including changing financial patterning, discovering the ideal vocation, programming to increase income, reversing poor financial planning, and help in recognizing early negative financial patterns. For winning the s lottery. [*Options, Mobius West, Off- Loading, Make Your Day*]

A tape with H-PLUS signals and no verbal instructions to provide a sustained, mindful, deep meditative state. [Once *Contemplation* is learned, using the Function Command accesses this kind of state.]

Functions for children in the areas of: sibling rivalry, obedience, learning to think, safety first, instilling good habits, and divesting bad habits. [*Relax, Attention, Let Go, Eight-Great, Mobius West, De-Hab*]

Tapes to improve pep level, auditory memory, and mechanical skills, read faster, and get up early in the morning. [*Reset, Imprint, Sensory: Hearing, Think Fast, Synchronizing*]

Exercises for no smoking, alcohol, drugs or abuse (for those tending to abuse spouses or children). [*De-Hab, Off-Loading*]

An H-PLUS Function for rejuvenation, a "Fountain of Youth." [*Regenerate, Eight- Great, Tune-Up, Mobius West]*

A tape to relieve psychological pain while simultaneously increasing endorphin production and allowing increased access to unconscious material. [*Let Go, Tune-Up, Recall, Off-Loading, Contemplation*]

World peace, communicating with animals, and understanding the earth, nature, and the universe as a whole. [*Mobius West, Empathizing Contemplation*]

A Function Exercise for invisibility. (This would remove the need for many others, wouldn't it?)

Thanks again for sharing these ideas. Your input is considered as we expand the H-PLUS repertoire. Remember, by utilizing the complementary Hemi-Sync tools offered in the GATEWAY EXPERIENCE® and MIND FOOD® series, the possibilities are limitless. Keep on Plussing!

Part 2: Exercises by Title

Gateway Experience®
Related Feedback
AIDS/HIV, Autism, Expanded Awareness, Fibromyalgia, Meditation & Spiritual Growth, Personal Growth / Self Improvement, Relaxation & Stress Management

Gateway Experience Wave I - Discovery – Album (Digitally Remastered)
Discovery introduces the Mind Awake/Body Asleep state (Focus 10) and other "mental tools" to help you experience states of expanded awareness. You are led from your physical waking state into deep relaxation and then into unexplored levels of your consciousness. Discover new potentials in thought and action as your total self becomes your personal gateway into profound forms of perception. Voiced by Bob Monroe. Includes a Guidance Manual and the following six exercises:
- Orientation - introduction and Focus 3
- Intro Focus 10 - establish the state of mind awake/body asleep
- Advanced Focus 10 - expand perception and learn greater control of personal energy
- Release and Recharge - detach from old fears and negative emotions
- Exploration, Sleep - techniques for expanding and exploring while asleep
- Focus 10 Free Flow - experiment with all tools learned in Wave I

Gateway Experience Wave II - Threshold (Digitally Remastered)
Learn more Focus 10 "mental tools" and benefit from exercises which take you to a state of expanded awareness known as Focus 12. Threshold opens new perceptual channels for expanding and integrating personal awareness while developing creative insights which assist in dissolving fear barriers. Voiced by Bob Monroe. Includes a Guidance Manual and the following six exercises:
- Intro Focus 12 - establish the higher energy state of expanded awareness
- Problem Solving - receive creative solutions to your questions
- One Month Patterning - reshape your life in desired directions
- Color Breathing - link mind and body to energize and support healing
- Energy Bar Tool - direct your nonphysical energies
- Living Body Map - balance and strengthen the physical self

Gateway Experience Wave III - Freedom (Digitally Remastered)
Enjoy Focus 10 and Focus 12 exercises developed specifically to make the methods for perceiving and controlling your nonphysical energy a comfortable and joyous experience. Voiced by Bob Monroe. Includes a Guidance Manual and the following six exercises:
- Lift Off - achieve ease with nonphysical experience
- Remote Viewing - tools for distant perception
- Vectors - reference points for easy movement
- Five Questions - answers from your total self
- Energy Food - absorb nonphysical energy
- First Stage Separation - explore nonphysical consciousness

Gateway Experience Wave IV – Adventure (Digitally Remastered)
Explore new experiences, new ideas, new places and new friends. This album provides you with the ultimate expression beyond Freedom - that of a personally controlled and directed adventure. Voiced by Bob Monroe. Includes Guidance Manual and the following six exercises:
- One Year Patterning - for designing your desired future

- Five Messages - gain insight into your total self
- Free Flow 12 - an unparalleled background for personal exploration
- NVC I - non-verbal communication, the language of intuitive thought
- NVC II - broaden perception in all states of your being
- Compoint 12 - establish a reference point for communication with higher consciousness

Gateway Experience Wave V – Exploring (Digitally Remastered)
(A Journey to Focus 15)

From the now familiar state of Focus 12, you will be introduced to Focus 15 - the "no time" state - the state of simply being. Here, far beyond your five physical senses, you can connect with the source of your intuition. Voiced by A.J. Honeycutt. Includes Guidance Manual and the following six exercises:

- Advanced Focus 12 - strengthen and reinforce your familiarity with this valuable state
- Discovering Intuition - use Focus 12 as a natural foundation for enhancing your intuitive abilities
- Exploring Intuition - further exploration of your intuitive abilities
- Intro to Focus 15 - be guided into Focus 15, the state of "no time," where time does not exist for you
- Mission 15 Creation and Manifestation - explore Focus 15 as a powerful state of creation and manifestation
- Exploring Focus 15 - a free flow opportunity for further exploration of this extraordinary state

Gateway Experience Wave VI – Odyssey (Digitally Remastered)
(A Journey to Focus 21)

Embark upon an odyssey of self-discovery. Wave VI features high adventure exercises in Focus 21 (the bridge to other energy systems). Explore realms of awareness that defy description in dimensions beyond physical time-space reality in this much-requested continuation of the Gateway Experience. Voiced by A.J. Honeycutt. Includes Guidance Manual and the following six exercises:

- Sensing - learn to control your energy body
- Expansion - reach out further from your physical body
- Point of Departure - project "out of phase" from your physical self
- Nonphysical Friends - meet your "helpers in energetic form"
- Intro to Focus 21 - travel the bridge to other energy systems
- Free Flow Journey in Focus 21 - brand-new territory for your exploration

Heart-Sync® Titles

Heart-Sync exercises feature frequencies that focus on opening ourselves to our heart's intuition and energy. This line of products was developed by Laurie Monroe, who had a wonderful ability to live from her heart and encourage others to do the same. Heart-Sync exercises incorporate verbal guidance and subtle sound effects along with specially blended Hemi-Sync frequencies.

Bridge to Paradise

(49 minutes)
Related Feedback
Expanded Awareness, Meditation & Spiritual Growth

Explore an otherworldly paradise in this guided Hemi-Sync heart-meditation voiced by Mark Macy. A miracle came to our world in the closing years of the 20th century, as scientists and researchers from different countries began to use technical equipment to get in touch with other worlds—the worlds of spirit. Remarkably, those spirit worlds began to get in touch with us though our TVs, radios, telephones, computers, and other technical devices. Mark Macy, a pioneer in this young field of research called instrumental transcommunication, or ITC, shares his vision of an extraordinary world in *Bridge to Paradise*.

Communicating with Animals

(42 minutes)
Related Feedback
Expanded Awareness

Learn to communicate with your animal friends in this guided Hemi-Sync exercise. Patty Summers, author of Talking with the Animals, shares her insights about animal communication and teaches us how to "tune in." We are all One and the wisdom of the animal kingdom has much to teach us about life, love and death. Track 1 features an informative narrative about inter-species telepathic communication along with some illuminating stories. Track 2 is a guided exercise for developing our innate abilities to communicate with our animal friends with whom we share the planet. A portion of the proceeds from sales of this CD is donated to the Almost Home Pet Adoption Center, a "no-kill" facility operated by the Nelson County SPCA, Lovingston, VA.

Partners Meditation

(38 minutes)
Related Feedback
Behavior Change, Meditation & Spiritual Growth, Personal Growth / Self Improvement

Enhance and deepen your meaningful relationships with this verbally guided Hemi-Sync exercise. The people who are important and central in our lives are here to be our teachers, guides and our loving support system. This exercise, created and voiced by Joe Gallenberger Ph.D., is designed to deepen the joy, appreciation and richness that you and your partner experience from your relationship. You can do this exercise by yourself or with your partner for highly beneficial effects.

Another title by Dr. Joe Gallenberger is *Manifesting with Hemi-Sync*.

Transforming Life's Challenges

(45 minutes)
Related Feedback
Aging, Anger, Behavior Change, Blood Pressure, Cancer Support, Energy,
Enhanced Well-Being, Frustrations, Immune System, Pain Management, Personal Growth / Self Improvement,
Problem Solving, Relaxation & Stress Management,
Sensory Integration Difficulties, Stroke Recovery, Surgical Support

Focus your energy toward health and vitality by reconnecting with the life force within. This powerfully guided Hemi-Sync meditation can help release emotions, invoke love, and generate life-giving energy to assist you in moving to a higher vibration. This, in turn, facilitates the activation of your body's natural healing abilities, allowing you to move beyond negative thought patterns and replace them with the positive energy of love and support. Know that you have the innate capacity to transform any physical or emotional challenge you may encounter.

Your Heart's Song

(63 minutes)
Related Feedback
Behavior Change, Enhanced Well-Being, Expanded Awareness, Personal Growth / Self Improvement

Obtain a greater sense of yourself and your life's purpose, live more gracefully and fearlessly, and radiate love as you attune to the vibration of your heart's song.

In this verbally guided exercise, Barry Goldstein teaches you how to connect with your heart's energy to recharge and replenish your physical and energetic bodies and clear your auric field. Features music from Barry's CD Ambiology 5: *Eden* combined with special blends of Hemi-Sync frequencies.

Other Hemi-Sync titles by Barry Goldstein include *Cosmic Consciousness* and *Wisdom of the Heart*.

Hemi-Sync® Series

These titles include multiple CDs in a series designed for specific applications. All include verbally guided exercises mixed and subtle sound effects or background music.

Cancer Support Series
Related Feedback
Cancer Support

The *Cancer Support Series* was developed to help you strengthen your mind-body connection and access inner resources to boost your immune system. Each selection of the series is also available individually on CD. This package contains:

Chemotherapy Companion - Support a positive outcome for your chemotherapy
Radiation Companion - Support a positive outcome for your radiation treatments
Journey Through the T-Cells - Strengthen and maintain your immune system
Sleeping Through the Rain - Journey from deep relaxation into natural, refreshing sleep

Going Home®
Related Feedback
Death & Dying, Meditation & Spiritual Growth

The entire series consists of two albums: Subject album for those in the last and irreversible stages of a terminal illness; Support Group album for those in close loving contact with the Subject, including caregivers. Developed in collaboration with the late Elisabeth Kubler-Ross, Robert Monroe and Dr. Charles Tart.

Elisabeth Kubler-Ross, MD, world-famous authority on death and dying, and Charles Tart, PhD, renowned researcher of altered states of consciousness, collaborated with Robert Monroe to create this unparalleled opportunity for personal growth and expanded awareness. The exercises carry you far along the continuum of consciousness to experience independence from the physical body. These rewarding journeys of discovery help you to know that death need not be feared and to resolve unfinished business so you can live more fully in the moment. Especially valuable for anyone with a life-threatening condition and for caregivers of the terminally ill.

Going Home Subject CD Album

11 Exercises on 7CDs - *Mind Awake/Body Asleep, Flying Free, Remove and Release, Edge of Here and Now, Touring Interstate, Moment of Revelation, Right of Passage, Homecoming, Freedom Flight, Return to Revelation, Relocation Theme*

Going Home Support CD Album

9 Exercises on 8 CDs - *Mind Awake/Body Asleep, Flying Free, Remove and Release, Edge of Here and Now, Touring Interstate, Moment of Revelation, Messages in 21, Recharge and Regenerate, Restorative Sleep, Death & Dying, Spiritual Growth*

Hemi-Sync Support for Journeys Out of the Body
Related Feedback
Expanded Awareness, Meditation & Spiritual Growth

The out-of-body-experience (OBE) is a state in which one's consciousness appears to depart the physical body allowing perception by means other than those of the physical senses. *Hemi-Sync Support for Journeys Out of the Body* is an in-home training series designed to provide Hemi-Sync audio-guidance to those who desire to achieve this state. With practice, one can be brought up to the borderland sleep state, and through it, to experience the out-of-body state with full conscious awareness.

6-CDs with Guidance Manual.

LEK - Learning Enhancement Kits
Related Feedback
Accelerated Learning, ADD / ADHD, Aging, Learning & Memory

The LEK is geared to facilitate the learning process of students working in a classroom or studying at home. The CDs included in these collections were specifically chosen to create whole brain learning, focused attention, relaxation and the perfect sleep; important elements to enhance cognitive functions.

The four separate packages are designed to promote success and assist all involved in the learning process: teachers, parents, and students of all ages. They are perfect for accelerated learning, students with special needs and their parents, and for teachers and students in elementary school, high school and universities.

LEK - Learning Enhancement Kit - Elementary Students

The CDs in this package are geared to the elementary student.

The CDs (each of which is also available as a separate purchase) included are:
Baroque Garden — Enjoy Baroque classics combined with Hemi-Sync concentration frequencies to make mental tasks easier and more efficient.
Remembrance — Focus with powerful Hemi-Sync and music designed for enhanced learning, peak performance and creative flow.
Cloudscapes — Music combined with Hemi-Sync; for deeper, more profound relaxation.
Dreamland — Tranquil melodies that allow you to flow with your own natural rhythms and Hemi-Sync frequencies carry you from deep relaxation into restful sleep.

LEK - Learning Enhancement Kit - Elementary Teachers

The CDs in this package are for the elementary teacher to play in the classroom.

The CDs (each of which is also available as a separate purchase) included are:
Remembrance —Focus with powerful Hemi-Sync and music designed for enhanced learning, peak

performance and creative flow.

Concentration — (non-verbal; utilizes pink noise with Hemi-Sync frequencies) Perfect for any mental task requiring focus and concentration.

Seasons at Roberts Mountain — This contemporary presentation of Vivaldi's Four Seasons combined with Hemi-Sync frequencies is ideal to focus attention for super-learning and creative flow.

Masterworks— Enjoy inner peace and relaxation as these classical performances mixed with Hemi-Sync relaxation frequencies.

LEK - Learning Enhancement Kit - High School/College Students

The CDs included in these collections were specifically chosen to create whole brain learning, focused attention, relaxation and the perfect sleep; important elements to enhance cognitive functions. The four separate packages are designed to promote success and assist all involved in the learning process: teachers, parents, and students of all ages. They are perfect for accelerated learning, students with special needs and their parents, and for teachers and students in elementary school, high school and universities. The CDs in this package are for the high school/college student.

The CDs (each of which is also available as a separate purchase) included are:

Breakthrough for Peak-Performance — Sail through challenging mental tasks with upbeat electronic music and Hemi-Sync.

Concentration — (non-verbal; utilizes pink noise with Hemi-Sync frequencies) perfect for any mental task requiring focus and concentration.

Guitarra Clásica — Sharpen your mental abilities, enhance memory and sustain focus and concentration with this beautiful collection of Latin-inspired classical guitar and Hemi-Sync.

Remembrance — Focus with powerful Hemi-Sync and music designed for enhanced learning, peak performance and creative flow.

LEK - Learning Enhancement Kit – Parents

The CDs in this package are particularly helpful for parents of children with learning challenges, and are designed to help them focus, relax, and experience a sound sleep.

The CDs (each of which is also available as a separate purchase) included are:

Lightfall for Focus and Concentration —A modern-day interpretation of R. Strauss' classical masterwork (Also Sprach Zarathustra) blended with J.S. Bach's Air on a G String and Prelude in C. Features Hemi-Sync concentration frequencies to support peak performance mental states.

Angel Paradise —Angelic harp music and Hemi-Sync frequencies for deep relaxation.

Catnapper —Enjoy a totally refreshing nap in only 30 minutes. Verbal guidance and Hemi-Sync provide you with a unique opportunity to obtain deeply restorative rest.

Sleeping Through the Rain —Journey across the border of wakefulness into refreshing sleep with soft, dreamy music and Hemi-Sync.

Lucid Dreaming
Related Feedback
Expanded Awareness, Personal Growth / Self Improvement, Sleep and Dreams

Lucid Dreaming provides a unique opportunity to benefit from states of expanded awareness during times we are not normally conscious. This four-exercise series on DVD is designed to teach you how to program and consciously participate in your own personal dreamscape. Clinical research suggests that focusing on the dream you wish to experience while remembering that you can consciously participate in your dream state can dramatically increase your chance of success. The Lucid Dreaming Series provides a substantial advantage for those interested in lucid dreaming by incorporating the Hemi-Sync sound technologies from Monroe Products®.

These exercises were designed to facilitate the brain-wave states found in naturally occurring sleep cycles. Accordingly, each of the first three exercises—*Mind Awake/Body Asleep, Creative Imagination, Flying Solo*—is 90 minutes in length. With the expanded capacity of DVD, Exercise Four—*Programming Your Dream State*—is designed for a full eight-hour sleep period to support your lucid dreaming practice.

Massage Therapy Collection
Related Feedback
Massage & Body Work, Relaxation & Stress Management

Relax body, mind, and spirit with the music and Hemi-Sync selections of the Massage Therapy Collection. Ideal for massage therapy, bodywork and energy healing. Help manage stress and balance subtle energy systems with this assortment of Metamusic CDs that promote deep relaxation and exquisite states of inner tranquility.

4-Metamusic CDs (also available individually on CD):

Dreamseed - Gain harmonic attunement with the low vibrational sounds of the didgeridoo
Gaia - Flute and guitar sounds blend exquisitely with the soothing sounds of water
Himalayan Soul - Enjoy a deep sense of well-being with enchanting flute music
Inner Journey - Ethereal sounds provide a deeply relaxing melodic flow to relieve stress.

Opening the Heart™
Related Feedback
Anger, Behavior Change, Expanded Awareness, Frustrations,
Meditation & Spiritual Growth, Personal Growth / Self Improvement, Self-Confidence

Love yourself and others, enrich your life and advance your spiritual growth. These soul-fulfilling exercises enhance relationships and release blocks that limit ability to love. Based on Heartline, a Monroe Institute residential program, this inspired experiential course helps enable you to deepen your emotional connections and open yourself to love. Exercise titles are: *Centered Calm, Remembering Love, Love's Power to Heal,* and *Opening to Love.* Guidance Manual included.

Opening the Way®
Related Feedback
Pregnancy and Childbirth

Enhance your deep pleasure in the miracle of childbirth as you move through psychological and physical stages of pregnancy, labor, and post-delivery.

A knowledgeable, caring, supportive guide for experiencing pregnancy and birth with confidence and serenity. For fathers, too.

8 tapes/14 exercises include:
Interview/Orientation, Healthy Pregnancy/Remove & Release, Deep Relaxation /Active Relaxation, Father/Supporting Late Pregnancy, Healthy Baby/Contacting Baby's Soul, Labor, Birthing/Pushing, and Postpartum Well-Being/Nursing Baby.

Guidance Manual included.

Available as a Digital Download only.

Out-of-Body Techniques by William Buhlman®
Related Feedback:
Expanded Awareness, Meditation & Spiritual Growth, Out-of-Body, Self Improvement, Shamanic, Sleep & Dreams

Learn techniques for out-of-body explorations from leading expert William Buhlman. Based on 40-plus years of experience, Buhlman found that each of us responds differently to various OBE induction methods.

Six separate CDs provide different approaches for achieving this state: Body of Light, Balloon, Count Down Globe, Target Technique, The Vortex, and Shamanic Method. Each track is approximately 45 minutes in length. Guidance manual included.

6-CDs with Guidance Manual.

PAL Executive Package
Related Feedback
Accelerated Learning, Focused Attention, Learning & Memory

This series was developed to help you improve your potential for learning. It incorporates selections with specially blended Hemi-Sync frequencies to guide you into focused, whole-brain states of consciousness. The Hemi-Sync sound patterns on these recordings help you achieve and sustain synchronized brain-wave activity in both hemispheres of the brain—an optimal condition for improving human performance. Focused attention, a prerequisite to effective learning is greatly facilitated by the Hemi-Sync process.

This package contains:

Concentration and Remembrance - enhance your ability to focus attention for peak performance and creative flow
Retain-Recall-Release - learn cues to retain, recall, or release information from memory
Catnapper - the ultimate pick-me-up; get a refreshing nap in only 30 minutes
Morning Exercise - plan a successful outcome for your day's activities
Deep 10 Relaxation - overcome stress.

Available as a Digital Download only.

PAL Student Package
Related Feedback
Accelerated Learning, Classroom, Focused Attention, Learning & Memory

This series was developed to help you improve your potential for learning. It incorporates selections with specially blended Hemi-Sync frequencies to guide you into focused, whole-brain states of consciousness. The Hemi-Sync sound patterns on these recordings help you achieve and sustain synchronize brain-wave activity in both hemispheres of the brain—an optimal condition for improving human performance. Focused attention, a prerequisite to effective learning is greatly facilitated by the Hemi-Sync process.

This package contains:
Concentration and *Remembrance* - enhance your ability to focus attention for peak performance and creative flow
Retain-Recall-Release - learn cues to retain, recall, or release information from memory
Catnapper - the ultimate pick-me-up; get a refreshing nap in only 30 minutes.

Available as a Digital Download only.

Positive Immunity Program
Related Feedback
AIDS/HIV, Cancer Support, Enhanced Well-Being, Fibromyalgia, Immune System

Strengthening the Mind-Body Connection

This experiential learning program reinforces the mind/body connection and has been reported to be helpful for Fibromyalgia, chronic fatigue syndrome, HIV and other immune disorders, as well as for maintaining wellness.

Positively Ageless
Related Feedback
Aging, Behavior Change, Energy, Enhanced Well-Being,
Personal Growth / Self Improvement

Enter into a timeless state of being while enhancing the mind-body connection with verbally guided Hemi-Sync exercises by Patty Ray Avalon. We have all heard "age is a state of mind." When we alter the way we have been conditioned to think about age, we are able to create new patterns that affect our physical and psychological selves.

Positively Ageless uses guided meditations, affirmations, creative visualizations, and other tools to help you rewrite the program of aging, allowing you to feel younger, healthier, stronger, and more at peace while enhancing the overall quality of your life.

A guidance manual and five exercises on four CDs are included: *Rejuvenation, Reconditioning, Lightbody, Clear and Balanced,* and *Renew Through H-Plus.*

Other titles by Patty Ray Avalon are *The Creative Way, Inner States: Dawning of Awareness; Healing Journeys Support,* and *Touching Earth.*

Support for Stroke Recovery

Related Feedback
Stroke Recovery

The primary focus of this series is to assist you in actively participating in your body's own natural healing process. A growing body of evidence supports the interconnectedness of mind and body, and medical research now shows that our words, thoughts, and feelings have substantial impact on our bodies. This series combines relaxation, affirmations, and guided imagery to help you rediscover your body's innate wisdom, and to maximize your body's natural tendency to heal and restore balance.

A guidance manual and four exercises (four CDs) are included: *Relaxation into Sleep, Healing Energie*s, *Support for Speech Recovery,* and *Support for Motor Skills Recovery.*

The 2012 Mindshift: Meditations for Times of Accelerating Change

Related Feedback
Meditation & Spiritual Growth, Personal Growth / Self Improvement

As the date 2012 approached, a growing circle of visionaries believed that the pace of change and transformation in the world was accelerating rapidly. What's the best way to adapt to these events? Noted scientist, lifelong meditator, and revolutionary futurist Peter Russell believes that the single most crucial technique is one of the oldest: meditation. Now on *The 2012 MindShift,* this expert on the 2012 phenomenon offers guided meditations that he personally designed to help anyone stay grounded through these turbulent times.

Peter Russell earned his master's degree in computer science from Cambridge University, and trained as a meditation teacher in India under the guidance of Maharishi Mahesh Yogi. He is the author of nine books including *The Global Brain, From Science to God,* and *Waking Up in Time.* Russell has consulted with IBM, Apple, American Express, Swedish Telecom, and Shell Oil about a variety of topics including self-development, creativity, stress management, and sustainable environmental practices.

The Creative Way ®

Related Feedback
Creativity, Expanded Awareness, Frustrations, Personal Growth / Self Improvement, Problem Solving, Self-Confidence

Reawaken your talents and creative abilities as you gain self awareness and expand your mind to live a more enriched, expanded and productive life.

The Creative Way uses guided meditations, affirmations, creative visualizations, and other tools to help you identify and overcome/transform blocks, stay open to new possibilities and ideas, and connect with your inner creative self and other sources of inspiration.

Other titles by Patty Ray Avalon, are *Inner States: Dawning of Awareness; Healing Journeys Support, Positively Ageless,* and *Touching Earth.*

The Network of Light Series

Related Feedback
Enhanced Well-Being, Relaxation & Stress Management

As a pioneer in the field of alternative medicine, Dr. C. Norman Shealy has helped medical practitioners to understand more fully the power of the mind-body connection and its relationship to maintaining wellness or restoring wellness following a trauma such as surgery or a life-threatening disease. Each of the four exercises in the collaborative Network of Light series has been voiced by Dr. Shealy. These exercises use a progressive relaxation technique, along audio signals embedded by Monroe Products, to gently guide you into a deep, receptive state of relaxation. You will use this receptive state of relaxation as a "switch" to turn on your inner network of light. A Guidance Manual and four exercises are included: *Mind and Emotions, Endocrine System, Immune System,* and *Nervous System.*

Another title by Dr. C. Norman Shealy is *Hemi-Sync Relaxation.*

The Shaman's Heart Program

Related Feedback
Expanded Awareness, Massage & Body Work, Meditation & Spiritual Growth,
Personal Growth / Self Improvement, Self-Confidence, Shamanic Programs

The first-ever comprehensive home learning program to develop your full capacity for soul-based and heart-centered living. A unique and practical integration of shamanic practice, transpersonal psychology, ancient wisdom, and various contemporary methods of spiritual growth, development and personal transformation.

Learn to live from a heart-centered and soul-based perspective with this unique and powerful combination of shamanic practice, ancient wisdom, various methods of spiritual growth, and Hemi-Sync. Dr. Byron Metcalf has created a comprehensive program to help you fully develop your authentic power, purpose and presence by exploring and developing the heart from a shamanic and transpersonal perspective. This program consists of four CDs containing six verbally guided exercises, a special version of Metcalf's award-winning Metamusic title, *The Shaman's Heart* CD, and a comprehensive guidance manual.

Other titles by Byron Metcalf are: *Deep Time Dreaming, Medicine Work, Spirit Gathering, The Shaman's Heart, The Shaman's Heart II* and *Spirit Gathering*.

The Surgical Support Series
Related Feedback
Cancer Support, Dental Pain, Heart, Pain Management, Stroke Recovery, Surgical Support

The Surgical Support Series was designed to ease the experience of illness, injury, surgery, chemotherapy, dental treatment and other physical trauma. By reinforcing the mind-body connection, these exercises help to strengthen the physical and mental components of the total healing process.

The first three exercises (*Pre-Op*, *Intra-Op*, and *Recovery*) are for use before, during, and immediately after treatment.

The last three exercises (*Recuperation*, *Energy Walk* and *Surf*) support healing and wellness. 6-CDs with Guidance Manual.

H-Plus® Titles

Experience peak brain states and personal development CDs

Human Plus, or H-Plus, is a means of utilizing the immense power of the subconscious to affect change in your life. Each H-Plus CD (or Function Exercise) contains precise combinations of Hemi-Sync frequencies that gently draw you into an extraordinarily receptive, whole-brain state while establishing the Access Channel—the ultimate communication channel to all levels of awareness—mental, physical, and emotional. By design, the Access Channel is opened during each Function Exercise, allowing you to learn a different Function Command (short, verbal cue) ranging from controlling your appetite to increasing your energy. Once the Function Command has become encoded while the Access Channel is open you can then call upon or 'activate' that Function at any time, on demand, in everyday life situations. The H-Plus series offers a different kind of pathway to new levels of freedom to becoming Human Plus.

Access to Energy

(71 minutes)
Related Feedback
Energy, Enhanced Well-Being, Fitness & Sports

Explore and experience the vast reserve of energy deep within you and learn to access that energy anytime you wish. Use *Access to Energy* to increase strength, agility, alertness, stamina, or to simply feel vigorous all over, and enjoy increased satisfaction and productivity.

Access to Information

(71 minutes)
Related Feedback
Enhanced Well-Being, Frustrations, Learning & Memory, Problem Solving

Enhance your ability to access your own personal library of information and knowledge. Bring wisdom, teachings, events, life experiences, or any other information you wish to retrieve into your waking conscious memory at any moment you desire. Use *Access to Information* to help you greatly improve your recall abilities and contribute to your overall well-being.

Attention

(60 minutes)
Related Feedback
Accelerated Learning, Behavior Change, Classroom, Creativity, Focused Attention, Heart,
Learning & Memory, Problem Solving

Sharply focus the mind and senses on a particular thought, action or event. Enhance any performance requiring concentration such as reading, writing, typing or studying. Increase productivity and improve information retention and recall.

Brain: Support & Maintenance

(60 minutes)
Related Feedback
Autism, Brain Injury, Enhanced Well-Being, Learning & Memory, Headaches, Multiple Sclerosis, Pain Management,
Sensory Integration Difficulties, Stroke Recovery

Enhance the body's natural ability to maintain optimal brain functioning, improve blood flow to the brain and normalize its chemical and electrical activity. Use to support mental clarity, improve memory, speed reaction times and stimulate sensory perception.

Buy the Numbers
(60 minutes)
Related Feedback
Accelerated Learning, ADD / ADHD, Financial Success, Frustrations, Learning & Memory

Sharpen your skills for working with numbers in everyday applications and improve your aptitude for defining and understanding numerical concepts. Use anytime to enhance your speed, accuracy, and ability to remember numbers and gain confidence in your mathematical abilities.

Circulation
(60 minutes)
Related Feedback
AIDS/HIV, Allergies, Blood Pressure, Brain Injury, Circulation, Enhanced Well-Being, Headaches, Hearing and Vision, Heart, Sensory Integration Difficulties, Stroke Recovery

Develop smooth and optimum blood flow throughout your body. Learn a simple method you can use anytime, anywhere to improve your body's circulatory system. May be used to focus upon critical areas or for general maintenance.

Contemplation
(60 minutes)
Related Feedback
Expanded Awareness, Frustrations, Meditation & Spiritual Growth, Multiple Sclerosis, Personal Growth / Self Improvement, Problem Solving

Access ideas, creativity, intuition and understanding from your total self. Expand your awareness to include all levels of consciousness and consider choices from a higher perspective. Supports an active rather than passive meditative state.

De-Discomfort
(60 minutes)
Related Feedback
Cancer Support, Enhanced Well-Being, Fibromyalgia, Fitness & Sports, Multiple Sclerosis, Pain Management, Pregnancy and Childbirth, Surgical Support

Use the mind/body connection to lower the volume of chronic pain signals. *De-Discomfort* teaches you a simple method you can use anytime, anywhere to reduce your perception of pain without losing the reminder that the area in question requires attention.

De-Hab

(60 minutes)
Related Feedback
ADD / ADHD, Addictions, Anger, Behavior Change, Enhanced Well-Being, Financial Success,
Frustrations, Personal Growth / Self Improvement, Self-Confidence, Weight Control

Eliminate or diminish undesirable mental, emotional or physical habits. Use anytime you are about to follow a behavior imprint you wish to change. Break free of anger or old emotional patterns, eliminate thoughts of failure or move beyond a cycle of negativity.

De-Tox: Body

(60 minutes)
Related Feedback
Addictions, Allergies, Enhanced Well-Being, Heart, Immune System, Multiple Sclerosis, Weight Control

Enhance your body's natural ability to cleanse itself of destructive substances. Reinforce the healthy functioning of your body's defense systems when a known toxicity exists or use daily for best results. May also be used to counteract the results of overindulgence.

Do This Now

(61 minutes)
Related Feedback
Behavior Change, Energy, Enhanced Well-Being, Personal Growth / Self Improvement

Move forward and increase your energy and enthusiasm for starting, continuing or completing actions and tasks any time you wish. Procrastination can result in increased stress, a sense of guilt, and a loss of personal productivity. *Do This Now* helps you tap into your positive life force flow, releasing all blocks within yourself resistant to energetic, effective action. Use this energy to access your full to be all of who you are, complete all that you wish to accomplish, and create all that you desire.

Eat/No Eat

(64 minutes)
Related Feedback
Behavior Change, Weight Control

Gain control over your desire for food with *Eat/No Eat*. Learn a simple method to regulate your brain's response to hunger signals and the sensory stimulation from aromas. Use to support a balanced diet and maintain your desired weight.

Eight-Great

(60 minutes)
Related Feedback
Anger, Autism, Behavior Change, Creativity, Depression, Enhanced Well-Being, Financial Success
Fitness & Sports, Frustrations, Personal Growth / Self Improvement, Problem Solving, Relaxation & Stress
Management, Self-Confidence, Stroke Recovery

Enhance calmness, confidence and self-esteem with *Eight-Great* and express your best. Use to focus your mental and physical states on demand anytime you wish to instill a positive and constructive attitude.

Heart: Support & Maintenance
(60 minutes)
Related Feedback
Blood Pressure, Enhanced Well-Being, Fitness & Sports, Heart

Improve the blood flow to your heart and enhance its functioning. Utilize the mind/body connection to increase flexibility of blood vessels and strengthen the heart muscle to optimize the performance of this vital organ.

Hypertension
(61 minutes)
Related Feedback
Blood Pressure, Enhanced Well-Being, Stroke Recovery

Utilize your mind/body connection to assist in balancing and adjusting your circulatory system and normalizing your blood pressure. Use daily for general maintenance and to support optimum functioning, or more frequently if a need is apparent.

Immunizing
(60 minutes)
Related Feedback
AIDS/HIV, Cancer Support, Enhanced Well-Being, Immune System, Multiple Sclerosis

Stimulate the mind/body connection to boost your immune system and strengthen your body's ability to defend against disease-producing organisms. Use to assist in regaining (or maintaining) a normal, healthy physical condition.

Imprint
(61 minutes)
Related Feedback
Accelerated Learning, AIDS/HIV, Financial Success, Focused Attention, Learning & Memory

Anchor information deeply into memory and develop whole-brain memory skills to facilitate easy recall. *Imprint* teaches you a simple method to recall information anytime or anywhere including "tip of the tongue" details such as names, dates or phone numbers.

Let Go
(61 minutes)
Related Feedback
AIDS/HIV, Addictions, Anger, Anxiety, Behavior Change, Enhanced Well-Being,
Frustrations, Heart, Personal Growth / Self Improvement, Relaxation & Stress Management, Therapy

Reduce or release overwhelming emotional reactions that interfere with calm or objective decision making with *Let-Go.* Control your response to difficult circumstances and counter destructive patterns. Use this simple method anywhere to relieve anxiety, overcome anger or alleviate depressed feelings.

Lungs: Support & Maintenance

(60 minutes)
Related Feedback
AIDS/HIV, Allergies, Asthma, Breathing, Cystic Fibrosis, Enhanced Well-Being, Fitness & Sports, Headaches

Strengthen your respiratory system and support the optimum performance of your lungs. Use your mind/body connection to improve lung capacity and oxygen intake and to breathe comfortably and healthfully. May also be used to counter the symptoms of asthma.

Available as a Digital Download only.

Möbius West

(60 minutes)
Related Feedback
Addictions, Anxiety, Autism, Behavior Change, Depression, Financial Success, Personal Growth / Self Improvement, Problem Solving, Self-Confidence, Weight Control

Create the reality you desire. Maximize your achievements and/or establish new directions in your life. Use *Möbius West* to program change in your thoughts, feelings, or behavior and to alter mental, emotional, or physical patterns.

Nutricia

(60 minutes)
Related Feedback
Behavior Change, Enhanced Well-Being, Personal Growth / Self Improvement, Weight Control

Increase or decrease caloric absorption. *Nutricia* teaches you a simple method to control your health and energy needs. Exist comfortably on a small amount of food by maximizing the calories and nutrients your body absorbs, or choose to reduce your caloric and nutrient intake.

Off-Loading

(60 minutes)
Related Feedback
AIDS/HIV, Anger, Anxiety, Behavior Change, Depression, Enhanced Well-Being, Financial Success, Frustrations, Heart, Personal Growth / Self Improvement, Problem Solving, Self-Confidence, Relaxation & Stress Management

Release restrictive or destructive mental, emotional and physical patterns which impede achievement of your goals. Use *Off-Loading* to overcome limiting beliefs, unwanted thoughts or undesirable behavior. Approach life from a fresh perspective.

Options

(60 minutes)
Related Feedback
Autism, Behavior Change, Creativity, Frustrations, Personal Growth / Self Improvement, Problem Solving, Self-Confidence, Relaxation & Stress Management, Therapy

Develop insightful analysis and creative solutions from a total, whole brain perspective. *Options* teaches you a simple method you can use anytime, anywhere to solve problems objectively and with confidence in your personal, professional or academic life.

Passages

(66 minutes)
Related Feedback
Enhanced Well-Being

Support and enhance your physical, emotional, mental and spiritual well-being as you experience normal fluctuations in hormonal balance. Hormonal changes occur periodically from puberty to old age, and imbalances can negatively affect one's quality of life. Use *Passages* to ease the effects of these imbalances, to feel more regulated and empowered, and to promote more peaceful and satisfying life changes.

Recall

(60 minutes)
Related Feedback
Accelerated Learning, Focused Attention, Learning & Memory, Problem Solving

Recall teaches you a simple method to retrieve information from your conscious or unconscious memory. Recall dreams, past experiences or facts long forgotten. Use this invaluable skill anywhere to improve your memory for personal, professional or academic purposes.

Recharge

(60 minutes)
Related Feedback
Energy, Enhanced Well-Being, Multiple Sclerosis, Sleep and Dreams, Relaxation & Stress Management

Feel refreshed and revitalized following a short catnap. *Recharge* teaches you a simple method you can use anytime, anywhere to restore energy and can help you cope with mental or emotional overload. Use to establish balance and equalization throughout your entire system and awaken fresh and alert.

Relax

(60 minutes)
Related Feedback
Anger, Anxiety, Behavior Change, Blood Pressure, Cancer Support, Classroom, Creativity, Enhanced Well-Being, Frustrations, Heart, Pain Management, Multiple Sclerosis, Pregnancy and Childbirth, Problem Solving, Relaxation & Stress Management, Self-Confidence, Surgical Support, Therapy

Obtain instant freedom from physical, mental and emotional tensions. Maintain a state of calmness and think clearly while coping with stress. Overcome nervousness before public speaking or exams. Use to counteract anger or frustration.

Reset

(60 minutes)
Related Feedback
Addictions, AIDS/HIV, Anger, Energy, Enhanced Well-Being, Fitness & Sports,
Frustrations, Problem Solving, Self-Confidence

Shift your mental, emotional and physical states from "down and out" to "up and energetic." Learn a simple method you can use anytime, anywhere to infuse your entire being with positive energy while helping you remain calm and confident. *Reset* is useful in countering depression or fatigue.

Restorative Sleep

(65 minutes)
Related Feedback
Allergies, Breathing, Cancer Support, Energy, Enhanced Well-Being, Fitness & Sports, Hearing and Vision,
Multiple Sclerosis, Pain Management, Sleep and Dreams, Stroke Recovery, Surgical Support

Easily enter into a deeply restorative sleep and support the process of healing. Use to assist your recovery from illness, injury, or surgery or to support the normal functioning of physical systems. Get a good night's sleep and wake up rested and refreshed.

Restorative Sleep is one of the exercises in the *Going Home* Series.

Sensory: Hearing

(60 minutes)
Related Feedback
Enhanced Well-Being, Hearing and Vision, Sensory Integration Difficulties

Amplify or decrease your sensitivity to sound. Learn a simple method you can use anytime, anywhere to control how you perceive sound. Use to compensate for hypersensitivity to sound or to hear low volume sounds more clearly.

Sensory: Seeing

(60 minutes)
Related Feedback
Enhanced Well-Being, Hearing and Vision, Multiple Sclerosis, Sensory Integration Difficulties

Improve and fine tune your eyesight. *Sensory: Seeing* teaches you a method you can use anywhere to sharpen your focus and enhance your sensitivity to light and movement. May also be used to ease eye strain, strengthen eye muscles, or help alleviate ongoing vision problems.

Sex Drive

(60 minutes)
Related Feedback
Behavior Change, Frustrations

Increase or decrease your sexual arousal. *Sex Drive* teaches you a method to gain control over your libido. Heighten your sensitivity and sexual pleasure with an intimate partner or diminish your sexual urges and state of arousal when circumstances are not appropriate.

Sleep

(60 minutes)
Related Feedback
Sleep and Dreams, Enhanced Well-Being

Move easily and comfortably into natural, restful sleep and leave your daily concerns behind. Learn a simple method with *Sleep* to counter insomnia, adjust to irregular work schedules or overcome disruptions to gain control over your sleep.

Speak Up

(60 minutes)
Related Feedback
Behavior Change, Self-Confidence

Address groups or individuals with ease and calmness. *Speak Up* teaches you a method to overcome shyness and enhance confidence when speaking in public. Use anytime to improve voice quality and achieve a better rapport with your audience in meetings, the classroom or social situations.

Sweet Dreams

(60 minutes)
Related Feedback
Personal Growth / Self Improvement, Sleep & Dreams

Program your dream state before going to sleep and unleash its creative potential. *Sweet Dreams* teaches you a technique to program the content of your dreams and helps you recall your dreams upon awakening. Also reported helpful with the induction of lucid dreaming.

Available as a Digital Download only.

Synchronizing

(60 minutes)
Related Feedback
Brain Injury, Fitness & Sports, Sensory Integration Difficulties

Strengthen and fine tune your mind/body coordination and ability to excel. *Synchronizing* teaches you a method you can use anywhere to enhance your precision, speed, agility and overall performance in activities such as sports, dancing, manual tasks or artistic creation.

Think Fast

(60 minutes)
Related Feedback
Accelerated Learning, Autism, Creativity, Focused Attention, Frustrations,
Learning & Memory, Multiple Sclerosis, Problem Solving, Self-Confidence

Speed up and clarify your thought processes with *Think Fast*. Develop greater confidence in your mental sharpness; stimulate or enhance creativity; improve memory and recall.

Tune-Up

(60 minutes)
Related Feedback
AIDS/HIV, Allergies, Blood Pressure, Breathing, Cancer Support, Energy, Enhanced Well-Being,
Fitness & Sports, Headaches, Hearing and Vision, Heart, Multiple Sclerosis, Pain Management, Immune System,
Positively Ageless, Pregnancy and Childbirth, Sensory Integration Difficulties, Relaxation & Stress Management,
Stroke Recovery, Surgical Support

Reinforce your body's natural ability to normalize its functioning. Speed recovery from illness, injury, or surgery. *Tune-Up* may also be used to provide relief from skin irritations, headaches, or muscle strain. Use daily for maintaining optimum physical condition.

Wake/Know

(60 minutes)
Related Feedback
Frustrations, Problem Solving, Sleep and Dreams

Wake/Know teaches you a simple method to use before going to bed to acquire knowledge from your total self during sleep. Requested information or guidance will flow into your awareness the following day to help you make decisions or solve problems.

Metamusic® Titles

Angel Paradise

(59 minutes)
Related Feedback
Massage & Body Work, Meditation & Spiritual Growth, Relaxation & Stress Management

Bridge the realms of heaven and earth with the angelic harp music of Erik Berglund and Hemi-Sync. Berglund's "angelic" compositions have garnered international acclaim as divine healing and transformation gifts for humanity. Celestial energy resonates through the crystalline sounds of Berglund's Irish harp creating an inter-dimensional communion with Spirit. Angels are beings of feeling and the healing melodies brought forth through Berglund's heartfelt composition act as a conduit for angelic feelings to touch the emotions of humanity during this time of transformation. Use *Angel Paradise* for massage or energy healing work or for deep experiential meditation. Instruments featured: Irish harp.

Angel Paradise is one of the exercises in *LEK - Learning Enhancement Kit - Parents.*

Ascension

(45 minutes)
Related Feedback
Expanded Awareness, Meditation & Spiritual Growth, Relaxation & Stress Management

Move beyond the boundaries of three-dimensional reality with the transcendent electronic music of J.S. Epperson and Hemi-Sync. Epperson's inspired "music of the spheres" composition is an intricate and subtle musical tapestry adeptly interwoven to support experiential meditative states. Access an exquisite state of mental calm and expanded awareness with *Ascension* and commune with higher aspects of Self.

Other Metamusic titles by J.S. Epperson are: *Einstein's Dream, Hemi-Sync in Motion, Higher, Illumination for Peak Performance, Indigo for Quantum Focus, The Lotus Mind*, and *Remembrance*.

Awakening Consciousness

(68 minutes)
Related Feedback
Behavior Change, Enhanced Well-Being, Expanded Awareness, Massage and Bodywork, Meditation & Spiritual Growth, Personal Growth / Self Improvement, Relaxation & Stress Management

Awaken your consciousness with this inspiring musical meditation.

Experience your consciousness emerging in this inspiring musical meditation by accomplished Spotted Peccary Music artists Howard Givens and Craig Padilla. Featuring an array of electronic instruments, from classic vintage and modular synthesizers to modern digital keyboards, this deep ambient work is about inward expansiveness. Combined with powerful Hemi-Sync frequencies, it is designed to lead you into a profoundly heightened state of awareness.

Other *Metamusic* titles with Craig Padilla are *Cycles* and *Land of Spirit.*

Baroque Garden

(46 minutes)
Related Feedback
Accelerated Learning, ADD / ADHD, Children, Creativity,
Focused Attention, Learning & Memory, Problem Solving

Enjoy Baroque classics performed by the Arcangelos Chamber Ensemble—combined concentration frequencies to make mental tasks easier and more efficient. Delight in music that stood the test of time, from composers like Bach, Vivaldi, Corelli and Albinoni. Use *Baroque Garden* at home, work or school while studying, reading, working on a computer or balancing a checkbook. Play or use with headphones to enhance mental capabilities while stimulating creativity and imagination. Produced by Richard Lawrence and Joshua Leeds.

Another *Metamusic* title by the Arcangelos Chamber Ensemble, with Joshua Leeds, is *Masterworks*. Another *Metamusic* title produced by Joshua Leeds is *Hemi-Sync Support for Healing*.

Baroque Garden is one of the exercises in *LEK - Learning Enhancement Kit - Elementary Students*.

Beneath the Moon

(57 minutes)
Related Feedback
Expanded Awareness, Meditation & Spiritual Growth, Relaxation & Stress Management

Explore the mystical realm between sunset and sunrise as the enchanting and emotive music of Deborah Martin and Hemi-Sync lead you on a profound inner journey. As you move through these higher dimensions, your consciousness soars beyond the stars to a place of connection, and inner peace washes over you. Awaken to the mysteries of the universe, and your own hidden self. Instruments include ambient electric and acoustic, bass, keyboards, orchestral textures, Taos drums and flute. Several tracks form the original album "*Under the Moon*" were used extensively on NBC's coverage of the 1996 Olympic Games.

Other Metamusic titles by Deborah Martin are *Convergence* and *Dimensions in Time*.

Between Worlds

(52 minutes)
Related Feedback
Expanded Awareness, Meditation & Spiritual Growth, Shamanic Programs

An extraordinary sojourn into a dreamlike shamanic landscape. The captivating shamanic music of Don Peyote and Naasko is combined to guide your inner journey. Sounds from the rain forest contribute to the surreal, organic ambience. Vivid images emerge as time blurs and the world disappears. For optimum results, listen to this experiential composition in one session—preferably in a darkened, meditative environment. Instruments featured: didgeridoo, flutes, mbira, synthesizer, indigenous chants, shamanic percussion and field recordings.

Another Metamusic title by Don Peyote and Naasko is *Dreamcatcher*, and another solo work by Don Peyote is *Eternal Now*.

Beyond the Golden Light

(46 minutes)
Related Feedback
Expanded Awareness, Meditation & Spiritual Growth, Relaxation & Stress Management

Feel the protection and nurturance of the Golden Light as you explore the outer reaches of consciousness. Matthew Sigmon's tender and fluid music combine frequencies to help immerse you in a place of unparalled beauty and peace. Instruments include: acoustic guitar, electric guitar, synthesizers, voice.

Other Metamusic titles by Matthew Sigmon (with Julie Anderson) are *Into the Deep* and *Sleeping Through the Rain.*

Breakthrough for Peak Performance

(44 minutes)
Related Feedback
Accelerated Learning, ADD / ADHD, Children, Creativity, Focused Attention, Learning & Memory, Problem Solving

Sail through challenging mental tasks with the upbeat electronic music of Michael Maricle and Hemi-Sync. The fast-paced tempo and driving-rhythms of Maricle's uplifting composition support faster beta Hemi-Sync patterns designed for peak-performance, super-learning and creative flow. Enhance your mental productivity, memory and aptitude for learning while enjoying this artistic creation. *Breakthrough for Peak Performance* may be helpful for ADD/ ADHD, dyslexia, and other learning challenges.

Another Metamusic title by Michael Maricle is *Elation*, and another featuring Michael is *Revelations for Heightened Creativity.*

Breakthrough for Peak-Performance is one of the exercises in *LEK - Learning Enhancement Kit - High School/College Students.*

Breath of Creation

Solo Huaca
(62 minutes)
Related Feedback
Massage & Body Work, Meditation & Spiritual Growth, Relaxation & Stress Management

Evoke timeless feelings and emotions with ancient sounds of the modern-day huaca and Hemi-Sync. "Huaca" is a South American native term for something holy or sacred and the hallowed sound of breath flowing through fired clay inspires this sense of sacredness. For thousands of years flute instruments from virtually every culture have been used for ritual and healing. The huaca is a radical innovation in this tradition with large chambers allowing for three-part harmony in a wind instrument for the first time. Alan Tower's hauntingly beautiful huaca compositions have an organic, primal sound quality that spans the ages of time. Instruments featured: solo huaca.

Another Metamusic title by Alan Tower is *Emergence.*

Celestial Meditation

(62 minutes)
Related Feedback
Meditation & Spiritual Growth, Expanded Awareness, Relaxation & Stress Management

Experience profound meditative states with the deep space music of Jonn Serrie and Hemi-Sync.

Dissolve into complete relaxation and allow yourself to be carried into other energy systems. Jonn Serrie is a master in creating electronic music suggestive of galactic vistas and open spaces, providing a perfect audio environment for exploring other realities. His deep space music, combined with powerful Hemi-Sync frequencies, will lead you into a profound and memorable meditative state.

Other Hemi-Sync titles that feature music by Jonn Serrie are *Into the Light* and *Maiden Voyage.*

Chakra Journey

(59 minutes)
Related Feedback
Enhanced Well-Being, Expanded Awareness, Massage & Body Work, Meditation & Spiritual Growth, Personal Growth / Self Improvement, Relaxation & Stress Management

Activate, clear, and align your chakras while expanding your awareness with the soothing, healing music of ThunderBeat and Hemi-Sync. A gifted shamaness and award-winning musician, ThunderBeat has created each musical track to focus on a chakra, from the root (key of C), to the crown (key of B), thus helping to relieve stress and emotional blockages. The final track is designed to balance and ground you. Use *Chakra Journey* for meditation; relaxation; massage and bodywork; or yoga. Instruments featured: keyboards, chimes, wind, rattles, ceremony drums, ocean waves.

Other *Metamusic* titles by ThunderBeat are *Chakra Journey DVD*, a visual meditation, *Egyptian Sun,* and *Mayan Winds.*

Chakra Journey DVD

(Region 1)
(33 minutes)
Related Feedback
Enhanced Well-Being, Expanded Awareness, Massage and Bodywork, Meditation & Spiritual Growth, Relaxation & Stress Management

Activate, clear, and align your chakras while expanding your awareness with the soothing, healing music of ThunderBeat and Hemi-Sync. A gifted shamaness and award-winning musician, ThunderBeat has created each musical track to focus on a chakra, from the root (key of C), to the crown (key of B), thus helping to relieve stress and emotional blockages. The final track is designed to balance and ground you. Use *Chakra Journey* for meditation; relaxation; massage and bodywork; or yoga. Instruments featured: keyboards, chimes, wind, rattles, ceremony drums, ocean waves.

Other *Metamusic* titles by ThunderBeat are *Chakra Journey, Egyptian Sun,* and *Mayan Winds.*

Cloudscapes

(30 minutes)

Related Feedback

ADD / ADHD, Aids-HIV, Alzheimer's, Behavior Change, Children, Creativity, Dental Pain, Expanded Awareness, Meditation & Spiritual Growth, Pain Management, Personal Growth / Self Improvement, Pregnancy and Childbirth, Relaxation & Stress Management

Break free and lift off—soar among the clouds and open your mind to a higher perspective with soul-stirring music inspired by Robert Monroe's passion for piloting gliders. Musical reveries abound when listening to this delightful homage. Use *Cloudscapes* for expanding awareness through musical imagery; for deeper, more profound relaxation; or simply for musical enjoyment. Composed and performed by Ray Dretske.

Cloudscapes is one of the exercises in *LEK - Learning Enhancement Kit - Elementary Students*.

Convergence

(55 minutes)

Related Feedback

Expanded Awareness, Meditation & Spiritual Growth, Relaxation & Stress Management

Gather with the ancients as culturally inspired music and Hemi-Sync weave you through time. Spotted Peccary Music artists Deborah Martin, Mark Rownd and Greg Klamt expertly blend lyrical instruments, rhythmic drums, rich atmospheres and harmonious melodies to awaken the spirit of diverse civilizations. As you open to these multidimensional states, the music evokes the essence of the heart and soul of these indigenous peoples, moving you into a place of reverence and unity. Use Convergence for transcendent inner journeys and profoundly deep meditations. Instruments featured: Native American and Chinese flutes, ocarinas, Taos drums, keyboards, turtle rattles, straws, cymbals, Tibetan hand drum, bells and bowls.

Other Metamusic titles by Deborah Martin are *Beneath the Moon* and *Dimensions in Time*.

Crossing the Abyss

(53 minutes)

Related Feedback

Expanded Awareness, Meditation & Spiritual Growth

Transform your awareness into a transcendental state.

A powerful mixture of electronic and acoustic ambient music by J. Arif Verner invokes a vast and expansive scene perfect for deep exploration. The addition of Hemi-Sync® frequencies offer support as your awareness transforms from an individualized state into a transcendental or enlightened state.

Cycles

(51 minutes)
Related Feedback
Expanded Awareness, Meditation & Spiritual Growth

This hauntingly beautiful and atmospheric music will take the listener deep inside while contemplating the very fabric of existence. Craig Padilla's *Cycles* (originally titled *Genesis*) was inspired by his awareness of the cyclical nature of life and the universe, and features electronic ambiences and vintage analog instrumentation with the addition of Hemi-Sync frequencies. Ascend to a higher plane, sit quietly, and listen for the message within.

Other *Metamusic* titles with Craig Padilla are *Awakening Consciousness* and *Land of Spirit*.

Deep Journeys

(57 minutes)
Related Feedback
Expanded Awareness, Meditation & Spiritual Growth, Relaxation & Stress Management

Features seven hypnotic musical tracks by internationally acclaimed recording artist Steven Halpern and the audio-guidance support of Hemi-Sync. The compelling meditative music is fashioned around an infrastructure of low tones to ground the body and higher frequency harmonics to crystallize the delicate textures you feel spiraling around in your head. *Deep Journeys* will immerse you in an inner peace that is uplifting and deeply restorative.

Another Metamusic title by Steven Halpern is *Seaside Slumber*.

Deep Time Dreaming

(73 minutes)
Related Feedback
Expanded Awareness, Meditation & Spiritual Growth, Shamanic Programs

Explore unknown spiritual realms with the ancient shamanic soundworlds of Byron Metcalf, Mark Seelig and Hemi-Sync. A portal for shamanic travel and divine communion, laced with mysticism, *Deep Time Dreaming* is sacred music in the truest sense. German-based flutist, Mark Seelig accompanies Metcalf's trancing, organic percussion in this awe-inspiring otherworldly sojourn with support from dreamtime maestro, Steve Roach. Originally released as Wachuma's Wave, this multi-textured shamanic masterpiece was recognized by Backroads Records as the number one release of 2003 across all genres. Instruments featured: frame drums, bass drums, clay pots, overtone singing, sacred chants and various soundworlds.

Other titles by Byron Metcalf are: *Medicine Work, Spirit Gathering, The Shaman's Heart Program, and The Shaman's Heart II.*

Desert Moon Song

(55 minutes)
Related Feedback
Meditation & Spiritual Growth, Relaxation & Stress Management

A 'classic' homage to the sacred and purifying energies of the desert combined. Dean Evenson's *Desert Moon Song* is one of the first ambient recordings to pay tribute to the desert. Native and silver flutes echo the distant call of coyotes. Harps and synthesizers evoke images of spacious landscapes creating a sense of mystery and inner calm. This delicious melding of instrumental and natural sounds completes the healing cycle at dusk with a chorus of mating frogs. The Indian rain chant is by Hopi elder Grandfather David Monoyne. Instruments featured: silver and Native flutes, harp, guitar, synthesizer, percussion and nature sounds.

Dimensions in Time

(62 minutes)
Related Feedback
Expanded Awareness, Meditation & Spiritual Growth, Shamanic Programs

Deborah Martin and Erik Wøllo subtly blend modern ambient textures and soundscapes with ancient and traditional instruments in this homage to the American Indian. Hemi-Sync frequencies deepen this listening experience as you embark on a journey between worlds. Vocals, lyrics, synthesizers, Taos drums, guitars, atmospheres, and additional sonic soundspaces by contributing artist Steve Roach mix with authentic American Indian instruments, on-site location recordings, Apache Crown Dancer songs and Apache drums, partial segments of Omaha and Kiowa Indian cylinder recordings from 1894, and live recordings of Kiowa powwow songs.

Other Metamusic titles by Deborah Martin are *Beneath the Moon* and *Convergence*.

Dreamcatcher

(55 minutes)
Related Feedback
Massage & Body Work, Meditation & Spiritual Growth, Shamanic Programs, Sleep and Dreams

Dreams are gateways to the soul. Drift gently into the mystical dreamstate with soothing ambient music, calming water sounds and Hemi-Sync. Don Peyote and Naasko bring their shamanic influence to bear in this versatile composition. *Dreamcatcher* supports deep, restorative sleep when used in continuous play. It may also be used for massage therapy, subtle energy healing work or for powerful meditations in the borderland sleep state. Instruments featured: harmonic chords, drones, synthesizer, and field recordings of water sounds and whale calls.

Another Metamusic title by Don Peyote and Naasko is *Between Worlds*, and another solo work by Don Peyote is *Eternal Now*.

Dreamer's Journey

(37 minutes)
Related Feedback
Expanded Awareness, Meditation & Spiritual Growth, Relaxation & Stress Management

Enjoy profound relaxation and inner peace as you journey through time. Enchanting melodies blend with subtle sound effects and Hemi-Sync for enlightening, dream-like experiences of exploration. Use *Dreamer's Journey* for expanding awareness through musical imagery; for deeper, more profound relaxation; or simply for musical enjoyment. Performed and written by Bob Volkman.

Another Metamusic title by Bob Volkman is *The Maze*.

Dreamland

(63 minutes)
Related Feedback
Cancer Support, Children, Enhanced Well-Being, Massage & Body Work, Pregnancy and Childbirth, Relaxation & Stress Management, Sleep and Dreams, Stroke Recovery, Surgery

Centered—balanced—serene. These are just a few of the states you may experience as the elegant and mesmerizing soundscapes of Laura Nashman and Michael Moon, and Hemi-Sync frequencies carry you from deep relaxation into restful sleep. The magic of this composition lies in the tranquil melodies, absent of direct rhythms that allow you to flow with your own natural rhythms as you drift into dreamland. Instruments include: alto flute, silver flute, Native flute, vibraharp, orchestra bells, wind chimes, and crystal chimes.

Another *Metamusic* title with Laura Nashman is *Lullaby*.
Dreamland is one of the exercises in *LEK - Learning Enhancement Kit - Elementary Students*.

Dreamseed

(53 minutes)
Related Feedback
Enhanced Well-Being, Expanded Awareness, Massage & Body Work

Access spiritual realms and gain harmonic attunement with the didgeridoo music of Amoraea Dreamseed and Hemi-Sync. Dreamseed transports you, experientially, into powerful mystical states using the low vibrational tones of the didgeridoo to resonate into all levels of your body, mind, and spirit. Bring balance to your subtle energy systems as you access the healing energy within. Instruments featured: didgeridoo, synthesizer, various drums, flutes, crystal singing bowls and nature sounds.

Another Metamusic title by Amoraea Dreamseed is *Touching Grace*.

Dreamseed is one of the exercises in the *Massage Therapy Collection*.

Ecstatic

(30 minutes)
Related Feedback
Energy

Stimulate alertness and energize your entire being with this upbeat piece by Steve MacLean. Wooden percussion instruments add dynamic vitality to this unusual creation. Speed your thought processes with a motivational jumpstart.

Available as a Digital Download only.

Egyptian Sun

(49 minutes)
Related Feedback
Creativity, Expanded Awareness, Meditation & Spiritual Growth,
Personal Growth / Self Improvement, Shamanic Programs

Feel your consciousness expand as your imagination takes flight with this combination of Middle Eastern inspired music and Hemi-Sync. Using her gift of activational music, ThunderBeat has crafted a powerful melodic experience that transports you to the Egyptian pyramids and temples—places she has personally explored and held sacred ceremony. Instruments include: flutes, violins, gongs, oud, sitar, guitar, cellos, bass, dumbek, tablas, timpanis, full drum set, keyboards, and chants.

Other Metamusic titles by ThunderBeat are *Chakra Journey, Chakra Journey DVD* (a visual meditation,) *and Mayan Winds*.

Einstein's Dream

(60 minutes)
Related Feedback
Accelerated Learning, ADD / ADHD, Aging, Behavior Change, Children, Creativity, Focused Attention,
Learning and Memory, Problem Solving

Enjoy the lively music of Mozart and the remarkable brain synchronizing effects of Hemi-Sync with this brilliant interpretation of Einstein's favorite music. *Einstein's Dream* can be used to enhance mental capabilities while stimulating creativity and imagination and may also be helpful for ADD/ADHD, dyslexia and other learning challenges. Interpreted and performed by J.S. Epperson.

Other Metamusic titles by J.S. Epperson are: *Ascension, Hemi-Sync in Motion, Higher, Illumination for Peak Performance, Indigo for Quantum Focus, The Lotus Mind,* and *Remembrance*.

Elation

(56 minutes)
Related Feedback
ADD / ADHD, Learning & Memory

Michael Maricle uplifting electronic music combines to facilitate a highly-focused state of attention while enhancing memory. Tend to tasks with confidence while balancing and sustaining energy, and experience clarity of thought in the absence of distractions. May also be helpful for ADD/ADHD and other learning challenges. Special thanks to Professor Barbara Bullard for her contributions.

Another Metamusic title by Michael Maricle is *Breakthrough for Peak Performance*.

Emergence

(70 minutes)
Related Feedback
Creativity, Expanded Awareness, Meditation & Spiritual Growth

Bring forth fresh ideas and insights while expanding your awareness with Alan Tower's unique sound of the solo Hang and Hemi-Sync. The Hang ("hung") is a truly remarkable evolutionary instrument invented in Switzerland by Felix Rohner and first introduced in 2001. The sound it produces is likened to a hybrid of the Steel Pan and Gamelan. Tower has invented a Triple Hang Altar that allows him to play two or three Hanghang together. Beautiful, melodic compositions will capture your heart and imagination, reawakening you to your divine nature and place in the Cosmos. Use *Emergence* for: quiet contemplation, creativity, or for establishing sacred space.

Another Metamusic title by Alan Tower is *Breath of Creation*.

Enchanted Forest

(57 minutes)
Related Feedback
Expanded Awareness, Massage & Body Work, Meditation & Spiritual Growth, Relaxation & Stress Management

Enjoy a magical respite with sounds of nature combined with the gentle and soothing ambient music of Jeffree Clarkson.

Gentle and soothing ambient music with sounds of nature is ideal for meditation, relaxation/stress reduction, massage and energy healing. *Enchanted Forest* features a compilation of specifically selected musical passages from eight different albums by Jeffree Clarkson. Jeffree solos on a wind-controlled keytar over music arrangements. Original music engineered/mastered by Alexia Clarkson.

Eternal Now

(55 minutes)
Related Feedback
Expanded Awareness, Massage & Body Work, Meditation & Spiritual Growth, Relaxation & Stress Management

All that Is exists in the present moment, and this moment is all that exists. Don Peyote's profound ambient music, combined frequencies, provide you the space to be fully present where you are now. Free your consciousness from the illusion of time, and allow memories from the past and worries about the future to dissolve as you move into the presence of Being. Instruments include: chimes, analog synthesizers, guitar, Tibetan throat singing, and singing bowls.

Other Metamusic titles by Don Peyote are *Between Worlds* and *Dreamcatcher*.

Eternity Within

(45 minutes)
Related Feedback
Expanded Awareness, Meditation & Spiritual Growth

Rendezvous with your eternal Higher Self with Frank Danna's heartfelt composition and Hemi-Sync. The ethereal music of *Eternity Within* was inspired by Robert Monroe's own experiences described in *Ultimate Journey*, the final book of his classic trilogy dealing with the out-of-body state. Monroe's encounters and communications with his Higher Self (which he referred to as his 'I-There') are the basis for a fundamental revelation to many on a path of self-discovery and personal transformation. Instruments featured: analog and digital synthesizers.

Another Metamusic title by Frank Danna is *Voyage to the Other Side*.

Flow

(73 minutes)
Related Feedback
Expanded Awareness, Meditation & Spiritual Growth, Shamanic Programs

Ride the current to a profound state of relaxation and exploration with the expertly crafted and dramatic ambient melodies of Jon Jenkins and Hemi-Sync. Using water as an analogy—its quality of instability, mobility, having no fixed shape but adapting itself to other shapes—Jenkins creates an elegant composition ideal for shamanic journeying, or for powerful meditative experiences. Instruments featured: keyboards, electric guitars, and percussion (including Taos drums).

Gaia

(43 minutes)
Related Feedback
Creativity, Expanded Awareness, Meditation & Spiritual Growth, Relaxation & Stress Management

A musical portrayal of Kokopelli, the Native American mythic hero who restores abundance by bringing forth the second summer rains. Deeply relaxing flute and guitar blend exquisitely with sounds of water in a soulful composition that stimulates imagination and creativity. Use *Gaia* for expanding awareness through musical imagery and self-exploration; for deeper, more profound meditation; or simply for musical enjoyment. Composed and performed by Richard Roberts.

Other *Metamusic* titles with Richard Roberts (aka Zero Ohms) are *Strand with Hemi-Sync, Land of Spirit*, and *Winds Over the World*.
Gaia is one of the exercises in the *Massage Therapy Collection*.

Golden Mind

(46 minutes)
Related Feedback
Aging, Accelerated Learning, ADD / ADHD, Focused Attention, Learning & Memory

J.S. Epperson's lively harpsichord interpretation of Bach's Goldberg Variations mixed is ideal for focusing attention, enhancing memory, and achieving states of peak performance. Epperson also incorporates the Golden Mean harmonics, the basis for the principle of information coding by the brain. May also be helpful for ADD/ADHD and other learning challenges. Special thanks to Professor Barbara Bullard for her contributions to *Golden Mind*.

Other Metamusic titles by J.S. Epperson are *Ascension, Einstein's Dream, Hemi-Sync in Motion, Higher, Illumination for Peak Performance, Indigo for Quantum Focus, The Lotus Mind,* and *Remembrance.*

Guitarra Clásica

(47 minutes)
Related Feedback
Aging, Accelerated Learning, ADD / ADHD, Children, Creativity, Focused Attention, Learning & Memory

Sharpen your mental abilities, enhance memory and sustain focus and concentration with this beautiful collection of Latin-inspired classical guitar and Hemi-Sync. Félix Rodriquez, a virtuoso guitarist from Puerto Rico, offers his renditions of classical pieces from composers such as: Agust'n Barrios Mangoré, Heitor Villa-Lobos, Francisco Tárrega, Mario Castelnuovo Tedesco, Heraclio Fernández, Stanley Myers, and Johann Sebastian Bach. Combined with special Hemi-Sync frequencies, this delightful selection may also be helpful for ADD/ADHD, dyslexia and other learning challenges.

Guitarra Clásica is one of the exercises in *LEK - Learning Enhancement Kit - High School/College Students.*

Heaven and Earth

(44 minutes)
Related Feedback
Relaxation & Stress Management

John Gregorius mixes acoustic and electric music with fingerstyle guitar and ambient textures, creating a peaceful space for you to contemplate the splendor of life.

Hemi-Sync frequencies harmoniously blend with this gentle and uplifting music, providing a perfect environment for quiet reflection and deep relaxation. Instruments include: acoustic, electric and ebow guitars, fretless bass, drums, udu and mallet drums, and electronic textures.

Hemi-Sync in Motion

(34 minutes)
Related Feedback
Energy, Fitness & Sports

Supercharge your dance or workout routines with upbeat electronic music and Hemi-Sync. J. S. Epperson's driving rhythms are combined with the innovative use of Hemi-Sync to give you added horsepower when you need it. Use this cutting-edge composition for dance, jogging, workout routines, or play in the background while cleaning house. Includes brief warm up and cool down tracks.

Other Metamusic titles by J.S. Epperson are: *Ascension, Einstein's Dream, Higher, Illumination for Peak Performance, Indigo for Quantum Focus, The Lotus Mind,* and *Remembrance.*

Hemi-Sync Support for Healing

(60 minutes)
Related Feedback
Cancer Support, Enhanced Well-Being, Massage & Body Work, Pregnancy and Childbirth, Stroke Recovery, Surgery

This unique restorative music collection, assembled from sound researcher and music producer Joshua Leeds' highly-acclaimed Essential Sound Series, features psychoacoustically arranged variations of Tchaikovsky's String Quartet #1. Designed to support recuperation, healing, and enhanced well-being, Hemi-Sync frequencies aid this process by moving you into a profound state of relaxation and helping to strengthen the mind-body connection. This soothing classical compilation is performed by the award-winning players of the Apollo Chamber Ensemble, featuring Lisa Spector, pianist.

Higher

(48 minutes)
Related Feedback
Expanded Awareness, Meditation & Spiritual Growth, Relaxation & Stress Management

Delicate, ethereal tones blend to focus you inward—to the source of creation. Enjoy a deep, sustained meditative state as the entrancing music of *Higher* transports you to illuminating levels of awareness. Use Higher for expanding awareness through musical imagery and self-exploration; for deeper, more profound meditation; or simply for musical enjoyment. Composed and performed by J.S. Epperson.

Other Metamusic titles by J.S. Epperson are: *Ascension, Einstein's Dream, Hemi-Sync in Motion, Illumination for Peak Performance, Indigo for Quantum Focus, The Lotus Mind,* and *Remembrance.*

Himalayan Soul

(43 minutes)
Related Feedback
Meditation & Spiritual Growth, Relaxation & Stress Management

Immerse yourself in an exquisite state of inner tranquility with the enchanting flute music of Ilona Selke and Hemi-Sync. The mystical, haunting music of *Himalayan Soul* provides a welcome refuge from the frantic speed of life today.

Another Metamusic title by Ilona Selke is *Romantic Wonder.*

Himalayan Soul is one of the exercises in the *Massage Therapy Collection.*

Illumination for Peak Performance

(51 minutes)
Related Feedback
Accelerated Learning, ADD / ADHD, Children, Creativity, Focused Attention, Learning & Memory

Creative flow and enhanced productivity seem effortless with J.S. Epperson's "designer" electronic music and Hemi-Sync. Develop a coherent and highly focused whole-brain state with Illumination for Peak-Performance and soar through any task requiring mental focus and concentration. This joyful composition may be helpful for ADD/ADHD, dyslexia and other learning challenges.

Other Metamusic titles by J.S. Epperson are: *Ascension, Einstein's Dream, Hemi-Sync in Motion, Higher, Indigo for Quantum Focus, The Lotus Mind,* and *Remembrance.*

Indigo for Quantum Focus

(71 minutes)
Related Feedback
Accelerated Learning, ADD / ADHD, Children, Creativity, Focused Attention, Learning & Memory, Problem Solving

Developmental states of peak performance. Features the electronic music of J.S. Epperson and designer mixes of Hemi-Sync concentration frequencies for super-learning. The whole-brain states made possible by *Indigo* are perfect for any mental task requiring focus and concentration and may also be helpful for ADD/ADHD, dyslexia and other learning challenges. Zero in on the task at hand with this extraordinary composition whenever you desire to enhance your mental performance and creative flow.

Other Metamusic titles by J.S. Epperson are: *Ascension, Einstein's Dream, Hemi-Sync in Motion, Higher, Illumination for Peak Performance, The Lotus Mind,* and *Remembrance.*

Inner Journey

(30 minutes)
Related Feedback
AIDS/HIV, Autism, Classroom, Expanded Awareness, Massage & Body Work,
Meditation & Spiritual Growth, Relaxation & Stress Management

Ethereal sounds and Hemi-Sync provide a deeply relaxing melodic flow to relieve stress and give free reign to your imagination—an ideal landscape for personal exploration. Use *Inner Journey* for expanding awareness through musical imagery; for deeper, more profound meditation; or simply for musical enjoyment. Composed and performed by Micah Sadigh, Ph.D.

Other Metamusic titles by Micah Sadigh are: *The Journey Home, Portal to Eternity, The Return, Spiral of Light, Transformation,* and *The Visitation.*

Inner Journey is one of the exercises in the *Massage Therapy Collection.*

Into the Deep

(29 minutes)
Related Feedback
Expanded Awareness, Meditation & Spiritual Growth, Pain Management, Relaxation & Stress Management

Many believe the ocean to be the origin of physical life. Inspired by this belief, Matthew Sigmon and Julie Anderson explore this silent world through the delicately textured music of *Into the Deep* for expanding awareness through musical imagery; for deeper, more profound relaxation; or simply for musical enjoyment.

Other Metamusic titles by Matthew Sigmon are *Beyond the Golden Light* and *Sleeping Through the Rain* with Julie Anderson.

It Dreams in Me

(45 minutes)
Related Feedback
Expanded Awareness, Massage & Body Work, Meditation & Spiritual Growth, Relaxation & Stress Management

Enjoy a deep and profound relaxation with this soothing and innovative soundscape. Musician Peter Jack Rainbird artfully coaxes truly unique and surprisingly full sounds from a single electric guitar, employing a special effect pedal and skillful use of harmonics to create a lovely ethereal composition. Combined frequencies, this exceptional recording makes for a memorable and peaceful contemplative experience.

Land of Spirit

(64 minutes)
Related Feedback
Expanded Awareness, Meditation & Spiritual Growth, Relaxation & Stress Management

Astral music carries you into the realm of spirit for a deeply comforting experience.

This elegant fusion of electronic space music is a perfect soundscape for deep meditation and exploration. Musical artists Craig Padilla, Richard Roberts and Skip Murphy have crafted a graceful musical landscape that, combined frequencies, holds you in a space of expanded awareness and peace. Instruments include analog synths and flutes.

Other *Metamusic* titles with Craig Padilla are *Awakening Consciousness* and *Cycles*.
Other *Metamusic* titles with Richard Roberts (aka Zero Ohms) are *Gaia, Strand with Hemi-Sync,* and *Winds Over the World.*

Lightfall for Focus and Concentration

(44 minutes)
Related Feedback
Accelerated Learning, ADD / ADHD, Children, Focused Attention, Learning & Memory

Also Sprach Zarathustra is frequently associated with the intellectual and technological achievements of humankind such as its use in *2001: A Space Odyssey. Lightfall* is a modern-day interpretation of R. Strauss' classical masterwork blended with J.S. Bach's Air on a G String and Prelude in C. Composed and performed by the talented Lenore Paxton on keyboards and Phillip Siadi on guitar, *Lightfall* features Hemi-Sync concentration frequencies to support peak-performance mental states and may be helpful to those with ADD/ADHD, dyslexia, and other learning challenges.

Other Metamusic titles by Lenore Paxton and Phillip Siadi are *Portraits* and *Prisms. Lightfall for Focus and Concentration* is one of the exercises in *LEK - Learning Enhancement Kit - Parents.*

Lullaby

(55 minutes)
Related Feedback
Children, Relaxation & Stress Management, Sleep and Dreams

This gentle and enchanting collection of the world's favorite lullabies carries you from deep relaxation into restful sleep. Perfect for children and adults alike, these selections feature Laura Nashman on flute and John Alonso on piano, blended with Hemi-Sync sleep frequencies.

Another *Metamusic®* title with Laura Nashman is *Dreamland.*

Maiden Voyage

(55 minutes)
Related Feedback
Expanded Awareness, Massage & Body Work,
Meditation & Spiritual Growth, Relaxation & Stress Management

Jonn Serrie says his electronic music "exists to help us explore a sense of ourselves and our place in the Universe." With the addition of Hemi-Sync to these relaxing, flowing melodies, get ready to embark on a fresh new journey into space while delving into the vastness of your own being.

Other Hemi-Sync titles that feature music by Jonn Serrie are *Into the Light* and *Celestial Meditation.*

Masterworks

(45 minutes)
Related Feedback
Expanded Awareness, Meditation & Spiritual Growth, Relaxation & Stress Management

Enjoy inner peace and transcendent relaxation as the Arcangelos Chamber Ensemble performs timeless gems. Use *Masterworks* for expanding awareness through musical imagery and self-exploration; for deeper, more profound meditation; or simply for musical enjoyment. Produced by Richard Lawrence and Joshua Leeds.

Another *Metamusic®* title by the Arcangelos Chamber Ensemble with Joshua Leeds, is *Baroque Garden.* Another *Metamusic®* title produced by Joshua Leeds is *Hemi-Sync Support for Healing.*

Masterworks is one of the exercises in *LEK - Learning Enhancement Kit - Elementary Teachers.*

Mayan Winds

(49 minutes)
Related Feedback
Expanded Awareness, Meditation & Spiritual Growth, Shamanic Programs

Authentic tribal rhythms, exotic jungle sounds and ethereal soundscapes invoke the atmosphere of ancient Mayan temples. Hemi-Sync frequencies combine to assist you in reaching higher states of consciousness. Enter into ceremony as these venerable predecessors call you to join them. Instruments include drums, flutes, bells, rattles, marimba, didgeridoos, and sounds of the rainforest.

Other Metamusic titles by ThunderBeat are *Chakra Journey, Chakra Journey DVD* (a visual meditation), and *Egyptian Sun.*

Medicine Work

(71 minutes)
Related Feedback
Meditation & Spiritual Growth, Shamanic Programs

A powerful shamanic musical journey to deep inner worlds with Byron Metcalf and Rob Thomas

This psychoactive composition is designed to guide and support you into deeper territories of your own inner worlds – far beyond the known and familiar. Award-winning shamanic-trance drummer Byron Metcalf and master didgeridoo artist Rob Thomas of Inlakesh combine their musical and personal medicines to create this powerful sonic experience, heightened by the addition of Hemi-Sync. The journey concludes with the safe return home to the harmonic resonance of the traveler's heart and true nature. Features Byron Metcalf on frame drums, buffalo drum, bass & ceremonial drums, hybrid toms, udu & clay pots, rattles & shakers, and Rob Thomas on didgeridoos, rattles and shakers, vocal chants and shamanic soundworld.

Other titles by Byron Metcalf are *Deep Time Dreaming, Medicine Work, The Shaman's Heart with Hemi-Sync, The Shaman's Heart II with Hemi-Sync, The Shaman's Heart Program,* and *Spirit Gathering.*

Another title with Rob Thomas/Inlakesh is *The Dreaming Gate.*

Midsummer Night

(28 minutes)
Related Feedback
ADD / ADHD, Autism, Behavior Change, Creativity, Learning and Memory/Learning Disabilities, Massage and Bodywork, Pregnancy and Childbirth, Relaxation & Stress Management

Drift into a forest dream as you listen to transcendent sounds of nature and Hemi-Sync designed for deep relaxation and heightened creativity. Sink gently into a state of inner peace and calm as rainfall and crickets blend with keyboards, strings, and classical guitar to provide an inspiring meditative experience. Use *Midsummer Night* for expanding awareness through musical imagery; for deeper, more profound relaxation; or simply for musical enjoyment. Composed and performed by Alan Phillips.

Mystic Realms

(43 minutes)
Related Feedback
Expanded Awareness, Meditation & Spiritual Growth, Relaxation & Stress Management

Hemi-Sync and the mesmerizing ambient music of Brad Allen beckon you into the transcendent stillness within. Inner guidance and a higher perspective await you as you experience the subtle nuances and ethereal sounds of *Mystic Realms.*

Oasis

(64 minutes)
Related Feedback
Creativity, Relaxation & Stress Management

Discover an oasis of serenity with the poignant music of Polish composer Andrzej Rejman and Hemi-Sync. Known for his international flavor and feel, Rejman blends a Central European romantic style with some neoclassical moods in this uplifting composition. Inspired by the beauty and mystery of nature, this timeless arrangement will provide safe harbor from your daily concerns. *Oasis* is also ideal for stimulating creativity and imagination. Instruments featured: keyboards, piano, synthesizer, strings arrangement, folk bells, electric and acoustic guitar.

Another Metamusic title by Andrzej Rejman is *Pearl Moon*.

Octaves of Light

(63 minutes)
Related Feedback
Enhanced Well-Being, Massage & Body Work, Relaxation & Stress Management

Sound and music have been used since ancient times for healing and transformation. International recording artist Eluv has created a unique blend of world music and sound based on her divine inspiration to help others. Combined frequencies to bring balance and harmony, this delicate and beautiful music also supports the benefits of energy and bodywork. Instruments featured: didgeridoo, tubular bells, crystal singing bowls (in the key of the heart chakra), Native American flute, Indian flute, keyboards, chimes, shenai, tabla, pipa, nature sounds, and Eluv's captivating voice as a celestial instrument on select tracks.

Another title by Eluv is *Chakra Meditation*, a verbally guided meditation.

Path to Peace

(46 minutes)
Related Feedback
Expanded Awareness, Massage & Body Work, Meditation & Spiritual Growth, Relaxation & Stress Management, Sleep and Dreams

Find your way to peaceful tranquility with this beautiful musical narrative.

This calming, peaceful and contemplative musical narrative invokes a pastoral locale – the perfect setting for an inner retreat. John Gregorius' tender and beautiful composition, with the masterful use of electric and acoustic ambient guitar, piano, cello, upright bass, drums, programming and vocals, carries you to a place of tranquility and peace. Hemi-Sync® frequencies help to deepen the relaxation process as you let go and flow.

Another *Metamusic* title by John Gregorius is *Heaven and Earth.*

Pearl Moon

(67 minutes)
Related Feedback
Massage & Body Work, Meditation & Spiritual Growth, Relaxation & Stress Management

Reveal your innermost feelings and subconscious self with the luminous sounds of Andrzej Rejman and Hemi-Sync. The moon is associated with the mind, habits, and emotions, and the pearl symbolizes innocence and a pure heart. Rich textures and ambient backgrounds create a flowing and peaceful sojourn to the depths of your soul, strengthening your innate abilities of perception while establishing self-acceptance and profound joy. Use *Pearl Moon* for meditation; relaxation; or for massage/body work. Instruments featured: piano, electric piano, analog and digital synthesizers, acoustic and electric guitar, real atmospheres, strings, flute.

Another Metamusic title by Andrzej Rejman is *Oasis*.

Portal to Eternity

(30 minutes)
Related Feedback
Meditation & Spiritual Growth, Relaxation & Stress Management

Imagine if Beethoven, Bach, and Mozart were to compose their timeless music with the technology available today. Lenore Paxton and Phillip Siadi of Lightfall share their inspired talents in this homage to these music legends. Enjoy lush blends of synthesizer, piano, cello, flute, and guitar as you experience a modern-day revival of classic compositions. Drift gently into a relaxed inner state as this fusion of classical music and Hemi-Sync transports you into an emotionally engaging experience.

Other Metamusic titles by Micah Sadigh are: *Inner Journey, The Journey Home, The Return, Spiral of Light, Transformation,* and *The Visitation.*

Portraits

(30 minutes)
Related Feedback
Classroom, Meditation & Spiritual Growth, Relaxation & Stress Management

Imagine if Beethoven, Bach, and Mozart were to compose their timeless music with the technology available today. Lenore Paxton and Phillip Siadi of Lightfall share their inspired talents in this homage to these music legends. Enjoy lush blends of synthesizer, piano, cello, flute, and guitar as you experience a modern-day revival of classic compositions. Drift gently into a relaxed inner state as this fusion of classical music and Hemi-Sync transports you into an emotionally engaging experience.

Other Metamusic title by Lenore Paxton and Phillip Siadi are *Lightfall for Focus and Concentration* and *Prisms.*

Prisms

(28 minutes)
Related Feedback
AIDS/HIV, Creativity, Expanded Awareness, Relaxation & Stress Management

Develop fresh perspectives and creative insights with this delightful New Age composition. Hemi-Sync sound patterns blend with guitar, flute, and keyboards to provide enchanting and deeply relaxing music to slow excess mental activity and stimulate a whole-brain creative process. Use Prisms for expanding awareness through musical imagery; for deeper more profound relaxation; or simply for musical enjoyment. By Lenore Paxton and Phillip Siadi of Lightfall.

Other Metamusic titles by Lenore Paxtion and Phillip Siadi are *Lightfall for Focus and Concentration* and *Portraits (Digital Download only.).*

Quest of the Mystic

(55 minutes)
Related Feedback
Expanded Awareness, Meditation & Spiritual Growth, Sleep and Dreams

A musical journey of self-transformation.

Chronotope Project's ambient dreamscapes and contemplative melodic sounds transport you to a mystical place of exploration. Hemi-Sync® frequencies enhance your journey as you delve deeper into the far reaches of consciousness. Instruments include analog and digital synthesizers, sequencers, various hand percussion, Tibetan and quartz singing bowls, Shakuhachi, Irish whistle, recorder, cello, koto, and more.

Radiance

(61 minutes)
Related Feedback
Enhanced Well-Being, Expanded Awareness, Massage & Body Work,
Meditation & Spiritual Growth, Relaxation & Stress Management

Immerse yourself in an ethereal "homecoming" of the soul with the frequency-raising music of Aeoliah and Hemi-Sync. Aeoliah is internationally known for his healing and uplifting music that nurtures body, mind and spirit. *Radiance* combines the harmonizing and transcendent effects of Aeoliah's music with powerful Hemi-Sync meditation frequencies to transport you into higher more expanded states of consciousness. The spiritual communions made possible by this divinely inspired composition are emotionally engaging; the feelings engendered deeply touching and profound. Use for massage and energy healing work or for deep, experiential meditation. Instruments featured: piano, synthesizers, flute, voice and angelic choir.

Another *Metamusic®* title by Aeoliah is *Serenity*.

Reflections

(60 minutes)
Related Feedback
Enhanced Well-Being, Expanded Awareness, Massage & Body Work, Meditation & Spiritual Growth

Tune-up the connection between body, mind and spirit with the music of Rick Borgia and Hemi-Sync. Therapeutic music is an ancient art. Greek and Roman spas incorporated such music to use in soothing cadence with the art of touch. Reflections mirrors this ancient practice of creating calming atmospheres to heighten one's energetic or healing connection. Immerse yourself in the delicate, floating rhythms of *Reflections* to support massage therapy, subtle energy healing work or for creating an ideal meditative space for inner reflection. Instruments featured: Synthesizer and nature field recordings.

Remembrance

(65 minutes)
Related Feedback
Accelerated Learning, ADD / ADHD, Aging, Asthma, Autism, Behavior Change, Brain Injury, Children, Classroom, Creativity, Depression, Financial Success, Focused Attention, Immune System, Learning and Memory, Personal Growth / Self Improvement, Relaxation & Stress Management, Stroke Recovery

Focus—with powerful Hemi-Sync and music designed for quantum learning, peak performance and creative flow. *Remembrance* is perfect for any mental task requiring focus and concentration and may be helpful for ADD/ADHD, dyslexia and other learning challenges. Play in the background or use with headphones to enhance mental capabilities while stimulating creativity and imagination. Composed and performed by J.S. Epperson.

Other Metamusic titles by J.S. Epperson are: *Ascension, Einstein's Dream, Hemi-Sync in Motion, Higher, Illumination for Peak Performance, Indigo for Quantum Focus,* and *The Lotus Mind.*

Remembrance is one of the exercises in three *LEK - Learning Enhancement Kits: Elementary Students, Elementary Teachers and High School/College Students,* and was part of the *Progressive Accelerated Learning (PAL) Student* and *Executive Packages. (The PAL Packages are no longer available.)*

River Dawn: Piano Meditations

(60 minutes)
Related Feedback
Meditation & Spiritual Growth, Relaxation & Stress Management

Experience the intimate piano meditations of Catherine Marie Charlton and Hemi-Sync. *River Dawn's* amazing depth and heartfelt emotion convey an exquisite combination of strength and tenderness that soothes and nurtures the soul. Charlton's artistic presence at the keyboard is intricately woven into her sensual and passionate performance as if it were intended just for you. Soft, but expressive, *River Dawn* is perfect for reducing stress and is an evocative sonic background for meditation. Instruments featured: solo piano.

Romantic Wonder

(50 minutes)
Related Feedback
Relaxation & Stress Management

Create a dreamy mood for those special moments with the romantic music of Don Paris and Ilona Selke combined. The passionate and emotionally engaging music of *Romantic Wonder* will speak to your soul. The haunting sounds of flute, guitar, and cello artfully convey every nuance of the tender and loving feelings expressed in this amorous composition.

Another Metamusic title by Ilona Selke is *Himalayan Soul.*

Sacred Realms

(57 minutes)
Related Feedback
Creativity, Expanded Awareness, Massage & Body Work, Meditation & Spiritual Growth, Relaxation & Stress Management

Enjoy this musical odyssey to mystical dimensions with the rich melodies of gifted musician Michel Genest. This inspiring musical soundtrack blends essential elements of earth and sky frequencies, aiding in the progression of a deeper state of consciousness. Michel uses a variety of computer software and electronic keyboards to create an exquisite tapestry of music and sounds, providing a truly unique listening experience.

Seaside Slumber

(74 minutes)
Related Feedback
Cancer Support, Children, Death & Dying, Enhanced Well-Being, Frustrations,

Massage & Body Work, Pain Management, Pregnancy and Childbirth, Relaxation & Stress Management, Sleep and Dreams, Stroke Recovery, Surgery

Drift gently into deep, restorative sleep with soothing ocean waves, solo piano, and Hemi-Sync. Studies have shown that the sounds of waves washing against rocks and beaches can enhance your sense of well-being. Combined with the healing music of Steven Halpern, the delta frequencies of Hemi-Sync lull you into a place of deep relaxation, tranquility and peace. Halpern performs on a Yamaha C-7 grand piano and Rhodes electric piano.

Another Metamusic title by Steven Halpern is *Deep Journeys*.

Seasons at Roberts Mountain

(67 minutes)
Related Feedback
Accelerated Learning, ADD / ADHD, Aging, Children, Creativity, Focused Attention, Learning & Memory

This 'classical-crossover' piece, a contemporary presentation of Vivaldi's *Four Seasons* performed by Scott Bucklin, is ideal to focus attention for super-learning and creative flow, and may be helpful to those with ADD/ADHD, dyslexia, and other learning challenges.

Seasons at Roberts Mountain is one of the exercises in *LEK - Learning Enhancement Kit - Elementary Teachers*.

Serene Sleep

(46 minutes)
Related Feedback
Enhanced Well-Being, Sleep and Dreams

Drift off into peaceful, restful sleep with the beautiful and relaxing music of Alpha Wave Movement and Hemi-Sync. Ambient textures, hypnotic soundscapes, nature sounds, Tibetan bowls and bells with hints of the Far East throughout gently create a place of tranquility, while the Hemi-Sync sleep frequencies carry you into deep sleep. Instruments include: Yamaha Motif, Ensoniq ESQ-1 + Modified VFX-SD, & Access Virus C. All compositions, programming and recording by Gregory Kyryluk.

Serenity

(63 minutes)
Related Feedback
Expanded Awareness, Massage & Body Work, Relaxation & Stress Management

Sit back, close your eyes, and allow this gentle and harmonious interlude to refresh and nurture. Aeoliah has been creating therapeutic music for almost 30 years. This collection of select compositions are combined frequencies to create a space of profound relaxation, soothing the mind and emotions to lift you out of the stresses of daily life. Instruments include orchestral and synthesizer sounds, harp, violin, acoustic piano, and nature sounds interwoven throughout certain pieces

Another Metamusic title by Aeoliah is *Radiance*.

Sleeping Through the Rain

(29 minutes)
Related Feedback
AIDS/HIV, Alzheimer's, Anxiety, Autism, Brain Injury, Cancer Support, Children, Classroom, Death & Dying, Dental Pain, Depression, Enhanced Well-Being, Pain Management, Pregnancy and Childbirth, Relaxation & Stress Management, Sleep and Dreams, Surgery

Journey across the border of wakefulness with soft, dreamy music and Hemi-Sync—from deep relaxation into natural, refreshing sleep. *Sleeping Through the Rain* is effective with headphones, earbuds or conventional speakers placed on either side or at the head of the bed. Composed and performed by Matthew Sigmon and Julie Anderson.

Other Metamusic titles by Matthew Sigmon are *Beyond the Golden Light* and *Into the Deep* with Julie Anderson.

Sleeping Through the Rain is one of the exercises in *LEK - Learning Enhancement Kit – Parents*.

Spiral of Light

(40 minutes)
Related Feedback
Expanded Awareness, Meditation & Spiritual Growth, Relaxation & Stress Management

Traveling to a higher vibrational landscape occurs in a spiral fashion. With each turn, we move upwards, but at times it seems as if we are where we started. Micah Sadigh has captured this sense with peaceful ambient music consisting of 10 overlapping movements depicting the journey of the soul to the presence of higher light and love. With each chord repeated — but with slightly different modifications, along with Hemi-Sync frequencies— you enter into a totally different realm, a higher dimension. It is at the end of the journey when we realize that what we perceived as light was indeed love, showering and guiding us onward.

Other Metamusic titles by Micah Sadigh include: *Inner Journey, The Journey Home, Portal to Eternity, The Return, Transformation,* and *The Visitation*.

Spirit Gathering

(73 minutes)
Related Feedback
Expanded Awareness, Meditation & Spiritual Growth, Shamanic Programs

Cross boundaries of time and space with the primordial shamanic percussion of Byron Metcalf and Hemi-Sync. Originally released as *Not Without Risk*, this multi-dimensional classic has been re-sequenced for its release as *Spirit Gathering*. The organic rhythms of this tribal tour de force will guide you to a center of primal power, from which all mysticism is born, and challenge you to push the boundaries of your own reality. Instruments featured: drums and percussion, flutes, ocarinas, didgeridoo, synthesizers & keyboards, voice, sonic atmospheres, and nature sounds.

Other titles are Byron Metcalf are *Deep Time Dreaming, Medicine Work, The Shaman's Heart Program.,* and *The Shaman's Heart II*.

Spirit's Journey

(36 minutes)
Related Feedback
Expanded Awareness, Meditation & Spiritual Growth, Relaxation & Stress Management

Embark on the adventure of a 21st century vision quest. Carefully orchestrated melodies and Hemi-Sync focus you within as you pursue that pearl of wisdom or guidance that is uniquely your own. Composer/musician Mark Certo's inspiring music is blended with changing Hemi-Sync signals to guide you into different states of consciousness throughout your journey of self-discovery. Use *Spirit's Journey* for expanded awareness through musical imagery; for deeper, more profound relaxation; or simply for musical enjoyment.

Star Spirits

(60 minutes)
Related Feedback
Massage & Body Work, Relaxation & Stress Management

An enchanting alchemy of Native American flute, deeply soothing nature sounds and Hemi-Sync. Stress and tensions melt away as you listen to the music of Gerald Jay Markoe's group, Ancient Brotherhood, against a background of ocean waves, babbling brooks and waterfalls. Crickets, tree frogs and other "sounds of the night" deepen your relaxation, as does a soft "heartbeat" medicine drum played at 60 beats per minutes. Use for massage and energy work or anytime you feel the need to relax and recharge. Instruments featured: Native flutes, synthesizers, medicine drum and nature sounds.

Another Metamusic title by Gerald Jay Markoe's group, Ancient Brotherhood, is *Where the Earth Touches the Stars.*

Strand

(56 minutes)
Related Feedback
Expanded Awareness, Meditation & Spiritual Growth, Relaxation & Stress Management

Relax and follow the thread from each track as it weaves a beautiful tapestry. Zero Ohms (Richard Roberts) and thunderjack (Tracy Chappell) join together to create an alchemical experience with ambient and introspective melodies. Hemi-Sync frequencies move you into deep relaxation for a powerful meditative experience. Instruments include: Zero Ohms on flute, bass flute, Nepali flute, bansuri, Bamboo Blue bansuri, bass bamboo flute, and Anasazi Native American flute; thunderjack plays Stratocaster and Les Paul electric guitars, and Fender acoustic bass guitar.

Other *Metamusic* titles with Richard Roberts (aka Zero Ohms) are *Gaia, Land of Spirit,* and *Winds Over the World.*

The Dreaming Gate

(59 minutes)
Related Feedback
Enhanced Well-Being, Expanded Awareness, Massage & Body Work,
Meditation & Spiritual Growth, Shamanic Programs

Enter a shamanic "dreamtime" with the entrancing didgeridoo music of Inlakesh and Hemi-Sync. Inspired by tribal cultures and ceremonial music from around the world, Rob Thomas and Tanya Gerard have raised the bar for fans of the spiritually evocative didgeridoo. Their masterful shamanic stylings are accompanied by other "dreamtime" tools to mystically weave the sonic portals of *The Dreaming Gate*. Step outside your normal reality and into a place of magic. Welcome to the Dream. Instruments featured: Didgeridoo, Tibetan horns, Gamelan gongs, cello, tabla drums, tambura, vocals (tracks 1 & 9), indigenous chants and highly textured soundscapes.

Another Metamusic title by Rob Thomas is *Medicine Work*.

The Journey Home

(45 minutes)
Related Feedback
Expanded Awareness, Meditation & Spiritual Growth, Relaxation & Stress Management

Celestial music and Hemi-Sync transport you on a poignant journey beyond space and time. Immerse yourself in this inspired musical depiction of a soul's journey to the realm of the Creator. Performed completely on analog and digital synthesizers, this enchanting soundtrack first characterizes the soul's yearning for 'home' followed by a musical recounting of the emotionally engaging journey. Bells sound in celebration of the soul's arrival in this spiritually uplifting piece which leaves you with a profound sense of inner calm. Composed and performed by Micah Sadigh, PhD.

Other Metamusic titles by Micah Sadigh are: *Inner Journey, Portal to Eternity, The Return, Spiral of Light, Transformation,* and *The Visitation.*

The Lotus Mind

(42 minutes)
Related Feedback
Expanded Awareness, Massage & Body Work, Meditation & Spiritual Growth, Problem Solving

The lotus grows in the murky water of still ponds and lakes. The magnificent blossom unfolds gradually in the sunlight, one petal at a time, and is seen as a metaphor for the development of the individual towards enlightenment. The ethereal sounds of J.S. Epperson's electronic mixed frequencies provide an ideal vehicle for stilling and opening the mind and heart, allowing for the evolving of consciousness. music

Other Metamusic titles by J.S. Epperson are *Ascension, Einstein's Dream, Hemi-Sync in Motion, Higher, Illumination for Peak-Performance, Indigo for Quantum Focus,* and *Remembrance.*

The Maze

(38 minutes)
Related Feedback
Creativity, Expanded Awareness

Stimulate your imagination and heighten your creativity with the captivating music of Bob Volkman and Hemi-Sync. Volkman's alluring and richly textured melodies seduce you at every turn as you wind your way through *The Maze*.

Another Metamusic title by Bob Volkman is *Dreamer's Journey*.

The Music of Graceful Passages

(74 minutes)
Related Feedback
Cancer Support, Death & Dying, Enhanced Well-Being,
Expanded Awareness, Massage & Body Work, Relaxation & Stress Management

From the best-selling CD-book *Graceful Passages*, this music by Gary Malkin will immerse you in your own private refuge of tranquility and reflection. The music was originally inspired by authentic spoken messages from many of the world's spiritual and humanitarian leaders; each spoke from a state of unconditional love, compassion, and a sense of Oneness with Source. As a result, when listening to this music, allow it to open your heart and offer healing for any wounds that might still remain. Since we're often most vulnerable during times of loss or change, experience this listening meditation as you traverse any significant transition in your life, so that you can remember who you are, live with an awareness of what matters most, and remember that you're never alone. The Hemi-Sync frequencies will deepen this experience, carrying you to a profound state of relaxation, allowing for calm and deep awareness of the beauty of life.

The Return

(46 minutes)
Related Feedback
Expanded Awareness, Massage & Body Work, Meditation & Spiritual Growth,
Relaxation & Stress Management, Sleep and Dreams

Embark on an inward passage that leads you into the arms of the Creator in this sequel to *Inner Journey* by Micah Sadigh, Ph.D. Ethereal sounds and Hemi-Sync gently guide you to a divine state of consciousness as you reconnect with the Source, finding comfort and peace in the beauty of oneness. Use *The Return* for deeper, more profound meditation; for crossing over into the sleep state; or for energy healing work.

Other Metamusic titles by Micah Sadigh are *Inner Journey, The Journey Home, Portal to Eternity, Spiral of Light, Transformation,* and *The Visitation.*

The Shaman's Heart

(73 minutes)
Related Feedback
Expanded Awareness, Massage & Body Work, Meditation & Spiritual Growth,
Relaxation & Stress Management, Shamanic Programs

Shamanism is an ancient spiritual system that helps one remain "heart centered" in the face of adversity— a hallmark of spiritual maturity that Don Juan referred to as traveling "a path with a heart." The spellbinding shamanic stylings of Byron Metcalf, and guest artist Steve Roach are combined with Hemi-Sync to transport you into the infinite heart-space dimension. For optimum results, listen to this experiential composition in one session—preferably in a darkened, meditative environment. Instruments featured: buffalo and frame drums, hybrid toms, didgeridoo, ocarinas, udu, shamanic rattles, and percussion.

Other titles by Byron Metcalf are: *Deep Time Dreaming, Medicine Work, Spirit Gathering, The Shaman's Heart II,* and *The Shaman's Heart Program.*

The Shaman's Heart II

(71 minutes)
Related Feedback
Expanded Awareness, Massage & Body Work, Meditation & Spiritual Growth,
Relaxation & Stress Management, Shamanic Programs

Enhance the heart's capacities for love, compassion, and strength with this entrancing shamanic journey crafted by Byron Metcalf with Steve Roach.

This powerful and potent shamanic journey invites the listener to make full contact with their heart, their own inner wisdom, and non-physical helpers and guides to reveal, heal and transform the habitual patterns and blocks that inhibit and stifle growth and creativity. Byron Metcalf's continuous heartbeat rhythm, medicine rattles, heart and soul activating trance drumming combines and Steve Roach's sonic mastery for a rewarding and memorable shamanic journey. Repeated use of this music in a personal ritual or ceremonial context will enhance the heart's capacities for love, compassion, courage, power, and strength.

Other titles by Byron Metcalf are: *Deep Time Dreaming, Medicine Work, Spirit Gathering, The Shaman's Heart,* and *The Shaman's Heart Program.*

The Visitation

(29 minutes)
Related Feedback
Expanded Awareness, Meditation & Spiritual Growth, Relaxation & Stress Management

Enjoy a deeply relaxing meditative state as you are transported by other-worldly music and Hemi-Sync to an encounter with a non-physical friend. Tabla drums and synthesizer are featured in this Eastern-influenced composition by Micah Sadigh, PhD. The enchanting experience of The Visitation can be an ideal stimulus for spiritual growth.

Other Metamusic titles by Micah Sadigh are: *Inner Journey, The Journey Home, Portal to Eternity, The Return, Spiral of Light,* and *Transformation.*

Timeless

(63 minutes)
Related Feedback
Expanded Awareness, Frustrations, Massage & Body Work,
Meditation & Spiritual Growth, Relaxation & Stress Management

This exquisite solo piano music of Pablo Peláez possesses a gravity and beauty beyond time. Allow yourself to be swept away by the enchanting and serene melodies to a restorative state of inner peace. Hemi-Sync frequencies facilitate a profound state of relaxation enabling you to look within for personal understanding and insight. Pablo plays the Shigeru Kawai SK7 piano of Infinity Studios (Madrid).

Touching Grace

(53 minutes)
Related Feedback
Enhanced Well-Being, Expanded Awareness, Massage & Body Work,
Meditation & Spiritual Growth, Relaxation & Stress Management

Connect with mystical realms with inspired music from Amoraea Dreamseed and Hemi-Sync. *Touching Grace* was originally released as *Antahkarana* in honor of the ancient healing and meditation symbol that has been used in Tibet and China for thousands of years. As a visual symbol, the Antahkarana was used in meditation to facilitate a connection to one's Higher Self. Similarly, Touching Grace is intended to facilitate a sonic connection to one's divine nature through music. Use for massage and energy healing work or for deep, experiential meditation. Instruments featured: flute, harp, percussion, singing bowls, didgeridoo, angelic vocals, soundscapes and nature sounds.

Another Metamusic title by Amoraea Dreamseed is *Dreamseed*.

Tranquility

(53 minutes)
Related Feedback
Meditation & Spiritual Growth, Relaxation & Stress Management

Mellow your mood with Paul Sihon's sensual fusion of East-West music combined. Richly composed and exquisitely played, Sihon weaves intricate textures of Indian music with Western music forms in this relaxing Hemi-Sync soundscape. The exotic rhythms of tabla drums blend with Paul Vornhagen's haunting flute passages, adding spice and a breadth of emotions to this enchanting composition. *Tranquility's* ultimate charm is its artful, unspoken appeal for East-West unity, spiritual awareness and world peace. Instruments featured: Paul Sihon on tabla drums, percussion and synthesizers; Paul Vornhagen on flutes, ocarina, clarinet, pennywhistle, and saxophone.

Transformation

(49 minutes)
Related Feedback
AIDS/HIV, Expanded Awareness, Meditation & Spiritual Growth,
Personal Growth / Self Improvement, Relaxation & Stress Management

Merge with the captivating music of Transformation and enjoy an enthralling transpersonal journey. Composed and performed by Micah Sadigh, PhD. Transformation provides a mesmerizing blend of Hemi-Sync and synthesizer music to move you beyond your sense of personal self. Let go of your thoughts and surrender to the deeply relaxing, wonderfully inspiring experience of Transformation.

Other Metamusic titles by Micah Sadigh are *Inner Journey, The Journey Home, Portal to Eternity, The Return, Spiral of Light,* and *The Visitation.*

Tribal Journeys

(57 minutes)
Related Feedback
Meditation & Spiritual Growth, Expanded Awareness

William Whitten's spellbinding use of ancient African instruments, and the audio-guidance support of Hemi-Sync transition you to a serene, otherworldly state where you are immersed in inspiring, dreamlike experiences.

Vision Quest

(67 minutes)
Related Feedback
Energy, Enhanced Well-Being, Meditation & Spiritual Growth, Shamanic Programs

You have entered the Sacred Circle and are surrounded by tribal elders as your vision quest begins—Spiritual drumming echoes into the depths of your soul as your energy merges with All That Is. "U-Tao-Chi" is a unique integration of sacred Native American drumming combined with newly translated rhythmic healing patterns from the ancient Chinese I-Ching hexagrams. Restore energetic balance and enhance your well-being with the harmonizing effects of this powerful fusion of Hemi-Sync and shamanic drumming performed by Kieran DeVerniero, an Elder in the Native American church. Instruments featured: udu, various drums & percussion, shekere, wood claves, shakers, and synthesizers.

Voyage to the Other Side

(43 minutes)
Related Feedback
Expanded Awareness, Meditation & Spiritual Growth, Relaxation & Stress Management

Enjoy deeply relaxing meditative states as you transition into ethereal realms beyond time-space. Daily burdens fall away as you listen to Frank Danna's emotionally engaging celestial music and Hemi-Sync.

Another Metamusic title by Frank Danna is *Eternity Within*.

Waves of Love

(65 minutes)
Related Feedback
Expanded Awareness, Meditation & Spiritual Growth, Relaxation & Stress Management

Inspired by the dolphins and composed from the heart, Frederic Delarue's gentle yet poignant melodies are combined frequencies to create a space of inner tranquility and deep reflection. Keyboards, dolphin-speak and ocean sounds work in harmony to help you reconnect with who you truly are as your heart opens, reminding you that your true essence is love. (Originally released as *Dolphins—A Message of Love*.) Frederic performs on a Korg Triton Extreme, Kurzweil K2500 and Roland JV-2080.

Where the Earth Touches the Stars

(47 minutes)
Related Feedback
Expanded Awareness, Relaxation & Stress Management

Relax to a calming blend of Native American and celestial music embedded. Native American flutist, A. Brent Chase performs with celestial soundscapes musician Gerald Jay Markoe to create music that is grounded in the earth yet connected to the stars. This delightful composition evokes the magic and mystery of a starlit night in the desert—the awe and wonder of nature and the cosmos. It inspires a sense of harmony and unity of earth with the universe. Instruments featured: Native flutes and synthesizers.

Another Metamusic title by Gerald Jay Markoe's group, Ancient Brotherhood, is *Star Spirits*.

Winds Over the World

(29 minutes)
Related Feedback
ADD / ADHD, Aging, Expanded Awareness, Meditation & Spiritual Growth, Relaxation & Stress Management

Aboriginal flutes and Hemi-Sync guide you through the world of musical imagery as you flow with this graceful expression of the spirit of life. Enjoy a sustained state of peace and calm as you journey within. Use *Winds Over the World* for expanding awareness through musical imagery and self-exploration; for deeper, more profound meditation; or simply for musical enjoyment. Composed and performed by Richard Roberts.

Other Metamusic titles with Richard Roberts (aka Zero Ohms) are *Gaia, Land of Spirit, and Strand with Hemi-Sync.*

Wisdom of the Heart

(59 minutes)
Related Feedback
Expanded Awareness, Massage & Body Work,
Meditation & Spiritual Growth, Relaxation & Stress Management

Based on his critically acclaimed series Ambiology, Grammy award winner Barry Goldstein has compiled the most conducive pieces for uniting the heart and mind. These pieces are all composed at a tempo that is consistent with the heart at a relaxed state, allowing the listener to reach a deep state of relaxation effortlessly. Ambient textures and soothing melodies work beautifully frequencies to create a peaceful environment for maintaining inner balance, nourishing body, mind and spirit, and remembering the splendor of life. Instruments include piano, keyboards and various synthesizers.

Other Hemi-Sync titles by Barry Goldstein include *Cosmic Consciousness* and *Your Heart's Song*.

Metamusic Atmospheres Titles

Metamusic Atmospheres is a new category to our product line, and features atmospheric music mixed for an enhanced experiential journey. While some of our *Metamusic* titles include atmospheric music, *Metamusic Atmospheres* titles contain atmospheric music exclusively. The absence of a discernible melody line lends itself to unreserved exploration, often enabling the listener to fall deeper into the frequencies for what is sometimes a more profound experience.

Cosmic Consciousness
(60 minutes)
Related Feedback
Expanded Awareness, Meditation & Spiritual Growth, Relaxation & Stress Management

Access higher awareness with the stellar music of Barry Goldstein and Hemi-Sync. Imagine floating in space, free from any physical tensions and the gravity of your mind. Surrender to the unknown and tap into the unlimited energy field where everything is possible. This exquisite composition by Barry Goldstein – with the addition of Hemi-Sync frequencies – is designed to balance and lift you into harmony. Instruments include ethereal textures, harmonic tones, keyboards and various synthesizers.

Other Hemi-Sync titles by Barry Goldstein include *Wisdom of the Heart* and *Your Heart's Song*.

Cosmic Traveler
(60 minutes)
Related Feedback
Expanded Awareness, Meditation & Spiritual Growth

Drift into dimensions of space and time with the atmospheric soundscapes of Max Corbacho. Hemi-Sync frequencies are expertly blended to carry you into a very deep, expanded state of consciousness. Enter into this powerful listening experience with an intention, and let go as you are carried into other realms of perception. Instruments: digital and analog modeling synthesizers, samplers and computer sound processing. Crickets and night sounds captured live in the county of Lleida, Spain.

Mind Food® Titles

Achieve brain synchronization with verbal guidance and sound wave methods.

Mind Food CDs do not contain music. These selections incorporate verbal guidance and/or subtle sound effects along with specially blended Hemi-Sync frequencies and sound patterns designed to help you achieve and sustain synchronized brain wave activity in both hemispheres of your brain. As with Metamusic recordings, Mind Food selections are available for a wide variety of uses ranging from meditations or focused attention to stress management and sleep enhancement, or for other practical everyday applications.

A Unicorn Named Georgia

(60 minutes)
Related Feedback
Children, Sleep and Dreams

Long ago and far away, in the land where magic and fairy tales begin, lived a very special unicorn named Georgia. As the only unicorn to be born with a golden horn, Georgia yearned to be like her friends, who often made fun of her, until one day her shiny golden horn saved the day. Track 1 features Georgia's magical bedtime story voiced by the author, Morgan MacKenzie-Perkins, along sleep enhancement frequencies to gently guide your child into a deep and restful sleep. Track 2 features the soothing sounds of ocean surf (pink noise) sleep enhancement frequencies.

Available as a Digital Download only.

Angels, Fairies and Wizards: A Magical Healing for Children

(60 minutes)
Related Feedback
Children, Enhanced Well-Being

In this enchanting story for young children, the Guardian Angel introduces the Fairy Ikier (for girls) and the Wizard Ikier (for boys) who can teach them how to participate in their own healing process. Using guided imagery, children can learn how to work with color, breath, positive affirmations, love, laughter and energy to encourage healing and better health (track 1). Track 2 features special Hemi-Sync frequencies to support a state of profound relaxation and transition into a deep restorative sleep. Created by Carmen Montoto, who has worked with children and special needs children utilizing the Hemi-Sync technology for learning and healing. *Recommended for ages 2-10, with separate CDs for girls or boys.*

Attention/At Ease

(58 minutes / 45 minutes)

Related Feedback
Energy, Enhanced Well-Being, Expanded Awareness, Relaxation & Stress Management, Sleep & Dreams

Created specifically for our armed forces, Monroe Products packaged two of its popular titles (*Concentration* and *Sleep Deeply*) to help meet the critical demands of military service.

This dual-purpose audio album is designed to help you stay focused during waking hours, and to fully relax and restore during down time.

Features two separate audio tracks/CDs:
Play **ATTENTION** (*Concentration*) to improve focus and concentration, helping you stay alert and sharp for any mental task. Features strong Beta frequencies, and has been tested and proven over the last 30 years to be helpful in sustaining attention for longer periods. 58 min.

AT EASE (*Sleep Deeply*) helps you power down for natural, restful sleep, allowing you to be more energetic and productive during waking hours. Features slower Delta frequencies associated with deep sleep. Play once to fall asleep, or repeat to stay asleep. 45 min.
Both are non-verbal and contain no music. You will hear soothing sounds similar to ocean surf or pink noise for optimum delivery of the frequencies.

Blue Moon Journey
(57 minutes)

Related Feedback
Breathing, Expanded Awareness, Meditation & Spiritual Growth, Relaxation & Stress Management

Recorded live near a wooded lake under a blue moon in the Virginia countryside, this captivating recording by A.J. Honeycutt features the sound of frogs, crickets, insects, and all sounds of the night.

Brief verbal guidance encourages you to relax and breathe in the fresh night air, exploring this realm in your mind and body. Connect with the earth, those elements you are made of, with this experience as rare and powerful as the blue moon itself.

Another title by A.J. Honeycutt is *Streamhaven*.

Breaking Free from Addictions
(42 minutes)
Related Feedback
Addictions, Behavior Change, Enhanced Well-Being, Personal Growth / Self Improvement, Weight Control

Disconnect from useless habits, achieve a broader range of options in your life, and let in a greater experience of joy. In this exercise Carolyn Ball, MA, LPC guides you with gentleness and compassion to unlock or address unwanted habits. As you go through the steps of healing your addictions, you will discover techniques to address the physical cravings, and how to achieve the emotions you want without the addictive patterns. You can repeat Track 2 (*Affirmations*) as a way to help reinforce and strengthen this process. Length:42 minutes.

This CD is for support in releasing addictions, and is not intended as a replacement for appropriate medical detoxification and treatment. If you are struggling with addictions, please see a medical or addictions specialist.

Other titles by Carolyn Ball are *Claiming Your Self, Creating Success, Emerging from Depression and Anxiety,* and *Weight Loss.*

Cable Car Ride

(16 minutes)
Related Feedback
Energy

Enjoy an infusion of cheerful energy as you awaken to joyful, uplifting rhythms and Hemi-Sync. Start your day in a positive mood or lift your spirits anytime with this delightful experience of *Cable Car Ride.*

Catnapper

(30 minutes)
Related Feedback
Addictions, Enhanced Well-Being, Pregnancy and Childbirth,
Relaxation & Stress Management, Sleep and Dreams, Therapy

Enjoy a totally refreshing nap in only 30 minutes. Verbal guidance and Hemi-Sync provide you with a unique opportunity to obtain deeply restorative rest. Benefit from *Catnapper's* proven effectiveness during work or study breaks or to re-energize for the evening. *Catnapper* is also effective for countering the effects of jet lag, coping with irregular schedules or as the ultimate pick-me-up anytime.

Catnapper is one of the exercises in *LEK - Learning Enhancement Kit – Parents,* and was part of the *Progressive Accelerated Learning (PAL) Student* and *Executive Packages.*

Chakra Meditation

(51/23 minutes)
Related Feedback
Enhanced Well-Being, Expanded Awareness, Meditation & Spiritual Growth,
Relaxation & Stress Management

Dolphin sounds and music combine to help align and balance each of the seven major chakras in this verbally guided Hemi-Sync exercise, created and voiced by Eluv. Located along the central line of the body, chakras receive and transmit life-force energy to our physical, mental, emotional and spiritual bodies. When we experience unreleased emotions such as fear, anger or guilt, the energy flows less freely and can become blocked. The affirmations included here will help to optimize each chakra for an overall sense of well-being. Features two tracks; Track 1 is a 51-minute extended meditation to fully open and deepen the process; Track 2 is a 23-minute abridged version for a quick balance and alignment.

A *Metamusic®* title by Eluv is *Octaves of Light.*

Chemotherapy Companion

(44 minutes)
Related Feedback
Cancer Support, Enhanced Well-Being

Support a positive outcome for your chemotherapy treatment. Verbal guidance and Hemi-Sync transport you to a profound state of total relaxation where you are immersed in feelings of inner peace and tranquility. Here, mental imagery and a series of positive affirmations are used in support of your return to physical well-being. You will also learn special encoding cues you may use anytime to reinforce the healing effects of your chemotherapy, or help you overcome the possible side effects of nausea.

Claiming Your Self

(68 minutes)
Related Feedback
Addictions, Behavior Change, Personal Growth / Self Improvement, Self-Confidence

Carolyn M. Ball, MA, LPC, takes you on two guided experiences geared to facilitate real changes in how you think and feel about yourself, helping you claim your Self by transforming mental and emotional "programs."

Track 1, *Thinking Empowering Thoughts*, helps you release negative beliefs about yourself and your life, replacing them with new perspectives and beliefs of confidence, self-appreciation, self-worth and self-empowerment. Track 2, *Healing Your Feelings*, guides you with affirmations for replacing negative emotions with love, compassion, self-acceptance, and peace. Gentle music and Hemi-Sync frequencies aid your process in expanding your awareness to a place of stillness, receptivity and wholeness. Music by Steve Sakellarios.

Other titles by Carolyn Ball are *Breaking Free from Addictions, Creating Success, Emerging from Depression and Anxiety,* and *Weight Loss.*

Concentration

(58 minutes)
Related Feedback
Accelerated Learning, ADD / ADHD, Aging, Asthma, Behavior Change, Children, Classroom, Creativity, Depression, Focused Attention, Headaches, Learning & Memory, Personal Growth / Self Improvement, Problem Solving, Therapy

Perfect for any mental task requiring focus and concentration—use at home, work or school while studying, reading, working on a computer or balancing a checkbook. Play in the background or use with headphones to enhance mental capabilities while stimulating creativity and imagination.

Concentration is one of the exercises in *Attention/At Ease,* two *LEK - Learning Enhancement Kits: Elementary Teachers and High School/College Students,* and was part of the *Progressive Accelerated Learning (PAL) Student* and *Executive Packages. (The PAL Packages are no longer available.)*

Connecting with Your Inner Guides

(35 minutes)
Related Feedback
Enhanced Well-Being, Expanded Awareness, Meditation & Spiritual Growth

Create a reunion and lasting communication with your personal inner guides. Lee Stone uses guided imagery along to facilitate this process, helping you to consciously connect and interact with those who love, protect and assist you.

Other titles by Lee Stone are *Exploring Other Lives, Exploring Our Future, Healing the Inner Child,* and *Inner Healer.*

Creating Success

(70 minutes)
Related Feedback
Addictions, Behavior Change, Creativity, Personal Growth / Self Improvement

Two verbally guided exercises assist you in overcoming limiting beliefs and opening the door to living your passion. With Defining and Believing in Your Success, Carolyn Ball, MA, LPC, guides you to create clear images and an understanding of your definition of success. The second track, Steps to Living Your Passion, will lead you through a progression of visualizations and positive affirmations for realizing your passion. Hemi-Sync frequencies support this process by assisting you in reaching those states of openness and receptivity.

Other titles by Carolyn Ball are *Breaking Free from Addictions, Claiming Your Self, Emerging from Depression and Anxiety,* and *Weight Loss.*

Deep 10 Relaxation

(64 minutes)
Related Feedback
Addictions, Anger, Anxiety, Blood Pressure, Cancer Support, Creativity, Death & Dying, Enhanced Well-Being, Frustrations, Immune System, Learning and Memory/Learning Disabilities, Personal Growth / Self Improvement, Pregnancy and Childbirth, Relaxation & Stress Management, Sleep & Dreams, Surgery, Therapy

Abandon your cares as verbal guidance and Hemi-Sync transport you to a blissful state of total relaxation followed by natural, restful sleep. *Deep 10 Relaxation* is a highly effective, time-proven means to counteract the negative effects of stress in your life. Anxiety and daily concerns seem to float away as you move into progressively deeper states of mental and physical calm. Track 1 contains verbal guidance; Track 2 continues your sleep cycle without words. Be kind to yourself. Use the popular *Deep 10 Relaxation* to rejuvenate both mind and body and leave your cares behind.

Deep 10 Relaxation - was one of the exercises in the *Progressive Accelerated Learning (PAL) Executive Packages. (The PAL Packages are no longer available.)*

Destination: Higher Self!

Related Feedback
Death & Dying, Expanded Awareness, Meditation & Spiritual Growth

Learn to become spiritually self-empowered and prepare for an enlightened transition.

We are all headed to the life-changing transition of consciousness that we call death. Are you and your loved ones prepared for your spiritual journey? William Buhlman, best-selling author and expert on the subject of out-of-body experiences, has created this program to assist those in the transition process to become spiritually self-empowered and prepare for an enlightened transition. Features three exercises: *Doorways to Your Higher Self, Waves of Light,* and *Affirmations to Experience your Higher Self.* All exercises are supported technology. This program can also be used for the exploration of consciousness. Music by Christopher Lloyd Clarke. Guidance manual included.

Other titles with music by Christopher Lloyd Clarke are *Into the Light: Meeting Your Guides, Into the Light: Exploring the Tunnel, The Gratitude Experience,* and *Total Relaxation.*

Please note: These exercises are designed to take you into highly expanded states of consciousness, and do not include frequencies for grounding at the end. Therefore, if you are not a person in transition, it is imperative to ground yourself after listening. See guidance manual for more information.

Emerging from Depression and Anxiety

(72 minutes)
Related Feedback
Addictions, Behavior Change, Enhanced Well-Being, Personal Growth / Self Improvement

In two exercises, *Dissolving Depression* and *Ending Anxiety*, Carolyn Ball, MA, LPC, helps you understand some of the underlying causes of these emotions, and gently guides you through empowering thoughts for transforming them into powerful and effective new perspectives. Hemi-Sync frequencies support this process by helping you to relax and open your mind to greater possibilities.

Other titles by Carolyn Ball are *Breaking Free from Addictions, Claiming Your Self, Creating Success,* and *Weight Loss.*

Energy Walk

(45 minutes)
Related Feedback
AIDS/HIV, Allergies, Anxiety, Behavior Change, Brain Injury, Cancer Support, Energy, Enhanced Well-Being, Fitness & Sports, Heart, Multiple Sclerosis, Pain Management, Immune System, Pregnancy and Childbirth, Stroke Recovery, Surgery, Therapy

Obtain greater vitality and personal strength with a verbally guided inner journey to natural sources of energy. Use *Energy Walk* to achieve greater balance and harmony and support the perfect functioning of mind and body. Hemi-Sync sound patterns facilitate deepening states of relaxation throughout your journey, until you drift gently into a restful sleep.

Energy Walk is an exercise in the *Surgical Support Series.*

Exploring Other Lives

(45 minutes)
Related Feedback
Enhanced Well-Being, Expanded Awareness, Meditation & Spiritual Growth, Personal Growth / Self Improvement, Self-Confidence

Knowledge of other lifetimes can bring clarity and insight to your present life, helping to remove blocks, discover unknown talents, cultivate new attitudes, and create a sense of well-being. Lee Stone, who has been conducting past life regression sessions and facilitating timeline therapy workshops for many years, guides you on an extraordinary journey to remembering these other significant incarnations. Hemi-Sync frequencies help you move beyond time and space to relax deeply into stillness as you expand your consciousness and gain insight into your life purpose.

Other titles by Lee Stone are *Connecting with Your Inner Guides, Exploring Our Future, Healing the Inner Child,* and *Inner Healer.*

Exploring Our Future

(58 minutes)
Related Feedback
Creativity, Expanded Awareness, Meditation & Spiritual Growth

Travel to the future to see how the world has changed geophysically, socially, economically, and technologically. Lee Stone guides you into states of relaxation as the Hemi-Sync signals assist you in moving into heightened states of consciousness, allowing you to explore the world in the selected year of your choosing. From there you will be directed to focus your attention on specific areas, moving about and noticing changes that have taken place.

Other titles by Lee Stone are *Connecting with Your Inner Guides, Exploring Other Lives, Healing the Inner Child,* and *Inner Healer.*

Freedom from Smoking

(74 minutes)
Related Feedback
Behavior Change, Enhanced Well-Being

Overcome your smoking addiction and restore optimum health with this life affirming Hemi-Sync exercise. Track 1 (*Freedom from Smoking*) uses verbal guidance and Hemi-Sync to strengthen your mind/body connection and focuses your total self—mental, emotional, and physical—on your goal of becoming a nonsmoker. Track 2 (*A New Life*) helps you control your weight and create a healthy new lifestyle following your decision to become a nonsmoker.

Guide to Serenity

(39 minutes)
Related Feedback
Anger, Behavior Change, Enhanced Well-Being, Frustrations,
Personal Growth / Self Improvement, Relaxation & Stress Management

Experience deep levels of physical and emotional comfort with this highly effective 10-point system of total relaxation. With Guide to Serenity you can achieve profound states of inner peace and calm and learn to recreate such states whenever you wish. Use *Guide to Serenity* to restore your strength and vitality. Hemi-Sync sound patterns support progressive states of relaxation until you drift gently into a natural, refreshing sleep.

Healing Journeys Support

(2 CDs)
Related Feedback
Allergies, Cancer Support, Enhanced Well-Being, Expanded Awareness, Pain Management, Immune System, Pregnancy and Childbirth, Sensory Integration Difficulties, Stroke Recovery, Surgery

Experienced energy healer Patty Ray Avalon, graduate and former faculty member of the Barbara Brennan School of Healing, offers her expertise in helping us take control of our own healing process. Four verbally-guided exercises on two CDs include: *Body Harmony*, for clearing your emotional, mental and physical bodies; *Chakra Tune-Up*, to become more aware of your chakras while learning to open and balance them with your voice and intentions; *Healing Helpers*, to bring in the assistance of a special non-physical helper (or team) to support your process; and *Heart Energy*, to help you access your heart's energy so you may live more fully, deeply and peacefully.

Other titles by Patty Ray Avalon are *The Creative Way, Inner States: Dawning of Awareness; Positively Ageless Way,* and *Touching Earth.*

Healing the Inner Child

(34 minutes)
Related Feedback
Children, Enhanced Well-Being, Personal Growth / Self Improvement

Assist your adult self in healing difficulties from childhood with compassionate verbal guidance and Hemi-Sync.

Return to a time in your childhood, where something occurred that was difficult, and still limits you in some way. With the aid of Hemi-Sync, Lee Stone guides your adult self to remember and witness this event in a safe and detached manner. As you observe this experience, allow the wisdom and skills you acquire to bring healing to your younger self through understanding and support, integrating this into your life. Repeated use of this exercise can be helpful for continued healing and inner peace. Music by Michel Genest.

Other titles by Lee Stone are *Connecting with Your Inner Guides, Exploring Other Lives, Exploring Our Future* and *Inner Healer.*

Healing Through Awareness

(40 minutes)
Related Feedback
Behavior Change, Enhanced Well-Being, Expanded Awareness, Meditation & Spiritual Growth, Pain Management, Personal Growth / Self Improvement, Relaxation & Stress Management,

A compassionate and effective meditation for healing emotional pain.

In this compassionate guided meditation, Geshe Tenzin Wangyal Rinpoche offers a deep practice for healing our "pain body, speech and mind." By being aware and connected to the inner stillness, inner silence, and spaciousness, we can open to our pain without trying to change, analyze, judge, or create stories around it as we heal. Hemi-Sync® frequencies help you relax and rest in an open, meditative state.

Track 1 is a four-minute intro explaining the focus of the meditation; Track 2 is the 36-minute meditation.

Himalayan Singing Bowls by Frank Perry.
Another title by Tenzin Wangyal Rinpoche is *Sacred Space: The Practice of Inner Stillness.*

Hemi-Sync Meditation

(45 minutes)
Related Feedback
Expanded Awareness, Meditation & Spiritual Growth

Connect with higher aspects of your Self with this extraordinary meditative tool. The deeply relaxing sound patterns of *Hemi-Sync Meditation* will gently lead you into powerful, free-flow explorations and leave you centered, focused and totally refreshed.

Hemi-Sync Nap

(25 minutes)
Related Feedback
Addictions, Enhanced Well-Being, Pregnancy and Childbirth,
Relaxation & Stress Management, Sleep and Dreams

It can be difficult to find the time to nap. In 25 minutes you can obtain the equivalent of a 90-minute sleep cycle, leaving you feeling refreshed, alert and ready to go. This non-verbal composition uses Hemi-Sync frequencies embedded in pink noise for optimum delivery. Delta frequencies quickly move you into a deep sleep state, while at the end of the session Beta frequencies awaken you restored and revitalized. Use during work or study breaks, to re-energize for the evening, or as the ultimate pick-me-up anytime. Also effective for countering the effects of jet lag, or coping with irregular schedules. Perfect for parents with newborns.

Hemi-Sync Relaxation

(50 minutes)
Related Feedback
Enhanced Well-Being, Relaxation & Stress Management

Experience total relaxation with this verbally guided Hemi-Sync exercise voiced by Dr. C. Norman Shealy. *Hemi-Sync Relaxation* uses a progressive relaxation technique along audio signals to gently guide you into a deep, receptive state of relaxation. While in this state, you will hear positive affirmations for health and well-being. As a pioneer in the field of alternative medicine, Dr. Shealy has helped medical practitioners to understand more fully the power of the mind-body connection and its relationship to maintaining or restoring wellness following a trauma such as surgery or a life-threatening disease.

Available as a Digital Download only.

Inner Healer

(33 minutes)
Related Feedback
Enhanced Well-Being, Expanded Awareness, Meditation & Spiritual Growth, Personal Growth / Self Improvement

Release emotions that limit you from a more positive life experience. Actualize your wholeness and fully align yourself to a higher level of emotional and physical health. With the aid of Hemi-Sync frequencies, Lee Stone guides you into a space of receptivity to connect with your inner healer. From there you will be directed to identify a recurring emotion, and to ask your inner healer to assist you in removing it.

Other titles by Lee Stone are *Connecting with Your Inner Guides, Exploring Other Lives, Healing the Inner Child,* and *Exploring Our Future.*

Inner States: Dawning of Awareness
Related Feedback
Expanded Awareness, Meditation & Spiritual Growth, Personal Growth / Self Improvement

With these Hemi-Sync exercises you will explore methods to activate the power within yourself, achieve inner peace, remain centered and calm in times of uncertainty, and transcend limiting thought patterns.

You will also learn to tap into an expanded source of knowledge and guidance for your life, find tools for initiating personal changes and transformational growth, become more aligned with your life's purpose, develop your intuition, bring more light into your body, and embrace a trusting, loving approach to living.

Co-developed with Patty Ray Avalon. Six verbally guided exercises on four CDs include: *Awakening Through Stillness, Equilibrium, The Limitless Self, Life Path Journey, Accessing Higher Guidance,* and *Luminosity.*

Other titles by Patty Ray Avalon are *The Creative Way, Healing Journeys Support, Positively Ageless,* and *Touching Earth.*

Into the Light: Near Death Meditations
(2 CDs)
Related Feedback
Enhanced Well-Being, Expanded Awareness, Death & Dying, Meditation & Spiritual Growth

This program features four expertly crafted guided exercises designed to give you a sense of what it is like to have a near-death experience. Created and voiced by near-death experience (NDE) researcher and speaker Scott Taylor, the program is based upon the analysis of more than 6,000 case studies of near-death experiences. The exercises — *Reunion, Life Review, Cities of Light,* and *Realm of Knowledge* —are designed to be used many times. You can expect a different experience each time, and you'll find your experience of the physical world will become richer as you gain more perspective from the nonphysical.

Will you have an NDE or NDE-like experience? No one can predict what another human being will do. However, you'll have every chance to enter altered states that will allow an experience of expanded awareness to happen. Guidance manual included.

Music by Jonn Serrie.

Metamusic® titles that feature music by Jonn Serrie are *Maiden Voyage* and *Celestial Meditation.*

Other titles by Scott Taylor are *Into the Light: Meeting Your Guides, Into the Light: Exploring the Tunnel,* and *Into the Light: Embracing Source.*

Into the Light: Meeting Your Guides

Near Death Meditations (2 CDs)
Related Feedback
Enhanced Well-Being, Expanded Awareness, Death & Dying, Meditation & Spiritual Growth

The second offering in Scott Taylor's *Into the Light* series, this album is designed to give you a sense of one aspect of a near-death experience—meeting your guides. *Into the Light: Meeting Your Guides* offers opportunities for exploration of a near-death experience as previously introduced in the popular *Into the Light with Hemi-Sync.* Scott Taylor has designed two new exercises to give you a sense of one aspect of an NDE—meeting your guides. The first exercise is a fully-guided exploration of how to prepare your body, mind, and energy body to make exploration possible, meet and converse with your guides, and learn the skill of bi-location—one of the forms of an out-of-body experience that is easy to learn and very helpful when exploring the nonphysical universe. The second exercise allows you more time to explore this expanded state of awareness. Detailed guidance manual included. Music by Christopher Lloyd Clarke.

Other titles with music by Christopher Lloyd Clarke are *Destination: Higher Self, Into the Light: Exploring the Tunnel, Into the Light: Embracing Source, The Gratitude Experience,* and *Total Relaxation.*

Other titles by Scott Taylor are *Into the Light: Near Death Meditations, Into the Light: Exploring the Tunnel,* and *Into the Light: Embracing Source.*

Into the Light: Exploring the Tunnel

Near Death Meditations (2 CDs)
Related Feedback
Enhanced Well-Being, Expanded Awareness, Death & Dying, Meditation & Spiritual Growth

The third offering in Scott Taylor's *Into the Light* series, this album is designed to address two opportunities for exploration. The first exercise, *Exploring the Tunnel,* is a fully guided exploration of the tunnel often encountered during a near death experience. During this exercise you will prepare your body, mind and energy body to make exploration possible. You will then explore the tunnel as you are guided to experience the colors, music and crystals found in the tunnel. You will connect with the tunnel itself, and discover its origins and significance. The second exercise is an open exercise, where you can revisit structures, people and energies you encountered during the guided exercise. Hemi-Sync® frequencies help to support this process. Detailed guidance manual included. Music by Christopher Lloyd Clarke.

Other titles with music by Christopher Lloyd Clarke are *Destination: Higher Self, Into the Light: Meeting Your Guides, Into the Light: Embracing Source, The Gratitude Experience,* and *Total Relaxation.*

Other titles by Scott Taylor are *Into the Light: Near Death Meditations, Into the Light: Meeting Your Guides,* and *Into the Light: Embracing Source.*

Into the Light: Embracing Source
Near Death Meditations (2 CDs)
Related Feedback
Enhanced Well-Being, Expanded Awareness, Death & Dying, Meditation & Spiritual Growth

In this fourth offering of the *Into the Light* series, you will enter the realm of the Black Light, the place of unmanifested potential where you can create with ease and merge with Source - the embracing, loving light that is the foundation of the Universe. In this exquisitely quiet place of complete and utter stillness, there is no ego, no future, no past, simply the eternal now. Features two exercises; the first is verbally guided, and the second is an open exercise where you can spend time in deeper exploration. Hemi-Sync® frequencies help to support this process. Detailed guidance manual included. Music by Christopher Lloyd Clarke.

Other titles with music by Christopher Lloyd Clarke are *Destination: Higher Self, Into the Light: Meeting Your Guides, Into the Light: Exploring the Tunnel, The Gratitude Experience,* and *Total Relaxation.*

Other titles by Scott Taylor are *Into the Light: Near Death Meditations, Into the Light: Meeting Your Guides,* and *Into the Light: Exploring the Tunnel.*

Journey Through the T-Cells

(31 minutes)
Related Feedback
AIDS/HIV, Cancer Support, Enhanced Well-Being, Immune System

Reinforce your mind-body connection with this verbally guided Hemi-Sync exercise. The whole-brain states made possible by Hemi-Sync are combined with positive imagery and health affirmations to assist you in strengthening and maintaining your immune system.

Journey Through The T-Cells is also sold as part of the *Positive Immunity Program* and the *Cancer Support Series.*

Joy Jumper

(46 minutes)
Related Feedback
Children, Sleep and Dreams

Children who have difficulty falling asleep at night will be thrilled to hear this delightful bedtime story about Kathy's newly discovered secret, "joy jumping." Track 1 features Kathy's fanciful bedtime story narrated by Morgan Mackenzie-Perkins along to guide your child into a deep and restful sleep. Track 2 features music and Hemi-Sync.

Manifesting

(74 minutes)
Related Feedback
Behavior Change, Enhanced Well-Being, Expanded Awareness, Financial Success,
Personal Growth / Self Improvement, Problem Solving

Conscious manifestation is not as simple as thinking about whatever you want and it will come true. The manifestation process involves all parts of us—as well as energies outside of us—and is most effective and rewarding when we have an open heart and a greater understanding of the process. Using his expertise in manifestation, Joe Gallenberger, Ph.D., has created verbally guided exercises, combined with special Hemi-Sync frequencies, to expand your awareness and energy to assist you in creating new or enhanced patterns that you may desire. Greatly enhance your ability to manifest positive elements in your life. Features two CDs; one is an overview from Dr. Gallenberger about the manifestation process; the other has two verbally guided exercises.

Another title by Dr. Joe Gallenberger is *Partners Meditation.*

Milton's Secret

(60 minutes)
Related Feedback
Children, Personal Growth / Self Improvement

This retelling of the popular children's book *Milton's Secret* is based on the bestselling *The Power of Now.* Eckhart Tolle and Robert S. Friedman have crafted an imaginative tale to teach kids how to live in the present, helping them to face difficult encounters at school, on the playground, and elsewhere in their lives. Using a variety of voices to portray the different characters, *Milton's Secret* is sure to delight young and old alike. Includes Hemi-Sync frequencies to help relax the body and focus the mind.

Moment of Revelation

(32 minutes)
Related Feedback
Expanded Awareness, Meditation & Spiritual Growth, Problem Solving,
Relaxation & Stress Management

Move beyond space, time and daily concerns as you ascend the spiral staircase to a wondrous place of peace and serenity. Deeply relaxing Hemi-Sync sound patterns and a guided visualization assist you on this delightful inner journey. Let go—release your expectations. The illumination of a peak experience—your moment of revelation—awaits you with this Hemi-Sync classic.

Moment of Revelation is one of the exercises in the *Going Home® Series.*

Morning Exercise

(19 minutes)
Related Feedback
Addictions, Anxiety, Behavior Change, Creativity, Depression, Financial Success,
Personal Growth / Self Improvement, Self-Confidence, Therapy

Pursue life to the fullest. Begin your day with *Morning Exercise* and plan a productive and highly successful outcome for the day's activities. By using this popular Hemi-Sync exercise, you can access your total self as you program your day for achievement. Positive images and messages are embedded deeply into your consciousness so that you might be your very best. Listen to *Morning Exercise* regularly to enhance your confidence and optimize your performance.

Morning Exercise was one of the exercises in the *Progressive Accelerated Learning (PAL) Executive Packages. (The PAL Packages are no longer available.)*

Pain Management

(44 minutes)
Related Feedback
Anxiety, Cancer Support, Death & Dying, Dental Pain, Energy, Enhanced Well-Being, Fibromyalgia, Fitness & Sports, Headaches, Immune System, Massage and Bodywork, Pain Management, Pregnancy and Childbirth, Stroke Recovery, Surgery

Listening to *Pain Management* can help you reduce pain signals until they no longer seem significant. You will also learn an effective, time-proven method to diminish pain signals anywhere. Use *Pain Management* to help restore the vitality and dynamic energy needed for the perfect functioning of both mind and body. This remarkable Hemi-Sync exercise helps you balance and equalize your mental, emotional, and physical self and guides you gently into a deeply, restorative sleep.

Radiation Companion

(45 minutes)
Related Feedback
Cancer Support

Support a positive outcome for your radiation treatment. Verbal guidance and Hemi-Sync transport you to a profound state of total relaxation where you are immersed in feelings of inner peace and tranquility. Here, mental imagery and a series of positive affirmations are used in support of your return to physical well-being. You will also learn special encoding cues you may use anytime to reinforce the healing effects of your radiation treatment or help you overcome the possible side effects of nausea.

Resonant Tuning

(30 minutes)
Related Feedback
Brain Injury, Breathing, Enhanced Well-Being, Expanded Awareness, Meditation & Spiritual Growth, Personal Growth / Self Improvement, Relaxation & Stress Management

Resonant Tuning combines a vocal/breathing exercise and Hemi-Sync to reduce your internal dialogue. This time-proven exercise may be used in preparation for entering meditative states or simply to quiet an overactive mind. It also promotes an accelerated gathering of your subtle life-force energies. Enjoy a heightened sense of these energies as they become revitalized with *Resonant Tuning* and benefit from their healthful influences on both mind and body.

Retain-Recall-Release

(32 minutes)
Related Feedback
Accelerated Learning, Focused Attention, Frustrations, Learning & Memory, Personal Growth / Self Improvement

Learn an easy method to improve your mental capabilities with this Hemi-Sync exercise. The more you practice the simple encoding cues featured in *Retain-Recall-Release*, the more proficient you become in controlling your memory. Use these cues whenever you wish to embed information more deeply and permanently into memory, bring desired information into consciousness, or release unwanted thoughts or memories. Retain-Recall-Release is a valuable tool for personal development. This easy method of memory enhancement may be used anywhere, at home, at work, at school or in social situations.

Retain-Recall-Release was one of the exercises in the *Progressive Accelerated Learning (PAL) Student* and *Executive Packages. (The PAL Packages are no longer available.)*

Robbie The Rabbit

(60 minutes)
Related Feedback
Children, Sleep and Dreams

Children will delight in the fanciful tale of *Robbie the Rabbit*. This comforting and soothing journey into Robbie's forest world is complete with nature sounds and the music of the night along to guide your child into deep and restful sleep.

Sacred Space: The Practice of Inner Stillness

(42 minutes)
Related Feedback
Expanded Awareness, Meditation & Spiritual Growth, Relaxation and Stress Management

Learn to connect with the sacred space that is the inner refuge in all of us. Revered spiritual teacher Tenzin Wangyal Rinpoche masterfully guides you inward to feel, connect, and become the inner stillness, releasing anxiety, fears, and confusion. In the sacred space there is a presence, an awareness, a sense of knowing. Discover and feel the presence of joy, warmth, and love in that space, which is your inner wealth. Experience it radiating through your body, speech, and mind in the world, transforming places, situations, and people. Allow it to manifest in the world, bringing balance to the workplace, the family, to all people and places. Repeated use of the meditation will deepen your experience with each listening.

Another title by Tenzin Wangyal Rinpoche is *Healing Through Awareness.*

Sleep Deeply
(45 minutes)

Related Feedback
ADD / ADHD, Aging, Children, Enhanced Well-Being, Focused Attention, Frustrations, Learning Disabilities, Massage and Bodywork, Personal Growth/Self Improvement, Relaxation & Stress Management, Sleep and Dreams

Sleeping better at night allows you to be more energetic and productive during your waking hours, and enhances your well-being and overall quality of life. This non-verbal composition can help you enjoy deep and restful sleep the natural way. Hemi-Sync frequencies — embedded in pink noise for optimum delivery — produce the slower Delta brainwave patterns associated with deep sleep. Play once to fall asleep, or repeat throughout the night to help you stay asleep.

Sleep Deeply is one of the exercises in *Attention/At Ease.*

Sleepy Locust

(60 minutes)
Related Feedback
Children, Sleep and Dreams

Big Freddy liked corn more than anything which is good because in Freddyville, everyone ate corn everyday—corn for breakfast, corn for lunch, even corn for dinner! Your child is sure to enjoy this whimsical bedtime story about Big Freddy and his big plan to outwit the locusts and save the corn. Track 1 features Big Freddy's tale narrated by Morgan MacKenzie-Perkins along sleep enhancement frequencies to gently guide your child into a deep and restful sleep. Track 2 features the subtle sounds of ocean surf (pink sound) and Hemi-Sync.

Soft & Still

(30 minutes)
Related Feedback
Aging, ADD / ADHD, Children, Creativity, Massage & Body Work, Meditation & Spiritual Growth, Relaxation & Stress Management

Enjoy the power and solitude of the sea with sounds of ocean surf, subtle music, and Hemi-Sync. Drift gently into mental and physical relaxation with the calming, natural energy of the tides. Allow tensions to melt away and open yourself to state of creative reflection.

Sound Sleeper

(70 minutes)
Related Feedback
Enhanced Well-Being, Relaxation & Stress Management, Sleep and Dreams

Enjoy the restorative benefits of a good night's rest with *Sound Sleeper*. On Track 1, verbal guidance relaxes you while Hemi-Sync sound patterns guide you into a totally refreshing Delta sleep. Track 2 features soothing sound effects embedded to continue your deep sleep cycle. You may wish to experiment with each Track separately, or play the entire title continuously. Use ear buds, headphones or speakers placed on either side of the bed.

Streamhaven

(60 minutes)
Related Feedback
Creativity, Enhanced Well-Being, Relaxation & Stress Management

This simple yet beautiful verbally-guided exercise offers a peaceful and refreshing respite from ongoing daily activities. Soothing live stream recordings combined frequencies create a sanctuary for a quiet retreat to use whenever you need to create some special time for yourself. Track 1 is verbally-guided; track 2 is a non-verbal 30-minute free flow for you to use anytime, or to extend your stay in the stream. Created and voiced by A.J. Honeycutt.

Another title by A.J. Honeycutt is *Blue Moon Journey*.

Super Sleep

(45 minutes)
Related Feedback

Aging, Children, Enhanced Well-Being, Focused Attention, Frustrations, Learning Disabilities, Massage and Bodywork, Personal Growth/Self Improvement, Relaxation & Stress Management, Sleep and Dreams

Super Sleep helps you produce the natural brain-wave patterns of the Delta sleep state and enjoy the benefits of totally refreshing, deeply restorative sleep. Use ear buds, headphones or speakers placed on either side of the bed. Play *Super Sleep* continuously to support uninterrupted sleep and get a good night's rest.

Surf

(46 minutes)
Related Feedback

ADD / ADHD, Aging, Anger, Autism, Behavior Change, Breathing, Cancer Support, Children, Classroom, Creativity, Death & Dying, Enhanced Well-Being, Frustrations, Immune System, Learning and Memory/Learning, Massage and Bodywork, Meditation & Spiritual Growth, Pain Management, Pregnancy and Childbirth, Problem Solving, Relaxation & Stress Management, Stroke Recovery, Surgery, Therapy

Relax—let your tensions ebb away with the soothing sounds of ocean surf and Hemi-Sync. *Surf* uses the gentle rhythms of nature to immerse you into progressively deeper states of relaxation until you are enveloped in a sense of inner peace and well-being. This Hemi-Sync favorite provides a welcome opportunity for inner reflection, and is ideal for inspiration and creativity.

Surf is an exercise in the *Surgical Support Series.*

The Gratitude Experience

(34 minutes)
Related Feedback

Energy, Enhanced Well-Being, Expanded Awareness, Meditation & Spiritual Growth, Personal Growth / Self Improvement

Raise your vibration by offering gratitude for everything in your life.

Feeling appreciation or gratitude is one of the most effective ways to bring high frequency energy and experiences into your life. The more you actively appreciate something or someone, the more you can shift into a positive state of being and attract similar experiences and relationships back to you. Patty Ray Avalon guides you through this experience as you list the situations, people, objects and qualities that you appreciate. Through this process you will become a more giving person and a powerful attractor of higher vibrational experiences. Hemi-Sync® frequencies help hold you in this higher vibration.

Other titles by Patty Ray Avalon are *The Creative Way, Healing Journeys Support, Inner States: Dawning of Awareness, Positively Ageless,* and *Touching Earth.*

Other titles with music by Christopher Lloyd Clarke are *Destination: Higher Self, Into the Light: Meeting Your Guides,* and *Into the Light: Exploring the Tunnel.*

The "SO" Chord

(45 minutes)
Related Feedback
Enhanced Well-Being, Expanded Awareness, Meditation & Spiritual Growth,
Relaxation & Stress Management

The *"SO" Chord* is one of many interpretations of the formative sound of Creation emerging from the "Void." When combined, Barry Oser's *"SO" Chord* provides an ideal sonic background to support experiential meditation. Any sound might appear as you listen to the powerful vibrational harmonics of the *"SO" Chord* (frequently one hears music that is not part of the recording). Restore balance and harmony to your mind-body with this extraordinary meditative tool. For optimum results, listen in one session—preferably in a darkened, meditative environment.

The Visit

(44 minutes)
Related Feedback
AIDS/HIV, Creativity, Expanded Awareness, Meditation & Spiritual Growth,
Problem Solving, Relaxation & Stress Management

Wonderfully relaxing Hemi-Sync sound patterns support the richly detailed verbal guidance of *The Visit* to transport you beyond time, into the presence of those who love and understand you. You may also enjoy using this long-time Hemi-Sync favorite to access knowledge not available in your waking state. *The Visit* will leave you totally refreshed and recharged.

The Way of Hemi-Sync

(29 minutes)
Related Feedback
Relaxation & Stress Management

This verbally guided demonstration exercise will introduce you to the extraordinary benefits of the whole-brain states of consciousness made possible by Hemi-Sync. You will hear, feel, and understand how Hemi-Sync works and then enjoy a relaxing and deeply restful experience.

Timeless Peace

(70 minutes)
Related Feedback
Enhanced Well-Being, Meditation & Spiritual Growth, Relaxation & Stress Management

Experience a deep state of infinite stillness with this verbally guided meditation by Lee Stone.

Experience a meditative state of infinite stillness, where thoughts fall away and you can be nourished by a profound eternal peace. Lee Stone's thoughtful guidance and Hemi-Sync frequencies help lead you into a place of timelessness, providing a deep, restorative sense of being. Features two tracks, each 35 minutes in length: Track 1 contains verbal guidance; Track 2 is a free-flow for you to create your own timeless experience. Music by Michel Genest.

Other titles by Lee Stone are *Connecting with Your Inner Guides, Exploring Other Lives, Exploring Our Future, Healing the Inner Child,* and *Inner Healer.*

Total Relaxation

(62 minutes)
Related Feedback
Addictions, Anger, Anxiety, Behavior Change, Blood Pressure, Cancer Support, Creativity, Death & Dying, Enhanced Well-Being, Frustrations, Immune System, Learning and Memory/Learning Disabilities, Personal Growth / Self Improvement, Pregnancy and Childbirth, Relaxation & Stress Management, Sleep & Dreams, Surgery, Therapy

Leave your cares behind with this verbally-guided exercise to relax and reduce stress.

Reduce anxiety and stress and move into a detached state of being. In this verbal exercise, Winter Robinson gently guides you into a deep state of relaxation. Experience inner peace and a serene mind, aided by Hemi-Sync frequencies and tranquil music. Features two tracks, 31 minutes each; track 1 is verbally-guided; track 2 is a free-flow.

Music by Christopher Lloyd Clarke.
Other titles with music by Christopher Lloyd Clarke are *Destination: Higher Self, Into the Light: Meeting Your Guides, Into the Light: Exploring the Tunnel,* and *The Gratitude Experience.*

Touching Earth

(34 minutes)
Related Feedback
Expanded Awareness, Meditation & Spiritual Growth

Deepen your relationship with Earth by entering into a heartfelt meditation to reflect on and celebrate this planet we call home. With the aid of Hemi-Sync, Patty Ray Avalon guides you to recall and feel gratitude for your exquisite earth-life experience, celebrate your connection in your heart, mind and spirit, and allow yourself to just be in quiet communion with all that is.

Other titles by Patty Ray Avalon are *The Creative Way, Inner States: Dawning of Awareness; Healing Journeys Support, and Positively Ageless.*

Transcendence

(73 minutes)
Related Feedback
Expanded Awareness, Meditation & Spiritual Growth,
Relaxation & Stress Management

Move beyond your thoughts and daily concerns as you listen to the deeply relaxing Hemi-Sync sound patterns of *Transcendence.* The verbal guidance and Hemi-Sync signals incorporated on Track 1 will lead you in the exploration of expanded states of consciousness. Create your own experiences with Track 2, an extended free flow exploration without verbal guidance. *Transcendence* will leave you centered, focused, and totally refreshed.

Turtle Island

(60 minutes)
Related Feedback
Children, Sleep and Dreams

A bedtime story by Patricia White Buffalo and Jane Ely, Ph.D. An American Indian "creation" story sleep enhancement frequencies. This delightful tale is about how "two leggeds" came to *Turtle Island*—the land most people know as North America. It is part of a revered Iroquois oral tradition for conveying spiritual and ancestral knowledge about the origins and history of their native culture. The narrative teaches children the importance of honoring Mother Earth and all of her creatures.

Track 1: *Turtle Island* voiced by Jane Ely, Ph.D. sleep enhancement to guide your child into sleep.
Track 2: soothing ocean surf (pink noise) sleep enhancement. Instruments featured: rattle, flute and drum.

Weight Loss
(43 minutes)
Related Feedback
Addictions, Behavior Change, Enhanced Well-Being,
Personal Growth / Self Improvement, Weight Control

Align yourself with your ideal body weight and change beliefs, perspectives and habits that previously perpetuated carrying extra pounds. Carolyn Ball, MA, LPC, helps you to replace these impressions with an inner knowing that can actually manifest a beautiful and healthy self on all levels. Powerful affirmations and new perspectives, along sounds, support your ability to overcome limiting beliefs that bring about an overweight condition. Put all doubts aside to confidently create a radiant, energetic, comfortable, and healthy body and mind. You can repeat Track 2 (*Affirmations*) as a way to help reinforce and strengthen this process.

Other titles by **Carolyn Ball** are *Breaking Free from Addictions, Claiming Your Self, Creating Success,* and *Emerging from Depression and Anxiety.*

Wisdom In Essence
(25 minutes)
Related Feedback
Expanded Awareness, Meditation & Spiritual Growth, Personal Growth / Self Improvement

Tune in to your inner wisdom, your true essence, with a verbally guided Hemi-Sync exercise voiced by futurist Peter Russell. Russell has been promoting the need for a spiritual rebirth if we are to survive the hurricane of change that lies ahead. Open to your innermost being and guidance to effectively and creatively deal with change as you experience *Wisdom in Essence.*

Sacred Geometry by LightSOURCE Arts

Experience personal development and enhanced well-being.

Sacred Geometry by LightSOURCE Arts products are visual aids (software and/or DVDs) of sacred geometry and other sacred symbols combined with a Metamusic soundtrack. These products may be used daily to manage stress and improve health and well-being. With appropriate intent, this vibrant mix of ancient wisdom and new technology may be used as an extraordinary tool for transformation. Regardless of how you choose to use it, you will always benefit from its calming, centering and rejuvenating effects.

Sacred Geometry is the blueprint of Creation and the genesis of all form. It is an ancient science that explores and explains the energy patterns that create and unify all things, allowing us to discover the balance and harmony in all manifest reality. The ancients believed the experience of Sacred Geometry was essential to the education of the soul. They knew these patterns and codes were symbolic of our own inner realm and the subtle structure of awareness. To them, the sacred had particular significance involving consciousness and the profound mystery of awareness—the ultimate sacred wonder.

LightSOURCE Arts products allow you to experience higher aspects of Self within the design of pure Source energy. As the blueprints literally come to life before your eyes, you are propelled into ecstatic play with the magic of the universe—the very heart of Creation. When you enter the world of LightSOURCE, you will recognize as never before, the wonderfully patterned beauty of the natural world.

Blossoming Lotus
Related Feedback
Accelerated Learning, Creativity, Focused Attention, Learning & Memory, Meditation & Spiritual Growth

Use *Blossoming Lotus* for powerfully focused meditation, daily stress reduction and serene ambience, as joyful upliftment at ceremonies and gatherings, and even for profoundly deep new experiences when giving or receiving massage.

Blossoming Lotus breathes light and life into mystical, sacred symbols of the Far East. Hypnotic animation and vibrantly brilliant color merged with the heart-opening *Indigo for Quantum Focus* Hemi-Sync soundtrack truly will inspire you to unparalleled new peaks of creative inspiration.

Blossoming Lotus presents twelve mandalas from the Taoist, Buddhist, and Hindu traditions that manage at once to be both ancient and contemporary. Mandalas include: Tao Yin Yang, The Blossoming Lotus, Dorje Sceptre, Endless Knot & Wheel of Life, Kanji Yin Yang, Lhasa Lotus, The Mahakala, Lotus Buddha, Om Devanagari, Mahamudra Buddha, Om Mane Padme Hum, and The Sri Yantra.

Blossoming Lotus is available in the following formats', CD-ROM Software, Software Download: Screensaver & Meditation, MP4 Video Downloads (4 different Sets)

Hanta Yo
Related Feedback
Expanded Awareness, Meditation & Spiritual Growth, Shamanic Programs, Relaxation & Stress Management

Hanta Yo! Is a Lakota Sioux invocation and prayer that calls upon the Great Spirit to clear the way and make the path ready for the seeker's spiritual evolution. Hanta Yo presents classic Native American shields, power symbols, and medicine wheels—finely illustrated and brought to life with scintillating color and LightSOURCE animation.

Included with HantaYo! is the award winning Metamusic title, *The Shaman's Heart* in 5.1 Surround Sound. The spellbinding shamanic music of Byron Metcalf and guest artist Steve Roach, will transport you to an infinite heart-space and remarkable binaural sonic dimension. Created by software designer and artist, Mika Feinberg, Hanta Yo offers a uniquely beautiful portal into Native American cosmology. The image gallery includes:

- Hopi Kokopelli Medicine Wheel
- Cheyenne Symbol of the Universe Shield
- Navajo Healing Snake Medicine Shield
- Comanche Buffalo Totem
- Mayan Tzolkin Mandala
- Cheyenne Four Winds Shield
- San Idefonso Pueblo Thunderbird Shield
- Pueblo Indian Rain Shield
- The Nazca Lines
- Papago Indian Sun Labyrinth
- Inuit Indian Mandala
- Navajo Hunting Shield

HantaYo! is available in the following formats', CD-ROM Software, Software Download: Screensaver & Meditation, MP4 Video Downloads (4 different Sets)

LightSOURCE 2nd Edition
Related Feedback
Enhanced Well-Being, Expanded Awareness, Meditation, Relaxation & Stress Management, Shamanic Programs

LightSOURCE 2nd Edition with Deep Time Dreaming and Hemi-Sync journeys to a zone beyond time and space where the mind becomes empty and Spirit becomes manifest. LightSOURCE doesn't just look and sound like a shamanic experience, it actually feels like one. Drawing on imagery that is both ancient and divine, LightSOURCE leaves little doubt that there is a Sacred Geometry which transcends and includes all spiritual paths. Influences from Mayan, Tibetan, Islamic/Judeo/Christian, Egyptian cosmologies—and Alchemy, too—all merge into Oneness with animation so beautiful it's entrancing.

LightSOURCE showcases 12 sacred geometries by digital alchemist Mika Feinberg, including classics such as: The Flower of Life, The Sri Yantra, The Endless Knot, Metatron's Cube, The Kabbalah Tree of Life, and The Vesica Piscis. There are also the extravagantly beautiful new forms, Cross of the Spheres and Nested Inscribed Polygons.

Deep Time Dreaming, a full-length Hemi-Sync Metamusic soundtrack, is a multi-textured shamanic masterpiece featuring ancient sound worlds from Byron Metcalf, accompanied by organic trance percussionist Mark Seelig. It includes designer Hemi-Sync frequencies that induce transcendent inner journeys and profoundly deep meditative mind states. LightSOURCE with Deep Time Dreaming and Hemi-Sync is a journey you will want to embark upon many times.

LightSOURCE is available in the following formats', CD-ROM Software, MP4 Video Downloads (4 different Sets)

Sacred Gaiametry
Related Feedback
Expanded Awareness, Meditation & Spiritual Growth, Relaxation & Stress Management

Crop circles are one of the most profound and mysterious phenomena of the modern age. Their enigmatic designs have had a powerful effect on thousands of people who have witnessed and studied them through the years. Irrespective of the origin, they have acted as a catalyst to spirituality as we strive to understand their true purpose and meaning. It has been said that crop circles are encoded with keys of great wisdom. Sacred Gaiametry—The Magic of Crop Circles offers a baker's dozen of these lush, powerful geometric designs, animated and vividly brought to life through exquisite technical artistry—connecting you with the very heart of this profound phenomenon. The soundtrack features an extended version of Richard Robert's classic Metamusic title, *Gaia*.

Sacred Gaiametry is available in the following formats: CD-ROM Software, Software Download: Screensaver & Meditation

Yantra Mantra Sacred Light - Sacred Sound
Related Feedback
Expanded Awareness, Meditation & Spiritual Growth, Relaxation & Stress Management

Yantra Mantra—Sacred Light Sacred Sound merges the ethereal splendor of Deva Premal's enchanting voice with relaxing Hemi-Sync binaural beats and the breathtaking beauty of LightSOURCE living mandalas. Together they form a potent spiritual cocktail that expands the mind, heals the heart, and uplifts the soul.

Yantra Mantra is a fusion of animated sacred mandalas—both ancient and new—and ageless spiritual chants with movement, rhythm, color and the Hemi-Sync frequencies. Yantra Mantra activates personal transformation, facilitates mental and physical relaxation, and leads to holistic spiritual awareness, resulting in a state of "peaceful awakening." Perfect for group meditation and for individually finding peace within.

Yanta Mantra is available in the following formats: DVD/Blu-ray, Software Download: Screensaver & Meditation, MP4 Video Downloads (4 different Sets)

Instrumentation and Title Index

MIND FOOD TITLES

SACRED GEOMETRY TITLES

ALPHABETICAL LISTINGS

A

B

C

D

E

www.ingramcontent.com/pod-product-compliance
Lightning Source LLC
Chambersburg PA
CBHW081348280526
45788CB00009B/2803